HARVARD EAST ASIAN MONOGRAPHS

81

THE DEWEY EXPERIMENT IN CHINA

EDUCATIONAL REFORM AND
POLITICAL POWER IN THE EARLY REPUBLIC

THE DEWEY EXPERIMENT IN CHINA

EDUCATIONAL REFORM AND
POLITICAL POWER IN THE EARLY REPUBLIC

by

Barry Keenan

Published by
Council on East Asian Studies
Harvard University

103704

Distributed by
Harvard University Press
Cambridge, Massachusetts
and
London, England
1977

This book is produced by the John K. Fairbank Center for East
Asian Research at Harvard University, which administers research
projects designed to further scholarly understanding of China,
Japan, Korea, Vietnam, Inner Asia, and adjacent areas. These
studies have been assisted by grants from the Ford Foundation.

Library of Congress cataloging in Publication Data

Keenan, Barry, 1940-
    The Dewey experiment in China.

    (Harvard East Asian monographs ; 81)
    Bibliography: p.289
    Includes index.
    1. Dewey, John, 1859-1952. 2. Education—China—History.
3. China—Republic, 1912-1949—History. I. Title. II. Series.
LB875.D5K4   370'.951   77-6682
ISBN 0-674-20277-5

FOREWORD

The encounter between John Dewey and modern China is one of the most fascinating episodes in the intellectual history of twentieth-century China. The effort made by Dewey's Chinese disciples to apply his ideas to the complex tangle of China's political, social, and cultural situation in the early twentieth century provides us with a unique perspective on the awesome dilemmas that confronted China's intellectuals during this period. Professor Keenan's penetrating and illuminating study of this episode should, however, be of profound interest not only to students of modern Chinese history but also to students of John Dewey and of twentieth-century American thought. It belongs to an area of inquiry which might be called the history of cultural-intellectual interaction in the twentieth century. While the influence in this case ran in one direction—from Dewey to China—Professor Keenan has clearly demonstrated that the implications run in two directions. When we view Dewey's ideas within the Chinese setting we suddenly become acutely aware of the unstated premises that lie beneath the manifest doctrine. We suddenly become aware of the degree to which Dewey's thought presupposes cultural, social, and political aspects of his American environment.

Professor Keenan has focused his main attention on the effort of both Dewey and his Chinese disciples to apply his educational and political philosophy to contemporary Chinese realities. In the course of this effort questions of the utmost urgency rose to the surface. What is the relationship of education to its socio-political milieu? What, after all, is the relationship of "scientific intelligence," which becomes almost a transcendental force in Dewey's thought, to the political and social democracy to which he was so ardently committed? In his biography of Hu Shih, one of John Dewey's most enthusiastic disciples, Professor Jerome Grieder has already addressed these and other questions as they were dealt with by Hu Shih. Professor Keenan considers Dewey's influence on an vi

entire group of intellectuals and educators who dealt with the master's ideas from a variety of perspectives.

Dewey's thought was, of course, not destined to achieve ascendancy in China. In the history of mankind it is, however, impossible to speak of definitive victories or definitive defeats. The questions raised by Dewey's encounter with China remain questions of enduring interest. Professor Keenan has provided us with a lucid study of this encounter.

Benjamin I. Schwartz

CONTENTS

ACKNOWLEDGMENTS

Appreciation for valuable assistance with this study must begin with Claremont Graduate School and University Center where it was conceived as a doctoral dissertation. It was my privilege to enjoy the experienced counsel and the instructive guidance of an excellent advisor, Professor Cyrus H. Peake. Professors John Isreal and George Beckmann added important critical advice and elicited expert opinion from Professor Michael Gasster. To Dr. Irene Eber, now of Hebrew University, I owe a lasting debt for introducing me to the Chinese source materials of the early Republican period. I should like to thank Professor Ch'en Shou-yi of Pomona College for introducing me to the late Professor Fan Chi-ch'ang and Dr. Ou Tsuin-chen (Wu chun-sheng), who became invaluable informants regarding the careers of Dewey's Chinese followers. I thank Professor Chow Tse-tsung for originally suggesting the topic.

The final chapters were written in the Columbia University community, where I was first employed. For his advice and for sharing his wealth of knowledge on Chinese history and society I shall remain indebted to a remarkable teacher and associate, Professor C. T. Hu. I also thank Professor C. Martin Wilbur and the East Asian Institute for a supporting grant on a related project, as well as the opportunity to test my initial findings with the China scholars assembled monthly for the Columbia University Seminar Series. I have learned much from Dr. T. K. Tong and Dr. Y. C. Wang as well as from my fellow researchers at Columbia, Ka-che Yip and Odoric Wou.

This study was selected for publication by the East Asian Research Center of Harvard University. For the encouragement that made this possible I must thank Professor John K. Fairbank and Dr. Charles Hayford. Professor Fairbank was kind enough to take time from a New Hampshire summer to read preliminary copy. Professor Charlotte Furth has also read a preliminary draft and made many constructive suggestions. Discussions with Professor

Jerome Grieder over a period of several years have been most helpful. I should like to thank the East Asian Research Center and its current director, Professor Ezra Vogel, for providing office space while revisions were under way. The steady hand of Professor Benjamin Schwartz touches all at the Center who venture into the area of Chinese intellectual history.

In Dewey scholarship, I owe valuable dissertation guidance to Professor Herbert W. Schneider. The outstanding Center for Dewey Studies at Southern Illinois University, and Dr. Jo Ann Boydston in particular, rendered professional assistance in locating Dewey source material. The John Dewey Foundation, directed by Sidney Hook, accorded me a much appreciated research grant while revision was in progress.

I should like to thank Mrs. Lucy Brandauer, the daughter of John Dewey, for her informative interview about the itinerary and other recollections of her trip to China with her parents. Dr. John L. Childs was kind enough to share his reflections upon Dewey's contacts in Peking. Professor R. Alan Lawson has kindly read over some chapters and provided helpful criticism. Finally, I thank the following for some important assistance in research and writing: Ichiko Chūzō of the Tōyō Bunko in Tokyo, Victor Kobayashi, Samuel Bowles, R. J. Wilson, Stephen Ellenburg, Sharon Libera, and John Lemly. The Faculty Grants Committee of Mount Holyoke College aided in the preparation of the manuscript, and I would like to express my heartfelt appreciation to a superb typist, Dorothy Kimball. Ms. Fay H. Y. Chen rendered valuable assistance with the index.

PREFACE

John Dewey's popular lecture tour of China following World War I was such a vogue among Chinese intellectuals that Dewey's ideas played a role in defining the content of liberal reform movements in the early Republican period. The frustrations encountered by these reformers, however, represented in many ways writ small what the problems of United States influence in China have more broadly been in the twentieth century. This book is about the attempts of Dewey's followers to make their ideas into effective reform tools in China.

Insofar as this study analyzes the plight of Chinese liberals in the early twentieth century, I would like to mention two works with which its conclusions are compatible in important ways. When this study was first completed as a doctoral dissertation, I had the delightful experience of picking up a recently published analysis of a political leftist from the same time period, and finding a largely similar interpretation of the weaknesses of the liberals. What I was discovering through an internal analysis of the writing and experiences of the liberals, the other author was deriving from the writings and the experiences of the contemporaneous left. This book was Maurice Meisner's *Li Ta-chao and the Origins of Chinese Marxism* (Cambridge, Mass., 1967). At another stage of research the pleasure was repeated on a second theme when Laurence Schneider published *Ku Chieh-kang and China's New History* (Berkeley, 1971). Professor Schneider's discussion of the New Culture movement liberals he studied in terms of the displaced intelligentsia following 1905 corroborated my own findings from the writings of the educational reformers discussed in this volume.

John Dewey's lectures were interpreted into Chinese as they were delivered, and the interpreted version published in Chinese journals. No English notes of Dewey's remain. His lectures have been translated back into English from the Chinese as part of an East-West Center project, and one volume of these was made available for the first time to English readers in 1973: Robert Clopton and Ou Tsuin-chen, trans. and eds., *John Dewey: Lectures in China, 1919-1920* (Honolulu, 1973).

   One matter of form requires explanation. Following the convention common in East Asian Studies publishing, Chinese periodical titles translated into English use the lower case for each word except the first, e.g., *Chiao-yü ch'ao* (The educational tide). If, however, the Chinese journal had its own English-language subtitle, that title will appear with capital letters and in quotation marks, e.g. *Tung-fang tsa-chih* ("The Eastern Miscellany").

INTRODUCTION

It was a philosopher's dream come true, that day in 1919 when Professor John Dewey stepped off the boat in China and was met by influential young intellectuals imploring him to extend his brief visit to lecture for a year. Over a thousand of the leading educators in central China were gathering to hear his opening address three days later. John Dewey arrived on the heels of the Allied victory over Germany in World War I and, as the dean of American philosophy, he was to lecture in China on the principles of democratic society.

John Dewey was a quiet, unassuming man with a droopy mustache. Nearing sixty, he and his wife had traveled across the Pacific primarily because they were living temporarily in San Francisco and thought it might be their last convenient opportunity to be tourists in East Asia. When they arrived, Dewey took an immediate interest in China and her problems. He was fascinated with the efforts of younger intellectuals to establish the first republican government in China's history. Although due to return to his position at Columbia University within a few months, he wrote for a leave of absence, and accepted a visiting professorship at National Peking University. Dewey lectured in China for over two years in the end, making tours throughout the country from Peking. Each lecture was interpreted into Chinese, and five book editions of his different lecture series soon appeared in Chinese. One went through ten printings before he had left China.

Chinese intellectuals closely followed currents of thought in the West at the time of the "European War." The Republic of 1912 had overthrown a 2000-year tradition of dynastic government as the war began. Open rejection of imperial institutions and the accompanying attack on Confucian values gave Chinese intellectuals in the second decade of the twentieth century an unprecedented interest in modern Western ideas and in learning how to make China into a strong democratic nation. Dewey's lectures addressed these interests, and he did not hesitate to present the United States as a

viable—albeit imperfect—model of a democratic society. Dewey
felt, in fact, some sense of mission to spread the internationalist
ideals for which the United States had so recently fought. He
described the purpose of United States intervention in World War I,
using President Wilson's phrase "to make the world safe for democracy"; and discernible in Dewey's lectures was the tone of a vindicated advocate of the internal strength of democratic societies.

Contemporaneous with Dewey's arrival a nationwide student
movement erupted opposing Japanese imperialism and domestic
Chinese corruption. The treaty provisions announced at the Versailles Peace Conference had set off this domestic upheaval. The
Chinese had joined the Allied side during the war with expectations
that conflicted with those of another ally, Japan. Despite Chinese
opposition, the Versailles Conference had not returned the rights
to German territorial concessions in China to the Chinese, but had
instead accorded them to Japan. Inflamed nationalist sentiment
burst out against the Peking cabinets that had made secret promises
assuring this arrangement during the war. Hatred was simultaneously
directed against the machinations of international power politics
exposed in this "shift" of foreign rights in China. Mass demonstrations, strikes, and boycotts spread throughout the country, politicizing the intellectual atmosphere during the entire two years
Dewey and his wife were there.

Dewey's lectures were reprinted in many of the hundreds of
new periodicals that stemmed from the nationalist movement.
Pragmatism, or "experimentalism" as it was usually translated in
China, became a significant current of thought in the political and
philosophic debates that accompanied the new political consciousness. Among intellectuals, the main competitors with Dewey's
reform ideas were the early Marxist proposals for change in China.
The Chinese Communist Party was organized from scratch during
the two years Dewey was in China, and held its first national convention the very month Dewey departed—July 1921.

Dewey argued against Marxism in his China lectures, although
he was sympathetic to other formulations of socialism. His own
political views derived from a description of democracy that

stressed the importance of a modern scientific understanding of human nature and social interaction. Dewey had been associated with the *New Republic* brand of Progressive Era reformism in the United States. The leading editors of that magazine, Herbert Croly and Walter Lippmann, acknowledged a debt to Dewey's pragmatic philosophy. From the authority of his professorship at Columbia, Dewey frequently contributed to the magazine. The *New Republic*'s political sympathies were with the centralized leadership of "democratic nationalism" subscribed to by Theodore Roosevelt. After its founding in 1914, the editors attempted to influence President Woodrow Wilson to adopt this program of Hamiltonian means towards Jeffersonian ends. Dewey's political articles had contributed to a reform trend that advocated the increased application of science to social policy. He wrote optimistically of the progress made in the new disciplines of social psychology and sociology; and felt the sciences of society held the promise of approaching the sophisticated level of the physical sciences, and of thereby assuring planned progress for the future.

Dewey's former Chinese students at Columbia University met him at the boat and arranged his visiting professorship in China. These "returned students" were already important young professors and professional educators when Dewey arrived and several became his loyal followers. Insofar as the ideas of these followers represented the democratic ideology associated with the industrial model of the United States, the reception of Dewey's ideas had political significance, and constituted an important episode in twentieth-century Sino-American relations. Dewey lived to see the establishment of the People's Republic of China in 1949, and watched his closest followers become refugees to Taiwan and the United States. Mao Tse-tung officially denounced Dewey's intellectual followers and the kind of cultural influence the United States had exerted in China: "For a very long period," Mao wrote, "U.S. imperialism laid greater stress than other imperialist countries on activities in the sphere of spiritual aggression, extending from religious to 'philanthropic' and cultural undertakings."[1] Mao identified Dewey's students with the United States in 1949 when that association meant support of Chiang Kai-shek's defeated Nationalists; and they have been condemned thereafter in the literature of the People's Republic.[2]

The People's Republic of China carried out an intellectual campaign in the 1950s specifically denouncing the influence of Dewey's educational and political ideas in China. A barrage of articles and a few book-length critiques of Dewey's theories appeared in 1951-1952, and again in 1955-1956 when Hu Shih, Dewey's prominent disciple, was under attack. Although, during the Great Leap Forward of 1958, two of Dewey's books were reprinted in Chinese translations, by 1963 another systematic critique of all aspects of pragmatism, and Dewey's epistemology and pedagogy in particular, was promulgated. This critique was revised for standard textbook use in schools during the 1970s.[3]

The fundamental incompatibilities of Dewey's pragmatism and the socialist needs of Mao's China, which were developed in these critiques, centered upon Dewey's piecemeal definition of the nature of science and, as importantly, upon his assumption that class distinctions could be subsumed within the operation of "democracy" in society. This latter "error" was considered by his critics to be the greatest oversight of the bourgeois educator and his Chinese followers. In assuming that economic class interests could be transcended, Dewey committed the error common to philosophically idealistic philosophies, it was argued, and in the end aided and abetted the class structure in power. His reformism therefore tended to be reactionary.

In Taiwan, John Dewey's works had a mixed but largely critical reception during the twenty-five years following 1949. His former followers wrote and spoke on his behalf. But the Communist victory had left most political writers very sensitive to Dewey's liberalism, and Dewey was under attack for his former influence in China, which was seen as too leftist—encouraging materialism and communism.[4]

These opposing criticisms of Dewey in China after 1950 portrayed him alternately as reactionary and leftist. But the critiques reflect more about the time in which they were written than the period when Dewey's ideas were given their real test in China, following World War I. Yet the criticisms indicate that Dewey's ideas did have a significant influence among some intellectuals in China. It was an influence that required systematic criticism in both Taiwan and Peking some fifty years later.

Nevertheless, despite certain propitious conditions in 1919, the reformist influence of Dewey's ideas in China was ephemeral. The careers of the Deweyites in China were beset by one crisis after another. Even during the two years he was there, his Chinese followers encountered obstacles they were without the means to overcome. Among professional educators, the effect of his ideas was lasting, but even these educators had little success practicing them outside academic institutions. The limited effectiveness of Dewey's reform ideas in China cannot be attributed to Comintern propaganda or Communist subversion. In fact his ideas underwent the same test of political and intellectual conditions as the earliest Marxist ideas in China.

PART ONE

YANKEE CONFUCIUS

In working out to realization the ideas of federation and of the liberation of human interests from political domination we have been, as it were, a laboratory set aside from the rest of the world in which to make, for its benefit, a great social experiment. The war, the removal of the curtain of isolation, means that this period of experimentation is over. . . That we should have lost something of our spirit of boasting about our material greatness is a fine thing. But we need to recover something of the militant faith of our forefathers that America is a great idea, and add to it an ardent faith in our capacity to lead the world to see what this idea means as a model for its own future well-being.

> John Dewey, "America in the World,"
> an address at Smith College,
> February 22, 1918.

Chapter I

JOHN DEWEY'S VISIT TO CHINA

Professor Dewey had taught at Berkeley for the first semester of his sabbatical leave from Columbia University in 1918. As the foremost proponent of pragmatism in the world, Dewey was at the pinnacle of his productive career at the time of World War I. Just as he and his wife were about to leave for a vacation in "the Orient," Dewey received a cable inviting him to lecture while in Japan.[1] A Japanese acquaintance from the University of Michigan, Ono Eijirō, extended the invitation, and had made arrangements at National Imperial University in Tokyo, where Dewey delivered a series of lectures during his two-and-a half month visit to Japan.[2] While in Tokyo a small delegation of Dewey's former Chinese students came to offer him a visiting professorship for the next academic year in China. Dewey proceeded to Shanghai after his lectures in Japan and had spoken in three cities when he received permission from Columbia University to remain in China for a year.[3]

The armistice ending World War I had been signed victoriously by the Allies in November 1918, but peace terms were still under discussion as Dewey set out across the Pacific in January 1919. His attitude towards lecturing in China was shaped by the immediacy of the war, and Dewey soon became self-conscious of his role as a spokesman for the democratic lessons he saw in the war. He did not want to be taken for a propagandist, he explained in Peking, "but I have just come from the United States at a time when a great World War has wrought greater damage than all the previous wars of history combined; and this has made me sensitive to the serious shortcomings of all antidemocratic systems."[4] At times Dewey saw himself taking part in the completion of a cycle of world cultural exchange going back to the ancient Mid-East. The United States had received the development of that early culture, Dewey noted, and was now transporting it back, in modern democratic form, to its homeland in Asia.[5] This questionable flight into the history of civilization did not preoccupy Dewey, but as he approached China he was quite conscious of the opportunity present for the cultural transmission of democracy, so unlike the violent conflagration recently fought in its name.

Dewey's Initial Reception

John Dewey received a thunderous welcome in China. His personal commitment to reform and progress and his authority as a philosopher of modern education and scientific thinking put him in tune with the interests of his large audiences. Furthermore, in the fall of 1919 a coincidence of history was given a symbolic meaning by some of his followers.

Dewey was informed by his Chinese friends that his sixtieth birthday on October 20 fell that year precisely on the day the rotating lunar calendar indicated as the birth date of Confucius. The fact that both philosophers were touring far from home as lecturers on their sixtieth birthdays was lost on no one. It was fitting that the President of National Peking University should draw out the comparison at the great banquet given Dewey on his birthday. Ts'ai Yuan-p'ei noted that Confucius had actually said some things not so dissimilar from Dewey's pragmatic formulation of experience and truth. "To learn (i.e., from the documents of the ancients) without thinking is a loss; to think without learning is perilous," described Confucius's caution about philosophizing which strayed too far from the practical experience of history.[6] Dewey never tired of insisting that thought must derive from actual experience.

But Ts'ai also stressed the critical differences between Confucius and Dewey, particularly regarding social issues: "Confucius said respect the emperor (*wang*), the learned doctor (*po-shih*) advocates democracy; Confucius said females are a problem to raise, the learned doctor advocates equal rights for men and women; Confucius said transmit not create, the learned doctor advocates creativity."[7] He might have added that the humanistic aims of both thinkers were posed from very different assumptions.

Confucius insisted that "a gentleman is not an implement." Dewey's contribution to the founding of functionalist psychology described the highest faculties of human beings as fundamentally implements for adjusting the behavior of an organism to its environment. So for Dewey human nature was instrumental to survival. Confucius was having his 2470th birthday, and Ts'ai questioned the applicability of his social ideas in twentieth-century China. In that sense celebrating only the sixtieth birthday of Dewey, he said, was actually more poignant, for his teachings were so directly related to the present.

Throughout the following two years of lecturing, the flattering comparisons with Confucius were frequently made in introducing Dewey.[8] There is little evidence of any attention to Dewey's life and works in China prior to the announcement of his visit in early 1919. Chinese scholarly journals published few, if any, articles written about Dewey; and none of Dewey's works existed in Chinese translation before his arrival. By the time of his departure in July 1921, however, there had been at least fifty articles about him and his ideas in journals of every persuasion, and translations began which continued throughout the 1920s. This enthusiastic reception was not because of Dewey's magnetic personality, for his lecture style was notoriously dull. In addition to the democratic ethos surrounding the end of World War I, and the modernity of his message, Dewey's crowds resulted from the active promotion of his former Chinese students.

By March 1919, when it became known that Dewey was going to visit China, even for only a month, announcements of his visit, biographical sketches, pictures, and introductory articles on his thought by his students began appearing in national journals and newspapers.[9] The most eminent of Dewey's former students was Hu Shih who interpreted for Dewey and made arrangements for his speeches and travel during the entire two-year visit. Hu Shih was a doctoral student of Dewey's in philosophy, and along with a second Columbia student, Chiang Meng-lin (Monlin Chiang), he had been the prime mover behind the invitation taken to Dewey in

Japan.[10] Hu had studied at Cornell and Columbia from 1910 to 1917, after which he returned to a position teaching philosophy at the foremost academic center in China, National Peking University. That university and Nanking Teachers' College were joined by the Ministry of Education in sponsoring Dewey's visit, and they requested that Hu give a series of four lectures on pragmatic philosophy before Dewey's arrival. These four were published in several leading Peking journals. By June 1919, Hu Shih had published three other articles on Dewey's philosophy and educational theory which appeared in national journals and major literary supplements.[11]

When the Deweys arose on May Day 1919 to spend their first full day in China, John Dewey was probably unaware of the extensive preparations which were underway for his talks two days later at the Kiangsu Provincial Education Association.[12] As Dewey adjusted to the buzzing commercial center of China, with its international concession full of foreign merchants, diplomats, and missionary organizations, his student Hu Shih on the evening of May 2, 1919 gave a preliminary lecture on pragmatism to a turnaway crowd of over 1000 people.[13]

The next day Dewey appeared before the crowded audience at 3:30 in the afternoon, and rose to the podium accompanied by a tall "returned student" already well known in Shanghai, Chiang Meng-lin. Chiang had spent ten years studying at Berkeley and at Columbia University's Teachers College. In 1917 he returned to China to work at the famous publishing house in Shanghai, the Commercial Press, and soon began to publish a progressive educational journal, *Hsin chiao-yü* ("The New Education"). In announcing Dewey's arrival, that journal had carried several articles introducing Dewey's educational philosophy. The April 1919 issue was, in fact, a special number dedicated entirely to John Dewey's thought.[14] Chiang interpreted Dewey's lectures on May 3 and 4, 1919, and had planned to continue on with the Dewey party to Hangchow and Nanking. Angry demonstrations in Peking on May 4 against the terms of the Treaty of Versailles initiated a student movement that changed his plans. He went directly to Peking to assume the Acting Chancellorship of National Peking University, where he would again welcome Dewey a month later.

Dewey proceeded to Chekiang province, south of neighboring Shanghai, to speak to an audience of 1000 students and teachers.[15] By mid-May he was at Nanking Teachers' College for a series of six lectures. John Dewey's reception in the culturally sophisticated Kiangnan region of central China, like that soon to follow in Peking, was inseparable from the presence of those bright young intellectuals who interpreted his lectures. The charisma of men like Hu Shih gave Dewey's lectures an effect which the near-sexagenarian would probably not otherwise have had with the students. As one of the recorders of Dewey's major series in Peking told the author, Dewey's lectures, like his books in English, were not clear to his Chinese audience—but Hu Shih was an excellent speaker, and his interpreted version was comprehensible to everyone. In Hangchow, a former student from Columbia's Teachers College, Cheng Tsung-hai, was singled out in press coverage for his oratorical talent in interpreting. In Nanking as well, where Dewey returned for the spring and summer of 1920, the interpreter's version of his lectures was re-called by some listeners just as Hu Shih's was in Peking—clearer and more eloquent than the quiet English version by Dewey.[16]

The procedure for interpreting Dewey's lectures into Chinese and recording them for publication in the Chinese press was es-tablished at the opening talks in Shanghai. Dewey typed brief notes of what he planned to say and gave these to his interpreters to study before every lecture. Interpretation was done consecutively, Dewey giving about a paragraph in English, then the interpreter turning this paragraph into Chinese. At times in the Peking lectures Hu Shih would stop interpreting to ask Dewey for clarification on some point, then continue the Chinese version.[17] Recorders who took down the Chinese interpreted version were selected by the Dewey students beforehand, and they often met with Dewey after the talks to clear up their notes. The recorders edited their tran-scriptions of the lectures and submitted them to the interpreter to check for accuracy. Even in the instances in which his English type-script was fairly detailed, Dewey often digressed so much from the typescript that it became no more than reference matter for him. The recorders' corrected notes appearing in the Chinese journals were a relatively accurate version of what Dewey actually said in China.[18]

"Returned Students" from the United States

The importance of United States trained students for Dewey's reception in China extended beyond the amplifying effect they had as interpreters. When he traveled to Nanking Teachers' College in the spring of 1920, Dewey said at the welcoming convocation that he had a special feeling about speaking at that institution because a great many of the faculty had been trained in the United States and many had been his "followers" (*ti-tzu*) at Columbia University.[19] The presence of Dewey's returned students from the United States in the world of education throughout China was one reason behind his warm reception. Dewey's renown at Columbia had drawn some of the best Chinese students in the United States to work with him. The fact that there were so many Chinese students to choose from in the United States at all was a reflection of broader trends in China's modern history. A brief analysis of the Chinese movement to study abroad will help explain the somewhat ambiguous social status and political position occupied by Dewey's promoters in China.

The Chinese movement to study abroad began in large numbers after the Japanese victory over China in 1895. China's defeat underscored the inability of the imperial examination system to provide training adequate to meet the challenge of the modern technology mastered by the West and Japan. The late Ch'ing dynasty reforms abolished the imperial system of recruitment in 1905, and instituted a modern school system for universal education. But many students at the level of higher education had already been attracted to the modern curricula offered in missionary colleges in China, and in colleges abroad. During the first two decades of the century, Chinese graduates returning from abroad composed a new intelligentsia, with the status of having received the most modern and advanced academic training since the scholar-official position of the literati had been formally eliminated.

The very strength that initially drew students to Japan to discover the secret behind victories such as the Japanese triumph over Russian forces in 1905 soon repelled Chinese students as Japan accelerated her expansionist policies in East Asia.[20] In 1910

Japan annexed Korea, and five years later presented the Twenty-One demands to President Yuan Shih-k'ai in China. These demands would have given Japan extensive economic and even administrative control in China; when the public became aware of them in the spring of 1915, national indignation spread throughout the country. Major loans continued to be exacted from the militarist cabinets in Peking, and student protests in Japan led to the departure of Chinese students from Japanese schools in both 1915 and 1918, and a redirection of funding to encourage students to go to Europe and the United States rather than Japan.[21] Anti-Japanese feeling reached a peak with the May Fourth demonstrations of 1919 when it was learned that Japanese claims to former German concessions in Shantung province had been incorporated in the Treaty of Versailles.

These political realities, along with some persuasive cultural diplomacy, increased the attraction of the United States as a training ground for Chinese students abroad. The Boxer remission of 1908 was one such policy of cultural diplomacy. In that year the United States Congress voted to return a major portion of the $24 million indemnity from the Boxer uprising of 1900 that was to be paid off annually by China up to 1940 for educational and cultural purposes. It was recommended that these funds go toward the expenses of Chinese students in the United States, and in 1910 in Peking a two-year preparatory college, Tsinghua (Ch'ing-hua), was established whose graduates had automatic grants to study in the United States. Hu Shih, the most eminent Dewey student, had come to the United States on a Tsinghua fellowship in 1910. From 1909 to 1925 some 1,031 Chinese students were sent to the United States on Tsinghua funds.[22]

By 1915, there was a shift in the movement to study abroad which made the United States the most important recipient country. Among the publicly supported students sent abroad between 1921 and 1925, the United States outpaced Japan and all other countries with 934 students. The closest competitor was Germany with 127, then came France with 89, and England with 29. Japan created fellowships to attract Chinese students but without great success.[23]

This shift was not unnoticed by American government officials in China, and they soon began to recognize the internal benefits these students might have for the increase of United States influence within China.

A cultural policy which met with great success after 1915 was to organize friendship clubs with the encouragement of the United States consulates in major cities within China. In 1915 the American Returned Students' Club of Nanking formed spontaneously with twenty-eight members. The American Returned Students' Association of East China was formed the same year in Shanghai. In Nanking, the energetic American consul, J. Paul Jameson, seized the initiative and worked to combine returned student groups with American residents in a non-discriminatory club with open membership. He quickly saw the possibilities of spreading this idea throughout China and suggested to Washington that a nationwide organization centered in Nanking be established.[24] Writing back to the Secretary of State in February 1917, Consul Jameson reported the successful organization of the Chinese-American Association. "I would call attention," Jameson noted, "to the fact that in other Chinese-American Clubs or Societies, it has been customary for the Americans to assume the leadership and condescend to admit the Chinese to their organizations. This is a bad feature which has been entirely eliminated. . . The association is to be extended throughout the whole of China with local organizations in all the large cities."[25] Consul Jameson enlisted the interest of eminent Chinese and could claim that "practically all the Chinese officials in Nanking" were charter members of the Association.

Jameson took his successful idea to Peking and spoke with the American Minister, Paul Reinsch. Reinsch endorsed the idea and said he would set up a similar organization in Peking. Further, Jameson wrote Washington, "The Minister authorized me to inform the Consuls General at Canton, Tientsin, and Hankow of the details of the proposed organization and to suggest that local organizations in each of these places be formed which would affiliate with Nanking and Peking to form a general association for the whole of

China."[26] Such an organization began forming in Canton just one month after Jameson met with Reinsch.[27]

The number of United States citizens in China grew rapidly during the same years that returned students came home in large numbers. The American population of Shanghai increased from 1,200 in 1914 to 3,000 in 1920.[28] There were several clubs for Americans in that city, including a women's club with 500 members in 1920. For the most exclusive, there was even a women's club for college graduates with 100 members. Among the ten Chinese women who were admitted to this club was its vice-chairperson, the future Madame Chiang Kai-shek, Miss Mayling Soong (Sung Mei-ling).[29]

The increased presence of United States residents in China, and particularly the growing importance of students returning from the United States, was observed anxiously by countries who already had vested interests in China. In January 1918 there were newspaper attacks against the President of Tsinghua College, Y. T. Tsur (Chou I-ch'ün), and rumors that the Ministry of Foreign Affairs was trying to replace him with the Japanese-educated Fan Yuan-lien. The American Minister in Peking wrote Washington that there was some fear, "that the appointment will introduce a political element incompatible with efficiency and that the Japanese who are extremely jealous of American educational influence in China would use their influence over Fan to the disadvantage of the college."[30] Secretary of State Lansing replied from Washington that a similar attempt had been resisted a few years before, so Minister Reinsch in Peking vigorously opposed the move. The result was a compromise; Chang Yu-chuan, who had been educated both in Japan and in the United States, was appointed as the new president.[31]

Following World War I, France sent a special mission, headed by the former Prime Minister, Paul Painlevé, to promote Franco-Chinese relations. His mission was established to give requested advice on university and railroad reorganization, and it succeeded in establishing academic ties through cultural institutes to be

formed in the two countries.[32] Painlevé's comments in Japan before
arriving in China reveal the broader aims of his visit:

> The young Chinese republicans are turning with sympathy
> toward the older sister republics, France and America. We
> know the influence and the attraction which Anglo-Saxon
> America exercises upon the imaginations of the Chinese. . .
> The peace of the world has nothing to gain from an American-
> ized or an Anglicized China. Without in any way meaning to
> offend our friends or allies, we feel that to the French belongs
> the moral obligation to encourage and develop the intellectual,
> scientific and technical relations which exist already between
> China and France.[33]

England as well was awakened to its relative loss of influence
in China. In the London paper, *The Daily Mail*, of June 17, 1921,
an article appeared from a correspondent who had just attended
Tsinghua College's tenth anniversary celebration in China. He
eloquently described the facilities and quality of the college, then
warned, "But is this China, or is it China Americanized?" He noted
that the 500 students in the school would later return from America
as leaders in China, while 500 more were still going through the
school, and continued, "Educated under the American system,
constantly reminded of the happy associations of their school days
through the influential alumni organization, aware that they owe
their scholarships to American justice, and saturated with American
sentiment by five to eight years' residence in the country, they
will look to the United States solely for cooperation in the troublous years to come."[34] The correspondent then emphasized, "*Why
should we not share an influence that we formerly monopolized
and that is now slipping away from us?*" He concluded that
England should return the Boxer funds as America had. *The Daily
Mail* endorsed his views in an editorial of the same issue, noting
that there were then 200 Chinese students in England while there
were 2,000 in the United States.[35]

The fact that many of the United States returned students
Dewey met had been at Columbia accurately reflected the tendency

of large numbers of Chinese students in the United States to gravitate toward that university. In 1909, when the influx of Chinese students to the United States was just picking up, there were 24 Chinese students at Columbia. This number grew to about 75 in 1916, and nearly 100 in 1918. In 1920 the Columbia Chinese Students' Club proudly claimed in the pages of *The Chinese Students' Monthly* that it led all other institutions with an enrollment of 123 Chinese students.[36] The *Monthly* began publication in 1905 in New York as a voice of the growing numbers of Chinese students in the United States, and by 1910 the national Chinese Students' Alliance in the United States had formed around it. The Columbia club continuously played a prominent role in the editorship of the *Monthly*. If attendance is calculated over the entire 100-year period after the first Chinese student graduated from an American institution in 1854, Columbia and its graduate school of education, Teachers College, led all other colleges and universities in Chinese graduates.[37]

Education and political science were the most popular majors among the Chinese students at Columbia. Many earned master's degrees from the graduate faculties, or diplomas and certificates from Teachers College. Some 208 Ph.D.'s were awarded to Chinese students up to 1954.[38] Teachers College conferred its first doctorate on a Chinese student in 1914 and continued to confer an average of one doctorate a year on a Chinese candidate throughout the 1920s. As Columbia's reputation grew in China, because degree-holders took influential positions at home, Chinese educators with experience as school principals and deans of normal schools began to appear at Columbia. A Chinese Education Club was started, whose activities gave members a direct link to pressing educational issues in China.[39] The club was subsidized by a foundation in China which later joined in sponsoring Dewey's visit, the Shang-chih hsueh-hui (The Aspiration Society). Its grants allowed the club to acquire books from China, host speakers from the Ministry of Education and other educational leaders who happened to be in the United States, and even to plan a publication series on the topics discussed at their meetings. Such topics included compulsory education in Kiangsu province, women's education, school hygiene, and vocational education.[40]

Dewey's former association with these students of education in a personal teacher-student relationship at Columbia reappeared when he met them again in China. Dewey had begun teaching courses at Teachers College during the 1904-1905 academic year when he arrived at Columbia, which coincidentally was the first year a Chinese student enrolled at Teachers College. The first two Doctorates of Education from that institution to Chinese were awarded to men who favored Dewey's educational philosophy the rest of their distinguished professional careers. The first was P. W. Kuo (Ed.D., 1914), who was president of the first Nanking Returned Students' Club and founded Nanking Teachers' College, and the second, Chiang Meng-lin (Ed.D., 1917), was Dewey's first interpreter in China and later Chancellor of Peking University.[41] The proportion of United States returned students who each year went into university teaching once back in China was well over one-third. Others went into government service or business and professional areas. They had generally been from families with good financial backgrounds and returned most commonly to the urban areas of the coastal provinces from which they had come.[42] When Dewey met them in academic centers he must have had the feeling that the educational influence of the United States was indeed taking hold in Chinese institutions. The problem for the Chinese intellectuals themselves, however, was that the transitional phase of early "Republican" government left them with an ambiguous social role. They were quite unlike the educated elite of pre-1905 China because they no longer were appointed to positions of power as officials. This would have been a satisfactory situation had a pluralistic democracy developed after the 1911 Revolution, so they could take their place as professional educators and critics as Dewey was able to do in the United States.

But in reality the parliament was a farce, and feuding factions of militarists rotated in and out of Peking, controlled only by opponents with superior force. These arbitrary and autocratic conditions characterized Chinese politics from the collapse of President

Yuan Shih-k'ai's attempt at imperial restoration in 1916 until
1926 when the Northern Expedition began the reunification of
China. In this time period John Dewey's followers were more like
the disciples of Confucius during the Warring States period than
they would have liked to believe. Confucius was a man out of office
and without power when he lectured to the warlords of the feuding kingdoms that composed the China of 500 B.C. He never did
succeed in influencing the politics of China in his own lifetime.
This unflattering part of the comparison was unfortunately valid
when applied to the floating intelligentsia of liberals who were
attracted to Dewey's ideas. They, as well, lacked a base of political
power, even though they enjoyed a certain social prestige; and
their vision of modern science and democracy for China was not
the vocabulary understood by militarists.

The May Fourth Movement and Dewey's Reception

The May Fourth demonstrations of 1919 were a shock to the
political and intellectual establishment of China during the first
year of Dewey's visit. Students had suddenly become a political
force, inciting merchants and workers to join in their nationalistic
attack on Japanese imperialism. When Dewey went north to Peking
at the beginning of June 1919, the city was full of commotion.
Since the incident on May 4, when protesting students had attacked
and burned the home of a pro-Japanese government official, police
had been trying to quell the student demonstrators. But as government pressure grew, protest grew, and student unions as well as
teachers' unions rapidly organized throughout China.[43] A general
strike had been called by Peking students in May, and in June
martial law was declared, and the mass arrest of students began.[44]
The law school of National Peking University was used as a jail
because police could not otherwise find room for the large number
of students arrested.

Dewey observed all of this with more than passing interest.
He was particularly struck by the fact that the "jailed" students
refused to leave the law school prison when police were withdrawn

unless they had an official apology from the government—which they received in early June.[45] The student-led protest also forced the resignation of three government officials whom the students had branded as pro-Japanese traitors. The upheaval became so widespread that it prevented the government from signing the Versailles Treaty which awarded German rights in Shantung to Japan. These political events were particularly significant because the students, utilizing the aroused public, had by-passed the corrupt entanglement of autocratic politics to achieve some political results.[46] They formed a new source of hope for some because they interrupted, at least temporarily, the continuous cycles of militaristic factions and power struggles dominating the political life of the country.

By June 1919, almost 200 new periodicals had mushroomed in the coastal provinces of Kiangsu and Chekiang alone as part of the nationalistic student movement.[47] During Dewey's years in China these popular journals reprinted his lectures and disseminated them into practically every academic center in China. New literary supplements added to the major newspapers were among the most far-reaching and effective of the new publications. Newspapers were often the first to publish Dewey's speeches, and other periodicals reprinted these texts. *Chueh-wu* (Awakening) was added as a supplement to the Shanghai newspaper *Min-kuo jih-pao* (Republic daily) in June 1919 to join the supplements of *Shih-shih hsin-pao* ("The China Times") of Shanghai, and *Ch'en pao* (Morning post) in Peking as the third major supplement in the country.[48] *Chueh-wu* and *Hsueh-teng* (Academic lamp), the other major Shanghai supplement, covered all Dewey's central China lectures and most that were given in Peking. The *Ch'en pao fu-k'an* (Morning post supplement) in Peking printed nearly all of Dewey's lectures in North China.[49]

Most of these journals carried Dewey's lectures because his opportune presence as a visiting professor made his ideas readily available to enter the stream of new thought introduced from abroad. The fervor of new ideas characterized the May Fourth period (1915-1924) with a sort of *esprit critique* reminiscent of

the French Enlightenment.[50] The surge of new publications and
the introduction of new ideas did not subside until about 1922.
Some magazines such as the influential *Hsin chiao-yü* ("The New
Education"), which Chiang Meng-lin, who invited Dewey to China,
had founded in February 1919, owed a direct debt to Dewey's
ideas. As Chiang put it in his autobiography, his journal advocated
"much that John Dewey stands for in his *Democracy and Education.*"[51] At Peking Teachers' College, *P'ing-min chiao-yü* ("Democracy and Education") was a journal founded in October 1919
specifically under Dewey's inspiration.[52] There was even a journal
of Neo-Confucian thought in Wenchow, Chekiang province, which
was dedicated to applying Dewey's pragmatism to the modernization of Confucian scholarship.[53] Whether specifically applying
Dewey's ideas to fields of scholarship, as these three journals did,
or simply printing Dewey's many lectures in China, these new
journals widely disseminated his ideas, as shown in the appendix
table of the published sources of his lectures.

While John Dewey definitely had a teacher-student relationship with his former students in China, there was one subject in
which he was the learner and they the tutors. The subject was China
itself. Dewey had, after all, originally intended to visit East Asia
only as a tourist. He was unfamiliar with China's history and
thought, and made no pretense to any mastery of China's current
affairs.[54] Yet his frequent articles on Chinese politics sent to *The
New Republic* and *Asia* magazine demonstrated that a rapid learning experience was going on, for which his Chinese associates de-
serve much of the credit.[55] Dewey was very close to Hu Shih and
Chiang Meng-lin during his two-year visit. Hu Shih not only made
all the arrangements for Dewey's lectures and trips, with Chiang's
help, but was with Dewey almost daily to discuss and interpret his
major series of Peking lectures.[56] Even by the time of his final
article sent to the United States, Dewey quipped that his debt to
"a close Chinese friend" for the contents of his comments on
Chinese society and politics was so extensive that it could make
him liable for intellectual theft.[57]

The debt Dewey owed his colleagues for the information he

reported back to the United States is particularly important to recognize. Dewey's description of the May Fourth upheaval, which has been used by scholars in the West as an important source for the events he viewed and their significance,[58] is basically a description of how Hu Shih and a particular faction of liberal intellectuals wanted the May Fourth movement to be. The intensely nationalistic upheaval that disseminated Dewey's works throughout China actually added to the difficulty his followers had applying their ideas, because it was different in character from the expansion of the cultural reform efforts Dewey described.

After his first three weeks in Peking, at the height of the student demonstrations, Dewey wrote an optimistic article to *The New Republic* concerning the new elements in Chinese politics. The militarist government had lost face in freeing and apologizing to the students it had imprisoned. Dewey was undoubtedly reflecting the hopes of Hu Shih and other returned students when he wrote, "It would be highly surprising if a new constitutionalist movement were not set going. The combination of students and merchants that has proved so effective will hardly be allowed to become a mere memory."[59] But Dewey soon privately admitted his disappointed realization that the liberal element did not appear strong enough to have any practical effect on politics.[60] Despite another victory on June 28, 1919, when the Chinese delegation in Paris refused to sign the Versailles Treaty, Dewey finally had to apologize to his *New Republic* readers for having anticipated substantial political changes when he first wrote of the student revolt.[61] By the end of July, the strikes of the students, workers, and merchants had all ended. No constitutional movement had developed, and no lasting effect on the structure of China's militaristic politics was evident. Dewey had reported the hopes of those around him, upon whom he was dependent for information on Chinese politics; but those hopes represented only one reform faction's interpretation of events.

In November 1919, when Dewey acknowledged that no popular political movement among the people had developed, he turned from his disappointment to a positive analysis of a deeper, hidden meaning in the student movement. In so doing, Dewey again reported the views of a certain cultural faction of reformers who claimed that the nationalist upheaval had represented a fundamentally non-political reform alternative for China, and was basically an intellectual awakening.[62] Dewey wrote: "A universal feeling operates that the comparative failure of the Revolution [of 1911] is due to the fact that political change far outran intellectual and moral preparation; that political revolution was formal and external; that an intellectual revolution is required before the nominal governmental revolution can be cashed in. . ."[63] Rather than a "universal feeling," Dewey was simply describing, almost verbatim, the contemporaneous views Hu Shih was publishing in Chinese.[64] The intellectuals Dewey was speaking for sought to salvage as much reform sentiment as possible from the national reaction to the Shantung question. But they did not want more political chaos, and they misrepresented the national crisis—which was highly politicizing—as basically an extension of their cultural reform efforts. Their interpretation claimed that the confrontation politics of the spring and early summer had not been political except in outward expression. Dewey wrote that the very spontaneity of the outbreak of student activism proved its deep, inevitable nature, "It was the manifestation of a new consciousness, an intellectual awakening in the young men and young women who through their schooling had been aroused to the necessity of a new order of belief, a new method of thinking. The movement is secure no matter how much its outward forms may alter or crumble."[65] This interpretation was fully consonant with the aims of those intellectuals who had dedicated themselves to cultural reform after 1917. Hu Shih and Chiang Meng-lin were leaders in this effort, and were fighting to perpetuate the priority accorded to cultural over political reform. Dewey was a good student in reporting what they said.

The cases of two other prominent leaders who argued for non-political reform after 1917 are instructive for they did so as much out of necessity as conviction. Both Ch'en Tu-hsiu, who founded *Hsin ch'ing-nien* (New youth) magazine, and Ts'ai Yuan-p'ei, the progressive Chancellor of National Peking University, had independent revolutionary experience as radical intellectuals in the publishing underground of Shanghai before 1911. They both had been frustrated in seeking changes in the corrupt and autocratic political structure of the opening years of the Republic, and had by 1913 become political fugitives from the monarchist-inclined government of Yuan Shih-k'ai. In 1917 they joined forces in Peking University to continue their battle for democratic principles. Warlord politics in Peking, however, allowed little room, even after Yuan's death, for the Kuomintang faction of 1911 revolutionaries.[66] Repressive publication laws led Ch'en to adopt an editorial policy dedicating his magazine against the active participation of intellectuals in politics under existing political conditions. As Dean of the Faculty of Letters after 1917, he worked with Ts'ai to be sure the prestigious National Peking University did not replace the old examination system as a recruitment mechanism for government officials. University policy actively discouraged students from participation in politics.[67]

Hu Shih had returned to China in 1917, and, like many other returned students, he viewed the floundering Republic for the first time with his own eyes years after having read of the Revolution. Hu agreed enthusiastically with *New Youth's* reform priority of building a new intellectual and cultural base before more political change was attempted, but Hu's rationale was grounded in his own definition of democratic politics, and had little to do with expediency.[68] He joined the staff of Ch'en's magazine, *New Youth.* As he reminisced years later, "I had suggested to my colleagues that this cultural movement, which was vaguely called a Chinese Renaissance, should essentially confine itself to the non-political sphere, should deliberately and consciously aim at the establishment of a non-political foundation for a new China; and in order to achieve this non-political basis for a new China, we should devote ourselves to the fundamental problems which we then regarded as predominantly intellectual, cultural, and educational. So I deliberately said that we should avoid politics for twenty years—*Erh-shih nien pu t'an cheng-chih; er-shih nien pu kan cheng-chih* (No political discussion for twenty years; no political activity for twenty years)."[69]

The joint cultural reform efforts of Ch'en and Hu had some success from 1917 to 1919. This was particularly true in their promotion of the use of the commonly spoken Chinese language instead of the classical language. This vernacular language movement—called the Paihua movement—had several reform aims. Its outcome was expected to unify China linguistically, establishing the Peking dialect as a national dialect to be taught in all provincial schools and providing a common base for national literacy. The democratic reform of social attitudes and thought patterns was a more subtle but no less important aim of language reform. Hu and Ch'en were opposed by conservatives who were sensitive to the implied threat to Confucian ethics if the literary revolution gained support.[70]

Other reformers, and other returned students, had elected not to give up the political battle and work only for cultural reforms. The editor of the magazine for which Ch'en Tu-hsiu worked briefly in Japan, before it was suppressed, was such a man. Chang Shih-chao, after working actively from Japan for Yuan's downfall, revived his suppressed magazine back in China as a daily newspaper in 1917 and rallied other more activist students returning from Japan to work with him. One was a man who later engaged Hu Shih in vigorous debate over political versus cultural reform priorities, Li Ta-chao. The editor Chang Shih-chao's attitude toward the literary revolution had been expressed in an exchange in his first journal in 1915. Hu Shih later noted that Chang had written, in opposition to the view Hu was to take, that "all social reforms must presuppose a certain level of political stability and oderliness [sic], and the promotion of a new literature cannot be an exception."[71]

Chang's political attacks did provoke repression. His daily newspaper was suppressed in 1917, the same year it began, by militarist authorities in Peking. Writers such as Li Ta-chao then joined the cultural reform group at National Peking University with Hu Shih and Ch'en. But this was a temporary retreat for Li and others, who were quick to perceive that the May Fourth demonstrations were a massively-supported demand for redress of grievances by direct political confrontation.[72] To the students around Li, as to so many who had taken an active part in the 1919 demonstrations, there was a lesson in the May Fourth Incident which was not forgotten throughout the 1920s. Demonstrations, boycotts, and strikes were shown to be *political* weapons which brought some results against the depredations of the militarists in power.

The cultural reformers, who composed the core group of Dewey sponsors, had rejected political confrontation as a tactic, and therefore found May Fourth activism unfortunate. Some of the New Culture movement intellectuals did not even mention the demonstrations in their writings.[73] John Dewey was delivering his opening lectures on the connection between democracy and education in Shanghai on May 4, 1919, and his most important followers were in his audience, missing the reaction in Peking altogether. Other returned students from Europe and the United States met separately from the rowdy masses of demonstrating students in the Peking "club house" of the European and American Returned Students' Club. They drafted telegrams of protest to the Big Four Powers in Paris as well as to the Chinese delegation. The "parade" they had announced for May 7, 1919, to present petitions from the returned students to the British, French, and Italian legations in Peking, was canceled because of the May Fourth demonstrations three days before and in order to "avoid any untoward incident." Instead, a "plain business-like meeting," which was conducted as a model for the country, was held, and twelve delegates, eight men and four women, were elected to "proceed by motorcar" (there were not many automobiles in all of Peking) with the petitions to deliver to the respective legations.[74] Dewey's sponsors among China's intellectuals never did endorse the activism of the May Fourth demonstrations; but, since the importance of the demonstrations was unavoidable, they did their best to use the aroused emotions to promote their program of cultural reform.

Throughout his visit, John Dewey reported back to the United States the interpretation of the May Fourth movement held by the cultural reformers. In his final article before leaving China he underscored the role of what came to be called the New Culture movement in Chinese intellectual circles. He noted that things were even more encouraging at the end of his visit because many students were pledged to non-official careers, confirming the anti-political bias of the movement.[75] Dewey's description of events in China for his American readers continued: "The two things that stand out today as active and dominant features of the situation are the need of reform in culture as antecedent of other reforms, and a tendency for leadership to revert to those who are distinctly Chinese in their attitude, as over against those who would introduce and copy foreign methods, whether from the West or from Japan."[76] This "native" leadership Dewey described as being the cultural reform faction. Their program was more consonant with tradition than those who copied materialistically from the West, because the native faction recognized the supremacy of intellectual and moral factors in guiding reform. Dewey even suggested that they retained a key notion from Confucianism, namely, "belief in the primacy of ideas, of knowledge, and in the influence of education to spread these ideas."[77] With regard to politics, Dewey said the movement was "stirred by democratic ideals, and is starting out with the premise that democracy must be realized in education and in industry before it can be realized politically."[78] Dewey's article was so competent a statement of the cultural reform position that his comments appeared in a Chinese translation the same month they were published in English.[79] Perhaps it was no wonder these comments on a Chinese social movement were translated, for it was at the beginning of this article that Dewey had admitted his debt for information about China to "a close Chinese friend." The imprimatur of Dewey's name was apparently assumed to make a difference to a reader of the Chinese article—accounting for his informant's words being turned back into Chinese by way of Dewey. Dewey's "description" to the West became advice to the East, for in actuality he was representing the wishful thinking of Hu Shih's reform group that needed much support.

The May Fourth movement had been very exciting to Dewey, and was undoubtedly one reason he and his wife accepted the invitation from National Peking University to stay for a second year.[80] The proliferation of journals had indeed spread his lectures to a wide audience in China, and his proponents succeeded in placing his thought at the crest of the wave of Western ideas within the New Culture movement. As *Millard's Review*, an American journal in Shanghai, wrote after his first year in China:

> Professor Dewey, by means of his lectures which are interpreted as they are given, has reached thousands of Chinese. These lectures are translated into Chinese and are published in the leading magazines and newspapers of the country. These printed lectures are carefully studied by many. It may be guessed that by means of the spoken and the written, or printed, word Professor Dewey has said his say to several hundred thousand Chinese.[81]

It remained to be seen, however, whether or not the May Fourth upheaval had perhaps been a mixed blessing for the reception of Dewey's ideas in China. Student activism had not been caused by, nor directed at, cultural reform. The spheres of cultural reform activity such as education were to find themselves politicized from within, and increasingly faced with more repressive governmental reaction from without.

The Lecture Trail and the Dissemination of Dewey's Works

When the Deweys sailed from Tientsin to Japan and returned to the United States in July 1921 they had been in China for a total of two years and two months. In that time John Dewey had addressed Chinese audiences from some seventy-eight different lecture forums, and several of these were for series of between fifteen and twenty lectures. Not only had major Chinese journals and literary supplements throughout the country reprinted the Chinese versions of these lectures; five book editions collecting different series were published. Nearly 100,000 copies of his principal series of lectures in Peking—a 500-page book—were in circulation throughout China in 1921.[82] Dewey lectured in the capitals of seven coastal provinces, as well as in six interior provinces.

The book edition of Dewey's Peking lectures included the lecture courses he gave at National Peking University, two of which were translated back into English from the Chinese texts for the first time in 1973: "Social and Political Philosophy," and "The Philosophy of Education."[83] He also gave a logic course on "Types of Thinking." Fifteen lectures on ethics, and lectures on James, Bergson, and Russell, complete this first volume. The other major Chinese book edition contained Dewey's three principal series of lectures at Nanking Teachers' College in the spring and summer of 1920. These *Three Major Lectures* were also published individually, and reprinted throughout the 1920s for use as classroom texts. "Experimental logic" was one of these three major series and had its fifth printing as a separate publication in 1923. In 1924 "The History of Philosophy" had its fourth independent edition, and in 1925 the final Nanking series, a technical treatment for professional educators of "The Philosophy of Education," had its fifth edition.[84] Meanwhile in Peking the 500-page *Five Major Lectures* had reached its sixteenth and probably final edition in 1924.

While centered at Peking and Nanking as lecture bases, Dewey made regular short trips into nearby provinces to lecture. During their first winter in Peking, the Deweys, recently joined by their daughter Lucy who had just finished a B.A. at Barnard College, traveled to the Northeastern Region (Manchuria), and soon after to Shansi, west of Peking.[85] In Shansi the Deweys were received by Governor Yen Hsi-shan, and watched "the model Governor" kowtow to Confucius in a midnight ceremony,[86] as the birthday of Confucius was approaching. Dewey himself lectured on October 10, the anniversary of the Revolution of 1911 founding the Republic of China. He spoke at Shansi University in Taiyuan, and soon afterward spoke to the major convocation of educators who opened the fifth annual convention of the National Federation of Education Associations (Ch'üan-kuo chiao-yü hui lien-ho hui) in Shansi. This was an important convention. Its resolutions owed a discern-

ible debt to the United States system of education.[87] Dewey then
returned to Peking for his sixtieth birthday celebration.

In the spring of the first academic year Dewey was in Nanking,
he began to take lecture trips to nearby towns in central China.
In June 1920 he received permission from Columbia for a second
leave of absence, and, before he returned to Peking in the fall, he
traveled for six weeks in the lower Yangtse valley.[88] Liu Po-ming,
a professor at Nanking Teachers' College, interpreted for Dewey
on most of these trips. He spoke in Yangchow, Shanghai, Hangchow, Nantung, Suchow, Wusih, and Soochow.[89] Much of his time
was spent at Nanking Teachers' College (Nankao) where a summer
school was in session. Nanking Teachers' College was the first
college in China to establish a summer school, and in 1920 there
were special institutes and expositions designed to give instruction
to both farmers and school teachers. The 1920 summer session at
Nankao was also a landmark because for the first time women
students were admitted on an equal basis with men. There were
eighty-six women students present, and it was perhaps appropriate
that Mrs. Dewey, whose occasional talks in China were predominantly on women's education and the feminist movement, was
made an Honorary Dean of Women.[90]

Alice Chipman Dewey often spoke to women's colleges and
groups when she was not waiting on the stage through the long
interpretation of her husband's speeches. In her talks she referred
to her own experience in the feminist movement in the United
States and exhorted her audiences to promote women's education.[91]
On one occasion in Hunan province where the Deweys were received at a dinner party by the warlord "governor" T'an Yen-k'ai,
Mrs. Dewey seized the opportunity of the brief after-dinner speeches
to instruct the governor that his province must adopt coeducation.
T'an replied, after a moment of shock, that he would seriously
consider the matter but that he feared the time had not come for
that in Hunan.[92] Unbeknownst to T'an, in that very month the
young Mao Tse-tung was organizing the first group of Communists
in T'an's capital city of Changsha.[93]

At the banquet given by T'an, John Dewey first met the

eminent British philosopher Bertrand Russell.[94] Russell had landed
in Shanghai a few weeks before, responding to an invitation by
the Chiang-hsueh she (Chinese Lecture Association) to spend a
year in China. He remained an acquaintance of Dewey's until they
both departed in July 1921.[95] Russell later collapsed with pneu-
monia during his stay and was so critically ill that his obituary
was printed in a British paper. Russell's lectures initially appealed
to a more radical element in Chinese politics than did Dewey's.
Many were frustrated, however, when Russell insisted upon the
value of China's great tradition of pacifist thought and praised such
men as Lao Tzu.[96]

Dewey's traveling and lecturing in China were extended to
the southernmost provinces for the first time in the spring of 1921.
From Shanghai the Deweys traveled by boat to Foochow, Amoy,
and Canton, lecturing in each.[97] Dewey's arrival in Canton happened again to coincide with significant events. Sun Yat-sen was
inaugurated as President of the Southern Government in the first
week of May 1921. The entire week was full of celebrations, including anniversary commemorations of the seventy-two martyrs
of 1911 on May 2, and then of the May Fourth Incident of 1919
two days later.[98] Dewey had met Sun Yat-sen during his first two
weeks in China. The two men thought highly of each other and
found a mutual interest in discussing philosophy.[99] Sun was writing
a book designed to stir the Chinese people into revolutionary
action, and he was interested in attacking what he called the over-
practical mentality traditional in China which made people see only
the difficulties of political change. Sun and Dewey agreed upon the
central role of human activity in the relationship between knowledge and action. In his lectures Dewey referred to Sun's position,
and Sun used Dewey for support in his book, *Hsin-li chien she*
(On psychological reconstruction). Their philosophic similarity
was really slight, but it was a credit to the activist Sun that he
engaged Dewey in arguments that made Dewey consider Sun a
philosopher.[100]

Dewey's popularity on his lecture trips far from Peking seems
to have continued to attract audiences as large as those that

originally greeted him in Shanghai and Hangchow. A month before
Dewey left China an article in the New York *Chinese Students'
Monthly* described some of the fervor surrounding his visit:

> Mr. Dewey's career in China is one of singular success. From
> the time of his arrival to the present, continual ovation
> follows his footprints. Bankers and editors frequent his resi-
> dences; teachers and students flock to his classrooms. Clubs
> compete to entertain him, to hear him speak; newspapers
> vie with each other in translating his latest utterances. His
> speeches and lectures are eagerly read, his biography has been
> elaborately written. The serious-minded comment on his
> philosophy; the light-hearted remember his name.[101]

Dewey became a fad; he was sought after in every province he
visited. In academic centers he was a quite serious fad, for many
intellectuals closely associated his thought with the very definition
of modernity.

Translations were one confirmation of this serious interest.
Chapters of Dewey's classic *Democracy and Education* began appearing in two different translations in 1920.[102] One scholar, Tsou
En-jun (Tsou T'ao-fen), published his full translation as a book in
1929. *Schools of Tomorrow* also appeared serially in periodicals
for several years after 1919. One translation appeared regularly in
the *Bulletin of the Ministry of Education* until it was completed
in October 1922. Another complete translation appeared serially
in the supplement of a major Shanghai newspaper in the fall of
1921. A book edition was published by Chu Ching-nung and P'an
Tzu-nien by the Commercial Press in 1923.[103]

As the dates of publication of many translations are not on
the volumes, it is difficult to determine how many existing translations came out while he was in China. Two other books definitely
translated in the 1920s were *How We Think* and *The Child and the
Curriculum*. The first was published in 1921 by Liu Po-ming, the
professor at Nanking Teachers' College who had interpreted for
Dewey throughout his tours in southern Kiangsu province.[104]

The Child and the Curriculum was translated by Dewey's former student and his interpreter in Hangchow, Cheng Tsung-hai. Cheng's translation was in its eighth printing in 1930.[105]

At the peak of Dewey's popularity in 1919 there were actually students who followed Dewey from city to city to hear his lectures. Professor Hsu K'o-shih, later of the Philosophy Department of National Taiwan University, belonged to such a group of "disciples" who regarded Dewey as a sort of modern-day sage, or saint, and followed him from Peking to Nanking and Shanghai.[106] They followed Dewey because he seemed to be a source of explanation for the modernity of the West and its trends in the future. In particular Mr. Hsu commented to the author that he was fascinated by Dewey's attention to the methods of attaining knowledge and truth, which contrasted with the assumptions of the Chinese classics. The five stages of thinking and the critical method described in Dewey's *How We Think* posed an alternative to the notion that fixed principles of truth lay in the accumulated experience of great men. It was this attention to process (*kuo-ch'eng*) in the methods of attaining knowledge that appeared to some intellectuals such as Hsu to hold the secret to understanding the modern West. Such ideas gave Dewey the aura of a sage. His name, Tu-wei in Chinese, incorporated a character *wei* (awe-inspiring) which some observers felt accurately described the atmosphere in his audiences.[107]

The facts of the enthusiastic response to John Dewey during his two years of lecturing are indisputable. The reception of this unassuming visitor with the droopy mustache as a Yankee Confucius must be attributed in large part to the context of World War I surrounding his visit. Viewed from the wartime ideals stated by the victorious Allies, the United States remained the most undamaged model of a strong, vibrant, democratic society in the world. John Dewey could be seen as the philosopher of the values and institutions which underlay the victory over autocracy. Within this context, the May Fourth student demonstrations, which stirred political consciousness throughout China, happened to occur at a time that enabled Dewey's message to catch the crest of a wave disseminating new ideas throughout China.

With these favorable conditions for Dewey's reception were mixed opposing tendencies and some marked weaknesses. The provisions of the Versailles Treaty caused an adverse reaction from intellectuals around the world, and brought charges of "might over right" in response to what appeared to be a punitive and self-serving victors' peace. Dewey's *New Republic* colleagues felt this disillusionment, as did many intellectuals in China. Pacifists in the United States attacked the pragmatic editors, as well as John Dewey, for justifying Wilson's intervention in the war.[108]

A more careful look at the May Fourth movement reveals that the swell of publishing activity which carried Dewey's works throughout China also contained the flood waters of political activism which soon battered the New Culture movement. Dewey's strongest advocates had accepted a priority for cultural reform that conflicted with the newly political atmosphere. They were led by a competent coterie of returned students from the United States. This group of reform-minded young intellectuals had, however, no effective power base in their roles as the new intelligentsia of the early Republic. The battle shaped up between their reform strategy and the militarists. As in the age of Confucius, the problem was how to make oneself heard.

Chapter II

JOHN DEWEY'S LECTURES IN CHINA

The corpus of Dewey's two years of lectures in China would
fill three volumes. These works represent a synthesis of much of
Dewey's writing, and include a few topics that do not appear at
any length in his previous work. There is an obvious concern with
his audience in the text of the lectures. At times Dewey goes to
great pains to fill in the historical context of his theme; and he
occasionally exaggerates and oversimplifies when contrasting
schools of thought to bring out his points. John Dewey's audiences
were, on the average, undergraduates with little background in
European thought. Dewey occasionally allowed himself to reflect
on the nature of Western society as a whole and its presuppositions.
Given the some seventy-eight lecture topics on which Dewey spoke
in all parts of China, it is remarkable that the collected body of
lectures is so self-consistent and interrelated. Three unifying themes
appear: modern science, democracy, and education. The close relationship among the three constitutes the message within Dewey's
lectures in China.

The Experimental Method and Philosophy
    Perhaps the most characteristic aspect of Dewey's lectures in
China was his insistence that the fields of philosophy, education,
and political theory incorporate modern science. He meant in
particular the methodological importance of testing hypotheses
with verifying evidence, and the implications of the Darwinian
theory of evolution. Dewey shared some views about history with
his colleague at Columbia, James Harvey Robinson, and stressed
the methodological importance of the scientific breakthroughs
made in Europe by the seventeenth century. Citing Francis Bacon,
Dewey defined the scientific method as basically the experimental
method, which required that a plan or hypothesis be the first
step made to give direction to experimentation. If the predictions

from that hypothesis were not verified by occurrences of natural
phenomena, then a new hypothesis would be made and predictions
tried.[1] The revolutionary significance of the advent of this simple
scientific method, Dewey explained, was that aristocratic claims
to esoteric knowledge, such as knowledge based on the command of
Greek and Latin classics, were gradually displaced by the universally
available scientific method of learning. Education could consequently
be more readily available to the common people, who might then
assume a larger role in society. The democratizing of society was
thereby linked by Dewey directly to the scientific revolution. His
audiences in China were introduced to democracy and the philosophy of experimentalism in the same breath, with both portrayed
as related developments in the history of Western thought.[2]

Dewey did not lecture directly on the philosophic "school"
of pragmatism. Instead he documented the re-definition of terms
which had been required historically when the scientific method
of learning was applied to traditional philosophic questions and
categories of analysis. Dewey noted that the influence of the
scientific method on philosophy and psychology did not become
wholehearted until the addition of the Darwinian theory of evolution in the mid-nineteenth century. Darwinism made the scientific
method directly relevant to psychology and philosophy by showing
that *homo sapiens* as a species was, after all, part of the animal
kingdom, and behaviorally was probably quite similar to other
animals. In Dewey's view, Darwinism contributed to such long-
standing philosophic controversies as the role that sense perception
—and experience more broadly—played in the acquisition of knowledge. Darwin demonstrated, said Dewey, that the rationalist and
empiricist schools of epistemology were both wrong in assuming
that the sense organs were passive recipients of sense data. Sense
organs, Darwin said, were instruments in the service of a living
organism, not in the service of obtaining abstract knowledge. Even
philosophical empiricism, which emphasized experience, had restricted the idea of experience to perception. Darwin showed that
sense organs, like wings or hands, are active instruments an organism needs in order to respond to its environment. They relate

functionally to the human organism and are not in the service of
any supposed faculties of thinking. This dynamic view of the
theory of evolution was joined, Dewey noted, by the new school
of motor psychology. Experience was much more complex than
mere perception or the accumulation of past sensations[3] and explained most human behavior traditionally attributed to some
faculty of "reason."

Dewey considered that this broader concept of experience redefined the concept of knowledge. Rejecting the existence of any
built-in faculties of reason or reflection in the human child, Dewey
considered knowledge to arise from the experience of the organism
in getting along in life. "Knowledge" in fact was false, Dewey felt,
unless it were relevant to concrete problems of living. Solving
problems on the basis of experience, and predicting likely occurrences, was all, in Dewey's terms, that could be expected of thought
and knowledge.[4]

In his lecture series on "Experimental Logic," Dewey continued his discussion of the pragmatic re-evaluation of knowledge
and human thinking. Dewey discussed the five stages of thought,
based on the model of the experimental method of thinking he had
formulated in 1910.[5] These stages explain what a simple mechanism
human thought is. The stages begin with some doubt or puzzlement
—a problem. Then reference material, mostly from one's experience, is brought to bear on the problem, and hypotheses are raised
as potential solutions. Finally verification proves one hypothesis
correct and the problem is solved. This experimental paradigm was
Dewey's view of how human beings think. These ideas had gradually
come to light from Bacon to Darwin. Their effect was to redefine
philosophic issues, as the pragmatists saw them anyhow, by eliminating such misleading dualisms as mind vs. matter which had plagued
Western thought from Plato to Descartes.

Dewey's explanation of the role of the development of modern science in the West emphasized some points that were particularly designed for his Chinese audiences. One of these was the effect
of science on human values and temperament. Dewey felt that the
two or three hundred years in which the West had materialistically

and morally undergone the effects of science accounted for the most evident differences between the East and West.[6] Where Dewey undertook to describe the moral or temperamental values science had made commonplace in the West, the reader of his lectures senses for the first time that Dewey felt he was presenting a full philosophy of life to his audiences. He outlined two important influences the development of science had on the outlook of people in the West. The first was the optimism and confidence a person could assume about his or her constructive role in the world.[7] Pre-scientific conceptions of nature, Dewey asserted, could not conceive of a person's role in controlling his or her environment, either because no order was suspected in nature, or because all the natural world was assumed to be determined by superhuman decision. This exaggerated description of the pre-modern West was then contrasted with the liberation of the modern era. The arrival of science had a positive moral effect, Dewey felt, by giving human beings confidence in the power of their own intelligence to correct ignorance and disorder in the world.

The second moral effect of science had been the production of what Dewey called a "new honesty." Science, by increasing the ability of human beings to distinguish truth from falsity, had given honesty a new meaning. Dewey pointed out that, when nature was assumed to be capricious or beyond man's control, facts about nature or any situation were easily sacrificed to the immediate requirements of persisting beliefs. However, perpetuation of error would finally prove disastrous and the social welfare would suffer. Scientific confidence in intelligence and the proliferation of tested and accurate information actually made it easier to tell the truth, and for others to discern that it was the truth. Aspects of scientific investigation involving publicity, public discussion, observation, and investigation made people more able and willing to observe the truth. In outlining the effect of the progress of science on human attitudes, Dewey fully endorsed the advantages inherent in the intelligent search for fact, as well as the honesty made possible in solving social problems.[8]

Dewey's discussion of values extended to some criticism of

the way ethics was taught in Chinese schools. In China the school system provided set courses on "ethical education" at the primary and secondary levels. Dewey attacked the theory behind such courses, namely, that morality could be presented as a body of facts and knowledge.[9] The error inherent in such courses was present in other practices in education, and had its origin in the idea that the role of the school was simply to impart a defined body of knowledge rather than to focus on the growth of the child's intelligence. Dewey's analysis of how best to modernize the "ethics" classes was directly related to his discussion of the effect of the development of modern science on man. Dewey suggested three values which could be taught to students through their participation in school activities, rather than through content courses. This learning process would have the effect of relating knowledge to morality rather than trying to teach knowledge alone. The three values were open-mindedness, intellectual honesty, and responsibility. Dewey claimed these were characteristic of a scientific view of the world; and without them it would be nearly impossible to be objective, reasonable, and thorough. Dewey contrasted open-mindedness with succumbing to its opposite—prejudice, pride, or selfishness. This virtue was actually the essence of being reasonable, he noted, precluding blind acceptance of the authority of tradition. Intellectual honesty and responsibility required being true to one's ideals, the admission of error, and a willingness to accept the consequences of one's actions.[10]

The modern experimental method had liberated epistemology and ethics from the binding restrictions of pre-Darwinian conceptions of knowledge and its acquisition. Dewey sometimes sounded like an Enlightenment *philosophe* attacking the *ancien régime* of imperial Confucianism: "The number one problem of society in the world today is how to use the 'Authority' of Science to replace the Authority of Tradition."[11] Basically, this meant an appeal to *fact* rather than authority based on myth, rewritten history, or speculation. The new authority to which he referred would depend on both extensive public dissemination of objective facts on social and political issues, and on widespread public examination and

political participation. Honest and extensive publicity would make
truth the possession of the majority, rather than the minority.
Even diplomacy, Dewey held in the spirit of Wilson's ideals, would
be more effective in the long run if it were made fully public. The
chief means for achieving the new authority of science in society
was through universal and popularized education which would provide the people access to fact.

Education

When Dewey's sponsors first met him in Shanghai, they encouraged him to speak on educational reform. His several series
of lectures on education usually dedicated as much as one-third of
their content to defining the revolution in knowledge that led to
the erosion of the authority of tradition. Dewey attacked the
notion of teachers' passing knowledge on to students, as if that
knowledge were ready-made and enshrined as permanent truth.
Education could be liberated from passive learning by conceiving
of knowledge not as an end in itself, but as an instrument for
intelligently directing human activity.

In his China lectures, Dewey felt it important to emphasize
the child-centered curriculum—a turning away from classroom
emphasis on subject matter to emphasis on the growth of the child.
He dedicated one of his first lectures in Peking to a discussion of
the natural instincts and inherent dispositions of a child, which he
considered "the natural foundation of education."[12] Child-centered
education should be a priority for China, Dewey felt, as a departure
from the stratified society or authoritarian tradition that tended
to promote the "pouring in" of accepted subject matter as education. If a child were being conditioned to occupy a predetermined
role and status, packaged knowledge might prepare him for the
future. But in the democratic society Dewey was told China was
trying to create, there had to be equal opportunity for each child
to develop his potentialities and become a participating citizen. It
was also important during a period of rapid social change, Dewey
noted, that the younger generation be able to adapt to new conditions.[13]

Dewey's comments on reform in China were undoubtedly guided by his coaches and spokesmen, Hu Shih and Chiang Menglin. Many references appear in his lectures relating his educational ideas to social change and "modernization" in China. Dewey, in fact, emphasized the role of "socialization" in the school as the progenitor of social reform. Socialization of the child should not only give him or her a critical attitude toward tradition, but also develop his or her critical judgment about contemporary social and political conditions. This critical perspective, Dewey thought, should form as the school incorporated current issues into the curriculum. The reproduction of social problems would be tailored to the needs of the growing child and "purified" so as to suggest how society would function without undemocratic impediments. A "miniature society" would be created in the schoolhouse and would socialize the child into reformist attitudes.

Dewey and his followers in China felt that the school should be the basic unit in the reconstruction of China. Other institutions of social reform and betterment such as law and political parties, Dewey pointed out, lacked the power of education to carry out deep and lasting change: "There are many other institutions such as the courts, law enforcement, politics, and so on, which cannot equal it [the school]. Although these are also units which reconstruct society, they have inherent obstructions, which can be conquered only in the school."[14] The inferiority of established legal and political reform tools, Dewey noted, was that they had to deal with adults rather than children. To vary the established patterns of behavior of an adult, and to provide the necessary environment in which new habits could operate, was often futile. In the case of the child, however, habits of thinking and feeling were flexible; and the environment of the schools could be changed and adjusted with ease, unlike society at large.

One goal of educational socialization that added to his lectures was his hope for a world prepared for international understanding and cooperation. The experience of going to school gave a child his first daily contact with an environment broader than the family. Dewey pointed out that it was the role of the school to present the world of human knowledge in order to extend the limits of the child's environment. Under world conditions of increasingly close contact among nations, it was Dewey's hope that teachers in different countries could convey a clear understanding of other cultures, so that international contacts could increasingly be on the level of cultural exchange and replace the past record of military conflicts. This need of understanding was critical in China, Dewey felt, partly because previous contact with the West had left suspicions of exploitation, and partly because adaptation from the West was still essential for the modernization of China. Although Dewey never developed this point at length, he assumed that China should utilize all the best points of the industrialized West on its road to reconstruction, being careful to adapt them to native environmental conditions so they could flourish.[15]

The concept of modern education Dewey presented in China began from the child's instincts and emphasized individual development through the child-centered curriculum. Socialization in the school selected appropriate elements of the present society for incorporation into school life to promote social progress. These characteristics of progressive education were aimed at preparing the child to participate in and help build an open, democratic society.

Political Thought

John Dewey's discussions of the nature of democracy in his China lectures were a kind of final equilateral component in the triangular connection of democracy, the experimental method, and democratic education. The democratization of knowledge by science had led historically to an increase in the role of the common people in society, as Dewey saw it, and the connection between scientific knowledge and democracy remained close. As he said soon after arriving in Peking, "A person in a democratic country must have the power of independent judgment, the power to think freely, and the actual opportunity to experiment. He must be able to use his own ability to choose the direction of his ideas and his behavior."[16] In such a society the dissemination of facts would be broad enough so that the common people, with the informed judgment that popular education could provide, would be intelligently prepared to choose policies to represent their interests and advance the progress of society. It was basically these concepts that Dewey developed into a science of politics in his lecture series on "Social and Political Philosophy."

Dewey began these lectures with an instrumental definition of theory, and of politics; then he discussed the characteristics of experimental politics. Political theories, like any theories, he noted, arose to account for and alleviate some difficulty that developed in the operation of established social habits and institutions. Thinking was a response to problems, and so was theoretical thinking. The specific conditions of the original habits and institutions, therefore, were primary, and the theories of how they operate derivative. After using this logic to discount devotion to theory, Dewey defined the discipline of politics itself as an instrument for diagnosing and curing social disorder. The relationship of politics to society was analogous to that of medicine to the body.

Dewey attacked the polarities that had formed in political practice between the radical and the conservative.[17] In times of crisis the weakness inherent in both positions came to the fore, and an exclusive "either-or" logic within their respective points of view construed everything as categorically good or evil. The radical group were those searching for complete liberation of the individual and ended up rejecting all existing institutions. The conservative group were those who always accepted the given set of institutions, but advocated purifying them to re-establish their original definition and meaning. The error in both positions, said Dewey, was methodological. They both insisted that their respective extremes of eradication or preservation were correct. Dewey was ready to propose a third school which suspended judgment in any given case, or problem, until the specific facts of the situation were clear. This third school relied on present experience, rather than assumptions or generalizations; it stressed emphasis on experimentation, on the study of individual events, and on the application of knowledge and intelligence to social change.

Dewey's "third school" was formulated as a science of society.

He pointed out that the applicability of science to the non-physical world was widely recognized but not fully practiced. Understanding the significance of the scientific method had allowed the rise of the social sciences, which claimed some power to shape events. This development permitted the rejection of "natural law" theories, like that of Malthus in social philosophy, Dewey said. Furthermore all ideals and theories like "national sovereignty" and "laissez-faire" had to be reconsidered in terms of the specific conditions in which they arose. None of these could be taken as a universal rule for guiding social progress. They should rather be conceived as hypotheses always subject to the review of new evidence. The science of society Dewey described held that progress could only be made step-by-step, in a piecemeal way according to specific conditions.[18]

The notion of using "interest groups" as the fundamental unit in understanding social problems was one feature of Dewey's moderate "third school." The old schools, held Dewey, whether supporting monarchy or socialism, had seen the central political issue as the strife between the individual and authority. This view had missed the point that the origin of social conflict was in some interest group. The social sciences provided data and tools of analysis only recently available for defining and analyzing interest groups, obviating the need to fight old battles that no one could win. If conflict were related to interest groups, those in power would not be forced into staunch conservatism, and those out of power need not become extreme radicals. Objective analysis could replace blind passions, and social ills could be objectively located and cured. Dewey assumed that old institutions in China could use a re-evaluation to be carried out by comparing the conditions which spawned them with present conditions. In this way step-by-step situation-oriented reform could be effected.[19]

In the process of formulating a pragmatic philosophy of politics Dewey discussed rugged individualism, Marxism, and socialism. He warned China to avoid the dangers of rugged individualism. Throughout his lectures Dewey endorsed the idea that individuals should be able to develop themselves to their full potential. But he had severe reservations about the nineteenth-century political philosophy of absolute free enterprise and free trade, supported by a faith in enlightened self-interest. Dewey's position was that the ideals of the French Revolution—liberty and equality—had proven mutually incompatible in the succeeding century and a half. Unrestricted liberty led directly to inequality and injustice. Dewey pointed out that unenlightened selfishness dominated what should be a system of equal opportunity unless moral principles were agreed to before competition. The problem was the same for free enterprise as for free trade: the inequality of the competing members increased naturally, no longer allowing for fair competition. The domination of capitalist managers over laborers was another symptom of the natural injustice arising from unbridled free enterprise. By the end of the nineteenth century, Dewey noted, these injustices had begun to be corrected by the intervention of governmental controls. The dangers of uncontrolled individualism were emphasized by Dewey because he feared China, in the throes of liberating itself from the authority of the state and the family system, would be prone to fall into its opposite extreme of radical individualism.[20]

Dewey was critical of Marxism in his lectures. He pointed out that Marxian theory had failed on two counts: 1) although capital squeezed out competition as predicted, the workers came to fare better and better—the poor did not become poorer and poorer; 2) the prediction regarding industrial nations being the first to change to socialism was erroneous and shed doubt on the rest of the theory. The question of labor discontent was taken very seriously by Dewey, but he addressed himself critically to Marx's theory of alienation. Dewey felt that the division of labor found in complex industrial societies became organic as it developed. The activities of any part affected other parts of society, just as the parts of a living organism operated interdependently. Dewey focused in one lecture on the faulty understanding and teaching of science as a main reason the worker could not feel the significance of the work he was doing. If scientific knowledge were disseminated so that it permeated all segments of society, workers could see the relationship of what they were doing to the other parts of the given system. Employers had intensified a needless alienation by intervening in the process of production themselves and reducing the workers' control over their own destinies.[21]

Dewey was not so critical of some non-Marxian types of socialism. Guild socialism in particular had several points Dewey thought appropriate to China's needs. The existence of guilds in China—for railroads, mines, forests, and roads—provided a natural organizational unit which could be useful in China's transformation from a handicraft to an industrial economy. Dewey advised that they develop internally to strengthen their respective craft groups; then they might also be used as a natural unit of representation in government—perhaps voting as units, replacing suffrage by individuals.[22]

Dewey's own vision of a fully democratic society was one characterized by what he called "associated living," encompassing contributions each person in the society was free and equal to make. Describing this goal, Dewey became euphoric: "Every element has the freedom to develop, the freedom of communication, mutual exchange of feeling; and there will be the opportunity for the mutual exchange of thought and knowledge."[23] Such conditions of freedom of thought and expression would lead naturally, he felt, to the open evaluation of conflicting ideas and claims. At this point one sees Dewey's vision of the integration of modern science and democracy. The open comparison of conflicting ideas and interests increased the opportunities for rational analysis of actual facts: "The more there is study and discussion, the clearer the principles of the matter will become. The more opinions there are, then there are that many more opportunities for improvement." The exercise of personal freedoms would thus act to allow reason a larger role in society. Scientific work itself would flourish under conditions of open investigation and publication. While such a society might appear to lack the strength of authoritarian societies, Dewey argued that, underneath, its democracy gave it unparalleled strength.[24]

Reform in China

The content of Dewey's lectures in China could have earned him the right to represent, incarnate, the "Mr. Science" and "Mr. Democracy" slogans current among liberal reformers since 1915.[25] The progressive aspect of experimentalism as a reform doctrine lay in the fact that it conceived of established social institutions in the same way it described any theory—that is, as a product of specific conditions, and as having no more necessary permanence than an hypothesis depending on available data. Old institutions would therefore have to be justified in terms of contemporary needs and conditions. The experimental method was a purging instrument in the service of reform. But this critical methodology was in no way a wholesale rejection of tradition. In fact it was in ways explicitly conservative, and Dewey called for Chinese reformers to retain a direct connection between the past and change. Dewey's views called for a re-evaluation of traditional customs and institutions, but not for their rejection. Intensive study of the past was encouraged, so that the indigenous cultural traits and institutions relevant to contemporary needs could be discovered and conserved. As Dewey put it, subjecting the cultural heritage to the test of experimentation simply required that the varied heritage undergo a sort of winnowing like the threshing of grain. The lighter chaff would rise to the top and be blown away, while the relevant substance of tradition would be retained like the kernels of grain.[26] In the schoolroom, that which was compatible with present social needs would be infused into the curriculum. Filtering the past for present use assured continuity with aspects of the past, which to Dewey was the stable way experimental change should operate.[27]

Experimentalism as a model for reform assumed that change should be directed at environmental conditions and should proceed at a gradual pace. It rejected sudden or revolutionary change as unstable, and strove to avoid any social conditions disruptive to the rational execution of planning for the future. Dewey's sensitivity to such disruptive features came out when, after being in China about a year, he expressed himself on the student movement.

His spring lectures of 1920 praised the many achievements accompanying the rise of public consciousness and social concern during the preceding year of activism. His judgments about these contributions repeated almost verbatim the evaluation Hu Shih made and published in Chinese at the time, and were undoubtedly written in consultation with Hu. Dewey then provided an argument why continued disruption from student strikes was counterproductive. Noting that there was an element of uncontrolled emotionalism which continued into frequent demonstrations and strikes even after the initial reaction against the crisis in foreign relations, Dewey argued that emotion was like steam—beneficial only if controlled. In fact, if the steam was not harnessed, or if the machine it ran was in poor condition, the machine would fall into disorder and ruin.[28] He pointed out that hyper-emotionalism and hyper-nationalism had inherently undemocratic elements in them. The value in democracy, on the other hand, was that people could be open-minded and take some responsibility for the public good over and above the personal interests of themselves or their families.[29]

Dewey expressed the hope that these weaknesses in the student movement would be transformed into constructive reform, taking advantage of the good features of the new nationalist feeling. The indignation and intolerance firing the movement could be reoriented toward knowledgeable and thoughtful action, he pointed out, and the negative commitment to repudiation of the government role in the Shantung negotiations could be turned into more positive and constructive activity.[30] Dewey reiterated that his point was not to eliminate emotion but only to put it under the control of intelligence. Strong feeling should be directed to fundamental questions where planning and construction were possible, such as literacy education, improvement of physical education, economic development, and the increase in the productive and consumer power of the people. Only when one's purposes were of longer range than emotionalism and anti-foreignism permitted, Dewey argued, could the values possible in a democratic society—

creativity, independent thinking, and open-mindedness—be attained.[31]

Dewey's comments on the student movement he witnessed were fully consistent with the science of society he advocated in his lectures on politics. They were probably aimed at aiding his interpreter, Hu Shih, and his reform group at the time. Dewey's advice was to undertake reform at a slow but sure pace. Stable progress could be achieved only through the piecemeal change of specific conditions—his scientifically moderate third alternative to radicalism and conservatism. The rational discussions proposed among interest groups, and the consequent resolution of conflict, would provide the foundation for intelligent social planning.

PART TWO

EDUCATIONAL REFORM

The good feeling entertained by the Chinese
toward New Russia is not so much for Russia's
Bolshevism as for Russia's stand for international
justice and equality, not in words but in action.
It is yet too early to forecast the influences of
this new friend upon our education. However,
one thing we are pretty sure of is that contact
with New Russia will make Chinese education
less favorable for further realization of imperialism and capitalism.

T'ao Hsing-chih, "China,"
Educational Yearbook, 1924

Chapter III

THE NEW EDUCATION REFORM MOVEMENT:
ITS ORIGINS AND DEVELOPMENT TO 1922

When John Dewey left China in July 1921, Hu Shih published
a short account of his two-year trip, summarizing the major ideas
Dewey expressed in China. In the history of China's contact with
the West, no Western scholar had enjoyed such a large influence as
Dewey, Hu wrote, and he added that in the coming decades it
would "be impossible for another Western scholar to have an influence larger than Professor Dewey's."[1] To support so bold a prophecy
Hu Shih pointed out that education was the field in which, during
the years ahead, the effect of Dewey's visit would continue to be
multiplied.

When Hu Shih and Chiang Meng-lin first thought of arranging
a visiting professorship for John Dewey they knew he would advocate the experimental method and the scientific spirit. They also
had a more specific reform aim in mind. They hoped that his
fresh educational philosophy would, as they put it, "awaken our
people, so everyone would become engaged in fundamental educational reforms."[2] Over the next two years most of Dewey's lecture
topics were, in fact, on education. Although the bankrupt condition of education under warlordism in 1921 prevented immediate
results, Hu pointed out in his farewell article that the seeds Dewey
had disseminated in those two years would germinate in time:

In the future, as "experimental schools" gradually arise, Dewey's
educational theory will have the opportunity for experimentation; and that will be when Dewey's philosophy blooms and
bears fruit! At the present time Dewey is just a famous name,
but ten or twenty years from now Dewey's name will be
attached to innumerable Dewey-style "experimental schools,"
directly or indirectly influencing education in all China. Will
not that kind of influence be one hundred thousand times
larger than it is now?[3]

55

These hopes went unrealized. Instead, Deweyan educational reforms were frustrated by dilemmas inherent in the reform strategy of his followers. The reformers who promoted Dewey believed in the Republic of 1912, and were trying to establish a democratic educational system appropriate to a republican form of government. The problems they encountered on the way to this goal were not conquered, and they were largely unsuccessful.

In a restricted sense, Hu Shih was right. Dewey's ideas found a reception among professional educators which had lasting consequences. In 1931 when a League of Nations team of educational experts surveyed China's schools, their report argued that the reliance on the United States system of education and philosophy of education had been excessive during the previous decade, and recommended a shift away from the United States model.[4] This influence was particularly evident at major academic centers where teachers were trained.

A word of background concerning these institutions will be appropriate. When the first modern school system was instituted in 1903 in China, "higher normal schools" were to be set up by provinces for the professional training of teachers to staff secondary institutions. When the Republic was declared in 1912, the six existing higher normal schools were put on the federal budget and subsumed under the Ministry of Education as national professional schools.[5] Most of them were later called teachers' colleges or affiliated with a university, as in the case of the most eminent—Nanking Higher Normal School.[6] Peking also had a higher normal school, which throughout the early Republic shared with its Nanking counterpart the responsibility for supplying the populous northern and central coastal provinces with teachers.[7]

The teachers' colleges in both Nanking and Peking became centers of Dewey's influence. Analysis of personnel and publications from these institutions reveals a confirmation, on one level, of Hu Shih's hopeful predictions. In Nanking Dr. Kuo Ping-wen (P. W. Kuo), the first Chinese Ed.D. from Columbia's Teachers College, became the dean of Nanking Higher Normal School (Nankao) in 1915, and its president in 1919. He succeeded in having his institution promoted to the status of a national university in 1921, with the new name, National Southeastern University.[8] It was widely recognized in overall quality as inferior only to National Peking University. The Nanking graduate school of education and later its science department could in fact claim to be the best in the country. From the year of his appointment as Dean of Nankao, Kuo systematically recruited highly recommended students returning from the United States; and he appointed an extraordinary number of these students before he left the presidency in 1925.[9] The faculty in education was almost exclusively chosen from those who had studied in the United States, and the majority came from Columbia's Teachers College. In 1917, for example, after visiting the United States as head of an educational commission, Kuo appointed T'ao Hsing-chih (then still called T'ao Chih-hsing) directly from Teachers College. T'ao later interpreted for Dewey's visit to Nankao, and as chairman of the Department of Education he helped sponsor and interpret for another of his former Columbia teachers, Paul Monroe, who came to China soon after Dewey.[10] From Teachers College Kuo also recruited Mr. Ch'eng Ch'i-pao, who later became a dean of Southeastern. At the World Conference on Education in San Francisco in 1923, Kuo telegraphed the surprised Mr. Ch'eng in New York and asked him to come to San Francisco for an interview. Ch'eng was appointed Executive Secretary of National Southeastern University in 1923 and remained in the administration, teaching concurrently.[11]

Three other major professors of education whom Kuo appointed after their graduate work at Teachers College also promoted Dewey's educational philosophy—Ch'en Ho-ch'ing, Cheng Tsung-hai, and Chu Ping-k'uei.[12] Mr. Cheng introduced Dewey in the pages of the pro-Dewey magazine, *Hsin chiao-yü* ("The New Education"), welcomed him in central China, and then interpreted for him in Hangchow. He continued to publish on Dewey a decade later.[13] In other departments Kuo appointed Columbia graduates with professional debts to Dewey. One was Lu Chih-wei who headed the Department of Psychology directly after receiving his Ph.D. from Columbia in 1920, and another Chu Chin who taught in the

Sociology Department.[14] In the humanities division, there was a philosopher, Liu Po-ming, who published on Dewey in *Hsin chiao-yü*, interpreted Dewey's philosophic lectures at Nankao, and translated *How We Think* into Chinese.[15]

Peking Higher Normal School (Peikao), the other major teacher training institution in North China, appears to have been taken by storm when Dewey's lectures were publicized throughout the world of education in China. Dewey spent much of his second year in China lecturing at Peikao, and two journals were founded at the college during his visit. Both promoted his ideas, and one, *Ping-min chiao-yü*, was the most avowedly Deweyan periodical of the May Fourth era.[16] Ch'ang Tao-chih, an advanced student who had published Dewey's class lectures in book form, edited the journal for five years until it ceased publication when he left for graduate work at Teachers College, Columbia.[17]

At the prestigious National Peking University there was another educational leader who was the single most important Chinese intellectual in the promotion of Dewey's educational principles. This man was Chiang Meng-lin. He assumed the acting chancellorship in the summer of 1919 after establishing his reformist views and remained a professor of education and top administrator at the university throughout the 1920s.[18] Before turning to Dewey's place in the educational reform movement Chiang was leading, it seems fair to conclude that Hu Shih's optimism in 1921 regarding Dewey's future influence was justified in the context of professional teacher training institutions. That is not all Hu Shih had in mind, which is a point to be examined; but considered within the restricted scope of these colleges and universities, the response to Dewey's visit and the reception of his ideas was enthusiastic. The personnel hired and journals founded at the Nanking and Peking colleges assured Dewey's ideas a significant influence on the professional educators produced by these seminal institutions in the coming years.

The New Education Reform Movement

Chiang Meng-lin and Hu Shih, in inviting Dewey to China,

were hoping to do more than capture the teacher training institutions. Achieving such a goal would have been a hollow victory. To their dismay, it was very close to what actually happened. But they originally envisaged Dewey fitting into the new movement for educational reform which consolidated at the end of World War I. They hoped his eminence, and indisputable authority as a voice of modern democracy and education, would serve to rally the world of education behind the new reform effort. Chiang Meng-lin spearheaded that effort through a national organization founded in January 1919, four months before Dewey's arrival, the Hsin chiao-yü kung-chin she (Society for the Promotion of New Education). The several educational bodies composing that organization were united in their opposition to the undemocratic course of the Republic since 1912, and were spurred by the wartime ideals of the Allies, which the reformers saw as the principles of a new era.

The democratic ideals of the Allies coincided with some of the unfulfilled aims of the revolutionary generation of 1912. The fundamental principle underlying the new education reform movement following World War I had, in fact, been well stated by the future chancellor of National Peking University, Ts'ai Yuan-p'ei, in 1912, when he was the first Minister of Education. In a declaration of principles as Minister of Education, he said:

> There are two great kinds of education: one is subordinate to politics, the other is above politics. During the monarchical period (I refer also to constitutional government of a monarchical nature) educators followed the policy of the government and considered the model education to be purely subordinate to government. In the republican period, educators can set up a standard based upon the situation of the people and thus we may have education beyond political control.[19]

In 1912 these words were directed specifically at the bureaucrats of the overthrown dynastic system. Overdue reforms had pushed discontented intellectuals into revolution. The republican system of government was seen by many as disestablishing the union of *cheng* (political affairs) and *chiao* (teaching, orthodoxy) which had bound the literati to the Confucian state. Ts'ai's attempts to institutionalize a certain independence of education from government, both ideologically and financially, had proven unsuccessful. Moralistic student societies were founded in 1918 as they had been in 1912, pledging their members not to accept government office. Following the First World War Ts'ai continued to argue for the independence of educational funding, but resigned twice from National Peking University because of injustice and corruption in the militarist cabinets running the country.[20]

The Society for the Promotion of New Education that formed in 1919 with Chiang Meng-lin as Editor-in-Chief of its monthly *Hsin chiao-yü* ("The New Education"), was committed to republican education as had been Ts'ai, but its goals and strategy had found new inspirations. The magazine was to be published in Shanghai, where Chiang had been a member of two of its five component organizations, the powerful Kiangsu Education Association (Kiangsu sheng chiao-yü hui) and the National Association for Vocational Education (Chung-hua chih-yeh chiao-yü she).[21] The other educational bodies joining this united leadership were National Peking University, where Chiang soon took up his administrative post, Nanking Higher Normal School, and Tsi-nan Institute, which included a middle school, normal school, and commercial school in Nanking.[22]

Throughout his two years in China, Dewey was closely connected with the activities and publications of these five sponsors of the Society for the Promotion of New Education. He figured prominently in the society journal and had much to do with defining the modern principles of progressive education that formed the specific content of the reform movement. Chiang Meng-lin acknowledged the debt his journal owed to Dewey.[23] The Deweyan educators mentioned above from the Nanking and Peking academic centers formed a core of *Hsin chiao-yü* contributors. Dewey's educational principles had thereby successfully attached themselves to a reform movement. The objectives of the movement were yet to be tested, however, in the years after 1919.

When the society became the vanguard of progressive educational reforms in January 1919, it had some predecessors and co-workers in its battle to establish democratic principles in education. In particular, it complemented and cooperated with one older national organization that was a natural ally. This was the National Federation of Education Associations (Ch'üan-kuo chiao-yü hui lien-ho hui) which had attempted to pull provincial educational associations into a national unit not long after the first provincial-level *chiao-yü hui* (public education societies) were established to disseminate knowledge in 1906.[24] The federation received official recognition from the Ministry of Education in 1914, and its annual conventions fit into the role of a "periodic deliberation and counsel" by public and private educational authorities institutionalized under the 1905 Ministry of Education.[25] Although it only gave advice once a year, from its first convention in 1915 on, the Federation increased its influence in proportion to the increasing decay of central control from the Ministry of Education.

When Yuan Shih-k'ai died in 1916, and the revolving cabinets of feuding militarists took over Peking politics, the central ministry of education was less able to control education in the provinces. From 1916 to 1926 there were twenty different Ministers of Education, an average of two shifts in that office every year.[26] These conditions did not allow the Ministry to continue its earlier pressure to centralize and unify education in the service of national strength. It also marked an end to monarchist success in securing any official sanctions for Confucianism by the state.[27] Regional and non-governmental educational leaders were provided a reprieve of relative freedom, albeit one based on neglect by those in power, to promote their professional standards of good education.

Reform Ideas in the New Education Movement

World War I was quite important in consolidating the new education reform movement. With the Allied victory in the fall of 1918 and the spirit of a Wilsonian world made safe for democracy, Chinese republicans pressed their case for a modern state whose strength was to rest on the strength of the individual citizen, rather

than upon a superficial increase in military power.[28] Only in 1919
did the Ministry of Education state that its emphasis on military
education since 1912 had been inappropriate.[29] In the fall of 1918
the Ministry of Education publicized a resolution from the annual
meeting of the National Federation of Education Associations calling for a restatement of the objective of Chinese education.[30] This
objective was endorsed by the ministry's own invitational conference of educators in April 1919. It was phrased as "cultivation of
a sound personality, and development of a republican spirit," and
established the democratic principle which was eventually to engender a new school system in 1922.[31]

The resolution of the ministry's invitational conference which
recommended the redefined objective of Chinese education was
signed by Chiang Meng-lin, the editor of *Hsin chiao-yü* ("The New
Education"), and the elderly Shen En-fu, an officer in the Kiangsu
Educational Association. This national recognition given reform
aims was a propitious launching for the new society and its journal.
The founding statements by the journal demonstrate the faith of
the "new educators" in the fundamental role they saw for cultural
reformism in attacking China's ills. This position associated *Hsin
chiao-yü* with the earlier *Hsin ch'ing-nien* (The new youth) policy
of avoiding political confrontation in order to get at the social and
cultural defects which allowed attempts at restoring the monarchy
to recur.[32] The movement for a new education became an important component of the New Culture movement which had been
forming since 1917. The opening issue auspiciously proclaimed
that the year 1919 was the "beginning of a new era, and [the
organizers] felt that education would be the foundation of the
prosperity of that era."[33] The magazine promised the introduction
of new currents of thought from throughout the world, with particular attention to democracy. The new China needed a citizenry
able to think independently, express themselves, and assume public
responsibilities. These characteristics relied on a wholesome individuality developed in each person, and this fundamental task was
achievable through one important means—the new education.

Chiang Meng-lin, as editor of *Hsin chiao-yü*, assumed the role of a chief ideologist of the reform movement. The ideas which recommended him to that position were expressed in his major articles published in large part in the nation's foremost educational periodical, *Chiao-yü tsu-chih* ("The Chinese Educational Review"), when he returned in 1917 from study in the United States. In these articles Chiang repeatedly described the inner strengths he felt characterized the democratic countries during the wartime crisis. He particularly admired the United States for the willingness of its people to rise in unison to the national cause, as reflected in the number of military volunteers.[34] He described the war as a victory of democracy over autocracy and militarism, so that democratic government would be safe to flourish thereafter. Looking at China through these lenses, he could not help attacking aspects of Chinese society he felt were clearly antithetical to the spirit of democracy sweeping the world. In particular he singled out the Confucian precept *jen* (benevolence), which, as a principle of governing, embraced the ideal of peace but treated the people as flocks of animals to be shepherded.[35] As Chiang saw it, the fundamental system of values required change.

The independent dignity of each individual must be recognized, he wrote, in place of the traditional deference required by the five Confucian relationships. Leaping into the national debate led by the monarchists on Confucianism as a possible state religion, Chiang attacked the hierarchy of social values based on the family system that extended outward to the emperor and his officials. In its place he recommended that all people be treated simply as "you," "he," and "she," giving each person his or her inherent dignity. Chiang noted that modern educators all agreed that the point of departure in educating a child should be to develop his or her individuality (*ko-hsing chu-i*, Chiang's translation).[36] This healthy individuality translated into individualism socially, which was, he argued, essential to the positive values of freedom and equality in modern democracy. As these concepts along with "sovereignty of the people" and "representative institutions" gained meaning in modern China, the special talents of each person would be liberated and contribute to the overall strength of a democratic society.[37]

The "new educators" never disregarded national strength as
a goal, but they were convinced its source lay in a less strongly
centralized state. They saw lasting strength in the individual citizen.
Chiang praised the scientific spirit pervading Western education
and scholarship because it seemed to provide systematic, clear,
and accurate knowledge. Such qualities would rectify the debilitating, vague thinking he felt characterized the moralistic education of the Chinese classical tradition. The new education
should relate the school to social strength indirectly, he argued,
through civic education, practical training for employment, and
voluntary groups. Remedial education (*pu-hsi chiao-yü*), vocational
education, and compulsory education[38] would be necessary com-
ponents of a progressive educational system for the democratic
republic of China.

*John Dewey and the Establishment of Democratic Educational
Aims*

In the summer and fall of 1919, Dewey's presence at Peita
(National Peking University) provided Chiang Meng-lin with
support for his efforts to democratize the administration of his
own institution. Chiang and Ts'ai Yuan-p'ei initiated an administrative reform to decentralize decision-making functions in the
fall of 1919. In encouraging student government as one dimension
of this change, Chiang publicly cited Dewey as his authority.[39] In
fact Chiang and Dewey went out together to Peking Higher Normal
School to address their students on the merits of an organized
student government. Chiang also frequently cited one of Dewey's
lectures arguing for the value of science in modern education. In it
Dewey attacked the ancient Greek disregard for using one's hands,
experimentation, and labor, as a source of the Greek failure to
develop modern science.[40]

Dewey's lectures were taken so seriously by progressive educators when he arrived that an analyst of the origins of the new
education reform movement of 1919 gave Dewey a fundamental
role in defining its content. In 1922 this professor of education at
Nankao described the disillusionment with the nominal "republic"

following the two monarchical restoration attempts of 1915 and 1917, and noted that at the time:

> There were several famous men who rejected political careers and turned their full energy to the academic and educational worlds. It was then that Dr. Dewey came to our country propagating his theories, informing us what the new education was, and what the way to the new education should be. Then educational thought in the entire country underwent a change, and this was the New Education movement.[41]

This article was written in the same year the School Reform Decree of 1922 incorporated several of the aims of the reform movement into a new school system. On paper this new statute was a significant victory for the reformers. The stamp of approval from the weakened Ministry of Education proved, however, something quite different from an affirmative national policy to carry out the changes. Verbal assent to some reformist aims in the Decree disguised the underlying ineffectiveness of a reform movement which lacked any real strategy for affecting power in the society, as would become evident.

The aims of the decree nevertheless are an indication of what the reformers wanted. The final provisions of the 1922 revised school system were largely the work of progressive educators who insisted upon them in hotly debated sessions with the Ministry of Education. The new objectives of Chinese education listed at the outset of that decree revealed that the reformers' point of attack was the rigidity of earlier school systems which had overlooked the development of the individual, and the relationship of the school to social progress. The "promotion of the spirit of democratic education," for example, established the cardinal principle of reform sentiment, which was to bring Chinese education into accord with the ideals of a democratic republic.[42] To do so required liberation from the pre-1905 mentality persisting from the Civil Service Examinations which sanctioned "education" conceived of simply as the mastery of a single body of classical

knowledge. The function of education in imperial times was
to allow the learner to pass from one level of examination to
the next, culminating in official appointment. Instead, the new
school system fostered the "development of individuality,"
which emphasized the growth of the child rather than emphasiz-
ing a fixed body of knowledge. The promotion of individuality
in the revised standards of 1922 included the promotion of
flexibility at the secondary level to introduce more practical,
vocational instruction—relating the training of the individual to
existing social needs.[43] The provisions of the decree have been
correctly interpreted as the high point of the influence of the
United States on Chinese education. Administratively the reorganization of elementary and secondary school years was legislated
to follow the United States model of a 6-3-3 system, with three
years each for junior and senior high school. Both John Dewey
and Professor Paul Monroe from Teachers College, Columbia, had
participated in meetings where Chinese reformers had drafted the
reform decree.[44]

The Decision for Cultural Reform

Before examining in detail the severe limitations of the reform
movement in practice, one may ask why its leaders subscribed to
the priority for cultural reform as an article of faith in 1919. Was
there a classical legacy traceable to the Confucian renunciation of
governmental service in times of corruption? Or did the modern
ideology these reformers promoted dictate their choice of reform
priorities?

The diversity of groups within the new education alliance
first merits attention. Ts'ai Yuan-p'ei's 1912 view that republican
government meant the freedom of education from political influence was shared by almost everyone, but this left considerable
space in which to define specific characteristics of what China's
progressive education should be. Ts'ai himself never argued precisely
along the lines of his former student from Shaohsing, Chiang Meng-
lin, for example, that a robust individualism was an essential ingredient in democratic education.[45]

The Kiangsu Education Association is another example of a progressive force in the reform effort, but one that did not derive directly from the United States formulation of progressive education. Its leaders were graduates of the imperial examination system, and had not studied abroad. Chang Chien, a *chin-shih* (doctorate) degree holder and an eminent industrialist as well as educator, had been its president since the Public Education Society of Kiangsu was established in 1906. The association had two representatives from each of some sixty-one prefectures in Kiangsu and was the foremost educational authority in the important Shanghai region. It had encouraged experimental schools, had underwritten the National Association for Vocational Education, and was a founder of the Society in 1919 and its journal *Hsin chiao-yü.* Yet when P. W. Kuo introduced coeducation at Nanking Higher Normal School in the summer of 1920, he did so against the opposition of Chang Chien, as well as Chiang Ch'ien, the first president of Kuo's institution.[46]

Huang Yen-p'ei was Vice-President of the Kiangsu Education Association. He was a *chü-jen* (second highest degree holder) who had fought for a replacement of classical studies with "practical" education early in the century, and had revolutionary credentials after seeking refuge in Japan when his progressive primary school of 1903 was under attack by Manchu authorities.[47] After 1912, as the provincial commissioner of education for three years, he reformed education in Kiangsu. Then, in 1915, he founded the National Vocational Education Association.[48] A sponsor of the Society for the Promotion of New Education in 1919, the Vocational Education Association had its own particular emphasis, which, among other aims, assumed a hand-in-glove cooperation between the educational preparation of skilled manpower and China's growing industries.[49] The rising business class during the war was a natural ally to educational reformers who assumed industrial capitalism was part of the modern development of Western democracies.

As a group, the reformers within the Society for the Promotion of New Education were all professionally dedicated to the field of education and as a rule steered clear of appointments within militarist administrations. The question might be raised as to whether the new educators, and perhaps the entire New Culture reform movement, were not choosing to reject political careers following the former literati practice of refusing service in a hopelessly corrupt state. This kind of classical legacy has led to fruitful historical analysis with some individuals, particularly regarding modes of thinking that passed unconsciously across the collapse of the Ch'ing dynasty into Republican times.[50]

In the case of the new education reformers of 1919 evidence suggesting the presence of some Confucian legacy in their program of cultural reform may be found, but it proves to be somewhat misleading. Dewey's article on the New Culture movement had noted that the cultural reformers retained a key notion from Confucianism, namely, "belief in the primacy of ideas, of knowledge, and in the influence of education to spread these ideas."[51] In his later life, Chiang Meng-lin also consciously associated himself with what he called "Confucian liberalism," which he felt was consonant with Deweyan pragmatism. The common feature was open-minded, tolerant thinking, which Chiang felt contrasted with the dogmatism of Chinese communism. Chiang placed the Communists in the tradition of the political competitor with Confucianism in China, Ch'in dynasty legalism—an attribution the People's Republic, interestingly, was to accept in the 1970s when the Ch'in dynasty (221-206 B.C.) was described as politically more progressive than the Confucian government that followed it.[52]

But there is a significant difference between these statements by New Culture advocates *intentionally* trying to connect the New Culture movement with Confucian liberalism and moderation, for whatever reasons, and the unconscious influence of Confucian modes of thinking upon their behavior. The specifically conscious, if not studied, use of references to Confucius by these modern rebels against tradition suggests the didactic purpose they had in mind each time Confucius was evoked against an evil they perceived as worse. The modern ideology of the new education reformers of 1919 was, it seems, at least as important in their choice of the educational reform alternative as was any hidden legacy, either to their social role as latter-day literati, or to the Confucian belief in the power of ideas.

Their modern ideology specifically required a rejection of the former social roles of the scholar-official class. The organ of the Society for the Promotion of New Education explicitly attacked the traditional notion of education as simply one division of the state, managed like the others, from the top.[53] Instead of serving government, education in a true republic was seen as producing and sustaining a democratic society. If the people were to initiate politics in a republic, then democratic education became the indispensable means of producing able citizens who could participate in representative government.

In rejecting the subservience of education to government, these reformers joined others in the New Culture movement who were trying to separate the intellectuals as a class from the former literati's service to the ruling political order. While there was uncertainty within the New Culture movement about the precise place of the intelligentsia in the new China, it was clear that the traditional social role had to be rejected. National Peking University, infused with Chancellor Ts'ai's belief that education should be separate from government, was spawning a generation of scholars like Ku Chieh-kang and Fu Ssu-nien who were committed to a new society wherein the intelligentsia demanded independence from the government.[54] The "new education" was one expression of the transformation of the educated class into new social roles—in this case, that of the professional educator, whose point was to be an independent contributor in a pluralistic democracy. The vision of this new social role, combined with the strong conviction that the Republic since 1912 had been a political failure, dedicated these educators to a program of social and cultural change to transform education and society in China below the superficial level of political forms.

Educational Reform in Practice

During the first year the Society for the Promotion of New Education and its journal *Hsin chiao-yü* were launched, the reformers encountered major resistance to their reform aims. Some of it—from existing political conditions—was foreseen although it proved more formidable than expected. Another kind of obstruction arose suddenly from the student activism of the May Fourth 1919 demonstrations and presented the educational reformers with their most immediate challenge. Both problems as they were posed to the educators were concerned with the influence of educational and cultural reform on political authority.

The opening issue of *Hsin chiao-yü* discussed how the reform movement saw its relationship to politics.[55] Chiang, as editor, insisted upon the responsibility of a professional educator in a democratic society to "discuss" political issues. In fact he criticized those intellectuals who seemed to be retreating into the world of education so as to remain unsullied by the corrupt politics of the early Republic. He argued that such a retreat would assure the failure of democratic government in the future.[56] What he meant by the "discussion of politics" was debate of current events in the classroom to produce well-informed citizens. Student self-government in the schools was also the kind of political involvement he felt appropriate.[57] The school was in these ways to be used as an ideal environment in which to develop the habits of popular government, with regional self-government the eventual extension of this training. He made it quite clear, however, that political discussion by teachers was not the same as involvement in politics. Being a politician would destroy the professional's independence and objectivity.[58]

Such a policy, while not exactly politically activist, was more ready to acknowledge political goals than Hu Shih's pledge not to talk politics for twenty years until new cultural conditions could be fostered.[59] Chiang Meng-lin, in fact, had some serious reservations about relying upon intellectual reform in itself. He warned how restricted the effect of the journalistic New Culture movement was—simply because its flurry of periodicals reached only those who could already read. He figured that no more than 2 persons out of every 100 in China's 400 million population were literate. He then used circulation statistics to show that only 25 out of every 100 literate people were reading May Fourth periodicals, so that, out of the whole population, this meant only 5 persons per 1000 were influenced by the New Culture publications.[60]

He concluded from this analysis that "social action education" must be an integral part of the cultural reform movement. He was convinced ideologically that popular education could provide the participation from the people which was necessary to avoid violent change. But he felt that the educated elite still needed to understand this point: "Social progress cannot be carried out by a minority in the intellectual class all the common people must be involved and only then can it be achieved."[61] In case this message did not get across, Chiang pointed out that, since the eighteenth century, the lower levels of society had been rising to create social progress. He continued, writing in February 1920, "You in the intellectual class, you make up the upper level of society. In the future when the suffering masses from below all begin to move, you will not be able to keep your feet."[62] He made specific reference to the Russian people's overthrowing their aristocracy and intellectual class.

Chiang had concrete suggestions for carrying out a cultural revolution at the bottom levels of society, and he presented them in *The New Education* journal. He noted that one out of every 800 people in the country was in secondary school or above. Instead of making each of these students responsible for educating 800 people, Chiang said he would be content to assign each literate person only 15 people (reaching a total of 7,500,000 at first).[63] To carry that out Chiang suggested friends could open night school programs at existing institutions. He noted that National Peking University then had 500 people in its night school, aged from 7 to over 30, and including both sexes. He said that any 3 friends united in such a cause could easily get 3 more apiece, and the 9 could again multiply into 27 committed to social progress. He further advocated the alliance of students and merchants and argued that a shop donating 100 *yuan* (dollars) could keep a night school going for nearly a year. With the help of only 2 students to run the school, 20 to 30 people could be educated for one hour every night.[64] Unlike the cultural revolution in the People's Republic of China in the 1960s, the ingredient missing in Chiang's plan was "politics in command." Political power was totally out of the reformers' control, in fact, and acted relentlessly to frustrate cultural reform efforts.

Before *Hsin chiao-yü* was half-a-year old, the May Fourth Incident took place and seriously affected the whole New Culture movement. As educators crammed into the hall of the Kiangsu Education Association on May 4, 1919, to hear the newly-arrived Dr. Dewey speak, no one suspected that the student movement exploding in Peking was to confront the reform movement with its first important challenge to the separation of education from politics. Some 3,000 students demonstrated in Peking. The uncontrolled student reaction against the government had led to Ts'ai Yuan-p'ei's resignation as head of National Peking University, and rumors were rife concerning government reprisal. The execution of arrested students and the dissolution of some universities in particular were anticipated. A campaign for justice spread to academic centers throughout the country.[65]

Hsin chiao-yü joined the campaign to defend the students, and proclaimed that a "new spirit" of reform and democracy now had its opportunity to arise. Chiang Meng-lin endorsed the May Fourth upheaval cautiously—hopeful that aroused student consciousness could be channeled into democratic reconstruction.[66] Chiang accepted his position as Acting Chancellor at Peita in July 1919 and worked to get the university functioning again. His interpretation of the spring disruption was the same as that of Hu Shih in 1919, and revealed that Chiang's stressing social action was just a difference in emphasis from Hu's more extreme rejection of political debate. Both men chose to describe the meaning of the student demonstrations as basically focusing attention on nonpolitical alternatives for change.[67] Chiang argued that a deep discontent with Chinese society and life underlay the widespread strikes and boycotts of 1919. The answer to this psychological crisis, as he described it, was the introduction of new thought and

cultural revolution. He offered examples of what he felt was required for the modern transformation in Chinese society—an intellectual adjustment from the simple to the complex life, from clan
to social life, from isolated to group life, and from an imitative
life following precedent to a creative life and freedom of thought.[68]
He fully subscribed to what he considered the real meaning of May
Fourth—a rejection of the prevailing "unfulfilling" definitions of
life and society.[69] For the next few years Chiang Meng-lin tried to
engineer an intellectual and social revolution that would divert
student activism from immediate political goals. He wanted a cultural revolution that would institute the educational practices he
felt underlay stable political change.

Unfortunately, the demonstrations were never successfully
channeled into social engineering and cultural reconstruction. A
political spirit was injected into the culture reform efforts in the
year following the incident. On the first anniversary of May Fourth
in 1920, Chiang Meng-lin and Hu Shih joined forces in the pages of
Hsin chiao-yü to sound the alarm that political activism had become excessive and was misdirected.[70] The two authors were react-
ing to a year of mass demonstrations, strikes, and boycotts, which
students refused to relinquish as instruments of power after they
had proved effective in forcing the cabinet ministers into resignation. Chiang and Hu confessed that they had missed the May
Fourth Incident itself because they were in Shanghai welcoming
John Dewey. They had learned of it only on May 6, the year before.
Having succeeded in convincing Dewey to lecture in China for the
past academic year, they noted that some of the fundamental reforms they hoped Dewey would stimulate had been quickened by
the May Fourth upheaval. But political activism had become
counterproductive, and the two professors lectured their readers
in May 1920 that, in matters of political ferment or renovation of
the political system affecting the overall quality of a society, one
must depend on the judgment of "mature people": "Those who
have still not matured" [which indicated, they noted, men and
women in their student years]"should have the right to pursue
their studies in peace. Society does not need them to engage in

activities outside academic life."[71] They concluded that the students should return to the classrooms, the playing fields, and the laboratories.

The lack of success of these views in controlling the politicized youth was frustrating for the new educators. Just two years later Chiang Meng-lin denounced the fugitive "cultural movement" whose influence he limited to from 1917 to 1920.[72] It had seemed of unlimited hope at the time, he noted, but the *hsueh-feng* (literally the "academic wind") had dissipated quickly. Despite their initial support for the May Fourth movement, both Chiang and Hu Shih eventually came to denounce it fully as an unwanted interruption in the effort to achieve deeper educational and cultural reform.[73]

The combination of political activism and the continuing repression from militaristic governments alienated many supporters of the New Culture movement, which began to appear powerless. Political parties such as Sun Yat-sen's Kuomintang made appeals to enlist students in the revolution against warlordism.[74] As Hu Shih later put it, "The strong desire of every one of these political parties to enlist the support of younger intellectuals had the effect of making almost everybody political minded, and directly and indirectly weakening what I had considered a non-political movement for intellectual and literary reforms."[75] Most symbolic of this change was the split between Ch'en Tu-hsiu, the founder of the leading New Culture journal *Hsin ch'ing-nien* (New youth), and his colleague, Hu Shih. Ch'en had a strong interest in John Dewey until early in 1920.[76] The conditions that led to Ch'en's radicalization included the immediate problem of repression by the Peking government. Ch'en had been arrested in June 1919 for distributing anti-government handbills and illegally left Peking in January 1920 while on parole, to lecture at Wuchang.[77] The police were searching for him when he returned, and he soon exiled himself to Shanghai and joined new political friends, the future founders of the Chinese Communist Party. Ch'en took the magazine with him and turned it into a political organ, which Hu Shih strongly opposed.[78]

The new education reform movement as well as the larger New Culture movement were ineffective in stemming the political activism of the May Fourth movement. That activism was countered head-on by other causes, the foremost of which was confrontation with the immovable force of autocratic militarism. In the very month when Chiang Meng-lin and Hu Shih pleaded with the students for a stop to the full year of strikes and demonstrations, the government in Peking passed the "Public Peace Police Law" whose twelfth article disbanded all student union organizations above the high school level in Peking.[79] This law came on the heels of increasing student demands. In February 1920 Peking students had pressed the government to refuse any direct negotiations with Japan on the Shantung question. In Tientsin, demonstrations had been vigorous since Chinese students returned from study in Japan in 1918 protesting mutual defense treaties and the Nishihara loans. In February 1920, speeches, parades, and a boycott of Japanese goods led to arrests in Tientsin.[80]

In December 1919, teachers and professors in Peking, under the leadership of a teachers' union, struck for the rightful payment of their salaries.[81] The strike lasted for over a month. In early 1921, demonstrations by teachers demanded the payment of salaries. This time students supported the faculty, and in June a massive march to the presidential mansion resulted in the beating and bayonnetting of both students and faculty.[82] Student demonstrations reverberated to Wuchang and Nanking in response to this incident.

The difficult lesson for educational reformers in the two years after their consolidation in 1919 was that governmental suppression and intransigence were actually an even greater enemy to their cultural reform efforts than uncontrolled political activism. The benign neglect of centralized control over education since the inception of unstable militarist government in 1916 proved to offer only momentary relief to progressive educators. Decentralization had allowed their provincial and professional organizations more voice in formulating democratic educational aims. But neglect soon proved financially painful, and arbitrary intervention by militarists turned out to be the reality behind the apparent decentralization of power.

After the first anniversary of May Fourth, Chiang Meng-lin and other leaders of democratic reform sentiment gradually began to see their plight more directly in political than cultural terms. Hu Shih and Chiang were the first signatories to the "Manifesto of the Struggle for Freedom" appearing in the summer of 1920 in *Tung-fang tsa-chih* ("The Eastern Miscellany") and signed by many intellectuals:

> Basically we are not men who talk about practical politics, but practical politics has always been our stumbling block. It has been nine years since the 1911 Revolution. Under the rule of the pseudo-republicanism of the last nine years we have experienced every kind of suffering known to those who are not free. These sufferings remain the same regardless of the political changes or the substitution of one political party in power for another. When politics brings us to such a dead end, we have to arouse ourselves and realize that genuine republicanism can never be achieved until politics is initiated by the people. In order to get the people to initiate politics, we must have as a prerequisite an atmosphere wherein a genuine spirit of free thought and free criticism can be nurtured.[83]

The last sentence states the dilemma then dimly visible to the cultural reformers: they assumed that political reform was possible only through deeper cultural reform; but cultural reform itself could not get started until political conditions were changed.

The dilemma was not easy for the educational reformers either to realize or accept. Sun Yat-sen, whom Chiang Meng-lin knew personally in 1918 and 1919,[84] had lectured to students in the fall of 1919 renouncing the priority of cultural reform.[85] Sun argued that the existing government of militarists and corrupt politicians would prevent cultural reforms from being accomplished. Liang Ch'i-ch'ao in the Chinputang (Progressive Party) was also sensitive to the problem and pointed out that it was a grave mistake to promote cultural activities without serious attention simultaneously to political affairs.[86] Cultural activities had to avoid obvious political obstructions. Even John Dewey, while touring fifteen Kiangsu towns in the summer of 1920, glimpsed the problem, though his advice did not change. Dewey had been interested in surveying the development of industry during his tour and came back shocked and disappointed by the "feudal social structure" he had witnessed, in which the developing elements of capitalism were being tied to militarism. He noted that being a bandit was almost as accepted as being a merchant, so that the well-to-do had to keep their homes as bare of furnishings as the poor because of their fear of theft. Soldiers were often part-time bandits, and officials used their soldiers to exact tribute from the people. Officials also blackmailed enterprises and reinvested their money in organs of financial control like banks.[87] In Anhwei province, Dewey wrote of an arbitrary military governor who had recently diverted a river from two cities to fill a canal leading to his mines. The same governor had dissolved the schools for a year in order to use the money for his army. After describing these adverse political conditions, Dewey wrote, "It is such facts as these that lead many to assert that any genuine industrial development of China must wait upon the formation of a strong and stabilized government."[88]

By 1922 continued political difficulties had brought the dilemma into sharper focus. The achievement of getting the weak ministry to promulgate the School Reform Decree in that year must have seemed a Pyrrhic victory to the frustrated reformers. The bloody faculty strikes of the year before literally gave Chiang Meng-lin nightmares as Acting Chancellor of National Peking University.[89] A national association for the independence of educational funds from arbitrary warlord budgets organized and met in futility.[90] One flicker of hope to release education from these crippling political influences had been the "Good Man Cabinet" which was dedicated to rescuing constitutional government from the existing reality of militarist power struggles. The frame-up which overthrew that cabinet in the fall of 1922 led to strikes and demonstrations at National Peking University and, eventually, to Ts'ai Yuan-p'ei's second disgusted resignation.[91] Chiang Meng-lin picked up his pen at the end of that year in a state of bewilderment and despair. In a painful essay he sounded the cry of other liberal reformers sensing the weakness of their position: "Politics are corrupt," he wrote, "how can we possibly not talk politics, yet if we discuss politics, how can the educational world avoid being used, being regarded as the enemy, and being overthrown by politics."[92]

As for new ideas to promote social and cultural reform more effectively, Chiang was confused and uncertain. After lashing out at the blind imitation of foreign ideas in the schools of the day, he fell back on his fundamental belief in political reconstruction through educational reform. He could only propose one suggestion for educators to try: *t'i-kao hsueh-shu* (to advance learning)—in the sense that the German university humanities movement had spread to all aspects of German culture in the beginning of the nineteenth century.[93] He admitted this method was slow and unlikely to produce a great new wave of active support. But, like the nineteenth century English movement in science which gave birth to the social sciences—another example he used for the argument—it would have to begin in the classrooms, laboratories, and libraries. Yet in 1922, before he could even finish this argument, the frustrated reformer-administrator burst into despair: "Ah! But why discuss it in such glowing terms! Our abused and deficient schools will not even last the year! There is no money . . . What is the use of talking about 'advancing learning'!"[94]

John Dewey, back in New York City, kept up with the plight of his followers in China. In 1922 Dewey articulated to his American readers the dilemma he had been unable to help his friends resolve during his visit:

> The difficulties in the way of a practical extension and regeneration of Chinese education are all but insuperable. Discussion often ends in an impasse: no political reform of China without education; but no development of schools as long as military men and corrupt officials divert funds and oppose schools from motives of self-interest. Here are the materials of a tragedy of the first magnitude.[95]

His only counsel in that article was addressed to the American missionary movement, whose schools he thought might possibly work to ease the plight of the reformers. It was a bad year even for such an unlikely possibility, however, for in the spring of 1922 a fervent anti-religious movement broke out in Peking.[96]

The new education reform movement promoted Dewey's ideas after 1919, and its supporters had hoped for an effect on society well beyond the halls of academe. To separate education from political control had been a principle shared by the reformers. But the repression of militarist cabinets was joined by May Fourth activism to close the gap between education and politics from both sides. The reformers hoped education could begin social and political change, but, under undemocratic political conditions, insistence upon reform by cultural subversion had created an insoluble dilemma.

Chapter IV

T'AO HSING-CHIH AND EDUCATIONAL REFORM,
1922-1929

T'ao Hsing-chih's Leadership

When Chiang Meng-lin openly aired his despair over militarist
obstruction of education in 1922, he had already turned over the
editorship of *Hsin chiao-yü* to the dean of National Southeastern
University, T'ao Hsing-chih. The change of editors occurred in late
1921 when Chiang left China to attend the Washington Naval Conference.[1] Foreign affairs unavoidably intruded into the priorities
of cultural reform leaders, despite their interest in not worrying
about the continuing problem of foreign intervention in China. As
Chiang told Paul Reinsch, the United States Minister to China in
1919, foreign countries had to give China "ten years' time—freedom
from outside interference—" which he said was an essential condition for the building of a democratic social foundation in China.[2]
A vigilant public opinion was needed to restrain government, Chiang
told Reinsch, and he saw the sprouts of that public opinion in the
student movement. But a lot more work building it into a steady
political force was needed, and was possible, in Chiang's mind, only
if foreign powers would not interfere.

The reality of foreign imperialism in China was, however,
something that could not be set aside in planning strategies. Chinese
government appeasement of Japan during and after World War I
fomented militant nationalism domestically, much as Manchu
appeasement of Russia had in 1903, following the Boxer uprising.
The Shantung decision at Versailles ignited the smouldering student
anger against foreign incursions in China, and a highly politicizing
anti-imperialist atmosphere engulfed Chinese intellectual life
after the May Fourth Incident. Chiang Meng-lin and many other
educational reformers did not give up their priority on cultural
reform. But in the winter of 1921-1922 he packed for Washington
to try and get the nine powers discussing East Asia to renounce

some of the privileges acquired over the previous eighty years of "unequal treaties." Pressure was brought to bear on Japan by several powers in these discussions, and the Shantung issue was partly resolved when Japan agreed to return the concession area, as long as she retained some economic rights in the Shantung peninsula.

T'ao Hsing-chih was five years the junior of Chiang Meng-lin, and had returned home from Columbia's Teachers College in the same year—1917. T'ao had passed his doctoral examinations, and arranged to send his Ph.D. thesis back to Columbia from China.[3] His first position on the Nanking Higher Normal School faculty had led to an encounter with his older colleagues. The dispute arose over some of T'ao's progressive educational views, and he was unable to assume the chairmanship of his department because of the conflict. It was Chiang Meng-lin who assured that T'ao's ideas were not eclipsed at the time by inviting him to publish an article on the disputed subject in Shanghai's *Shih pao* (The times).[4]

T'ao contributed to the opening issue of Chiang's *Hsin chiao-yü* in 1919, and helped formulate the initial positions taken by the Society for the Promotion of New Education.[5] In the years before he took over the editorship, it is clear that T'ao's views agreed well with those of Chiang Meng-lin. In particular, T'ao was deeply interested in John Dewey's educational ideas, and worked to introduce them to the Chinese public.[6] He later acknowledged that Dewey's ideas had been the inspiration behind the major progressive educational proposals he had made during his first teaching jobs in China.[7]

By the end of the 1920s T'ao found himself turning many of Dewey's principles upside down in a somewhat drastic reformulation of Dewey's educational philosophy.[8] In 1929 T'ao criticized the hitherto popular slogans of Dewey's thought such as "the school is society," and "education is life," by arguing that educators in China accepted them uncritically and refused to acknowledge their inapplicability. "Now I am going to give it ['education is life'] a half-somersault and change it into 'life is education,'" said T'ao, as he transformed Dewey to conform with social conditions so unlike those in the United States. The change was based on much

painful applied experience during the 1920s. His whole attitude
towards Western models for Chinese education had, in fact, undergone a transformation by the end of the 1920s. A volume of his
own essays edited in 1928 noted in the preface: "As I was selecting
from my old manuscripts, I suddenly had a realization. All those
[manuscripts] written about Western educational systems pulling
an Eastern cart were being eliminated forthwith. Those which remained were those [ideas] which had been personally tried."[9]
The changes in T'ao's educational ideas during the 1920s eventually
pulled him in a direction away from the views of his first sponsor,
Chiang Meng-lin.

When T'ao took over the editorship of *Hsin chiao-yü* and became a major spokesman for the reformers in late 1921, he shared
one article of faith with all his colleagues in the new education
reform movement—the assumed connection between educational
reform and broader political changes. As he put it to his fellow
provincial, Hu Shih, one night under the stars in 1920, "I wanted
to use a vigorous, openly-disseminated (*ssu-t'ung pa-ta*) education
to create a vigorous, openly-communicating society."[10] This
sounded much like Dewey's ideal of "associated living," with education as the point of departure in bringing about new social conditions. In the three years following that serious talk with friends,
Tao's dedication to new teaching techniques, coeducation, and
common people's education had not been simply to make everyone educated; he rather had the "ultimate aim of bringing a healthy,
renewed society to pass."[11] He believed in educational reform as
an indispensable first step in bringing about lasting social and
political change—a position we have seen Dewey also advocated.
At the time he took over the magazine, he was concerned
about the effectiveness of the reform effort and launched a new
phase of the movement. He insisted that energies be turned
toward "investigation," which meant practical surveys of existing conditions, and the implementation of the successfully
established philosophic aims of the movement. His arguments
for this new phase of the movement were supported by the visit

to China of Professor Paul Monroe, one of Tao's teachers at Columbia and an eminent educator.

When it was learned that Monroe planned a brief visit to China at just about the time Dewey was to leave, professional educators formed a special organization to invite Monroe to make a three-month survey of Chinese educational conditions.[12] Several of the organizers had recently returned from surveys of European and American educational conditions. T'ao Hsing-chih was one of the founding members of the Shih-chi chiao-yü tiao-ch'a she (Practical Education Survey Society), and he interpreted for Monroe when Monroe toured South China in the fall of 1921.[13]

T'ao took him to Canton where a distinguished congress of provincial educators passed the resolutions that later became the School Reform Decree of 1922. It was also at this meeting that foundations were laid, on Monroe's advice, for the unification of all non-federal educational associations into one efficient national association.[14] In Monroe's final meeting with educators in Peking, this organization was named The Chinese National Association for the Advancement of Education (Chung-hua chiao-yü kai-chin she, abbreviated hereafter CNAAE), which absorbed the older Society for the Promotion of New Education, and retained *Hsin chiao-yü* as its professional organ.[15] T'ao Hsing-chih became its Director General and soon announced that the new phase of the reform movement would stress data collection and statistical analysis of existing conditions in education. The intent of this action was to move a step beyond the initial phase in which Dewey's ideas had made a marked contribution—definition of the principles of democratic education. T'ao hoped that scientific investigation of educational conditions carried out carefully and publicized by the association would promote concrete reform.

In 1922 T'ao's new emphasis on implementation seemed to him quite compatible with accepting the advice of educational authorities from the United States. When Paul Monroe left China, two specialists from the United States were sponsored by the association for prolonged periods of investigation and consultation. Professor William H. McCall arrived in 1922 from Columbia's

Teachers College to be the Association's Director of Psychological Research for a year. McCall set up projects that resulted in Chinese intelligence tests and other educational tests to standardize education in China.[16] The other specialist was hired following Monroe's recommendation that some expert in the teaching of science spend two years surveying school conditions and lecturing on the significance of science education and modern methods of science instruction. In June 1922, George R. Twiss from Ohio State University arrived to become Director of Science Education for the Association.[17]

Twiss's trip somewhat paralleled Dewey's earlier visit, although he was more occupied with conferences and talks to organizations than giving university courses. He spent his first winter in Peking and traveled in the north. The next spring (1923) he followed Dewey's first-year schedule by traveling throughout the southern Kiangsu region and teaching during the summer at National Southeastern University.[18] He then returned to Peking. By the time he left China, Twiss had presented a total of 176 lectures and roundtable conferences, and had inspected 190 schools in some 24 cities in 10 provinces. *Hsin chiao-yü* began carrying some of his lectures and translated reports in its April 1923 issue, and continued to do so for about a year. He left hundreds of pages of special reports with different educational organizations that had requested his services, and he published a comprehensive final report of his two years' work.[19]

It might be noted that T'ao and the association were not the only educational organizations with a markedly pro-American orientation. In addition to the association's connections, the resolutions of the annual convention of the National Federation of Education Associations also reflected this influence. In 1921 the federation called for the adoption of William Kilpatrick's Project Method in elementary schools in China, and in 1923 for the adoption of Helen Parkhurst's Dalton Plan.[20] Parkhurst and Kilpatrick had their own brief lecture tours in China in 1925 and 1927 respectively.[21]

T'ao's attention to advice from educational leaders in the

United States contrasted somewhat with the tone of intolerant nationalism pervading the student community after 1919. But T'ao praised international standards of progressive education as precisely the kind of goal China should reach. He recognized the problem of cultural imitation, and lectured his *Hsin chiao-yü* readers not to make that mistake.[22] The superficial borrowing from abroad which characterized the initial Ch'ing response to Western encroachment was partly owing, in his view, to the fact that China had no "first-rate item of trade" to offer in exchange. T'ao was extremely self-critical. His perspective from what he had learned abroad made him dissatisfied with existing standards at home. For China to learn anything from international education, T'ao wrote in the spring of 1922, she had first to get to work at home, and only after achieving an understanding, produced through rigorous research and field work on her own educational conditions, could she expect to benefit from the major conferences in world education which were proliferating each year.[23]

When Dewey left China he gave his audiences the following advice, with which Monroe concurred: "The program of educational development for China must be worked out on the spot by those engaged in actual educational work. Prescription and detailed borrowing will both be fatal. Moreover the program must not only be worked out on the spot but it must be developed experimentally, and be flexible and not uniform."[24] T'ao did not violate that counsel, nor any other fundamental guidelines of Dewey's thought. But following this advice had an unexpected effect: it gradually turned him against some of the most often repeated principles of educational philosophy Dewey had professed in China.

T'ao's Educational Ideas, 1922-1924

When T'ao first began his educational career on returning home from the United States, the immediate conflicts he faced were not caused by his perception of imperialist encroachment, but rather by his perception of the backward state of Chinese education. The first point that rankled was the age-old separation of the supplicating student from the voice of authority and wisdom, the teacher: "When I returned from abroad, I noticed that our school teachers were concerned only with professing, and students were concerned only with receiving what was taught; so I was convinced of the need for reform."[25] This attitude was the source of his initial disagreement with his colleagues at Nanking Higher Normal School in 1917, and the topic remained a fundamental theme in T'ao's philosophy of education the rest of his life. In 1917, he proposed in a two-hour staff meeting that they eliminate the notion of "instruction" and "teaching methods," so that a less passive, mutual-learning environment could be created between teacher and student. Although he was defeated in his proposal, the May Fourth movement two years later created such a wave of liberal opinion that his colleagues could no longer resist, and the wording throughout the entire curriculum was changed to replace "method of instruction" with "teaching-learning method."[26]

During the 1920s T'ao expanded this idea, and it became one of his most important educational innovations. T'ao argued that, because the way one learns depends directly on how one does things (the method of doing), the notion of "teaching" should conceptually include the notion of "doing." By 1926 he called it "the union of teaching, learning, and doing" (chiao-hsueh-tso ho-i), and gladly approved when one normal school accepted his idea and varied it slightly to call it "the union of doing, learning, and teaching."[27] T'ao's new formulation had significant implications for the traditionally accepted roles of teacher and student. "We must teach from doing," T'ao wrote, "and study from doing . . . Regarding the relationship of teacher to student: to teach is to do." Presumably this meant one taught not by lecturing alone but by active involvement, which would certainly change the style of many professors. T'ao continued, "Regarding the relationship of student to teacher: to study is to do."[28] So, finally, the old relationship was totally redefined with doing, or *practice*, as the new common denominator. Those who could do, could then teach, which had shocking social implications. Later T'ao applied this principle to the peasantry, but in 1922 he was more modest, and simply suggested the use of children as "little teachers," instructing their parents in the written characters they had practiced all day until the parents learned them too—an idea he developed more fully in the 1930s.[29]

The first national association of education was auspiciously launched with this vigorous innovator in charge. The association planned actively to sponsor conferences, to publish statistics on scholars, students, and finances in every province of the country, and to provide a constant channel of progressive ideas to educators through its journal. Besides attacking authoritarian concepts of the teacher, T'ao turned the association's attention to literacy education and a concern for the millions of citizens who were untouched by the faltering system of schools under warlordism.

Despite these hopes in the summer of 1922, governmental neglect and obstruction quickly reasserted their stifling effect on formal education.[30] Chiang Meng-lin's plaintive cries to "advance learning" could not even be articulated at the end of 1922 without the accompanying gasps of despair and defeat. The first Chihli-Fengtien War in the spring of 1922 pitted against one another the former allies of the northern faction of militarists who had worked together in 1920 to succeed Yuan Shih-k'ai. Meanwhile, in the southern provinces, which had been in various stages of secession ever since 1913, the local Cantonese power figure rebelled against Sun Yat-sen in June 1922. These military facts meant hardship for all secondary schools in the war regions because their finances were generally taken from provincial treasuries. Finances for university facilities and salaries in the north came from the Peking federal budget, and had long been inadequate. Now neglect by provincial treasuries spread this debilitating condition to the secondary level. Teachers' salaries were commonly months in arrears.

In January 1923 Ts'ai Yuan-p'ei's second resignation at National Peking University began a year as disastrous as the preceding one for Chinese education. The frame-up of Lo Wen-kan in the "Good Man Cabinet" case of November 1922 was tried in the courts, and four days after Lo's release in January 1923 he was re-arrested by a new cabinet who claimed it would rehear his case itself regardless of the judgment from the judiciary.[31] Ts'ai resigned, and the presidents of four national institutions of higher education in Peking followed suit. A student movement proceeded through-out the year against the Minister of Education, P'eng Yun-i, who had suggested the move. He finally resigned in August 1923.[32] By November, the eight national institutions in Peking, whose students had worked for P'eng's resignation, were meeting to proclaim that nine months of insufficient financing would soon force them to close their doors.[33]

It is not surprising that under such conditions T'ao should have been led to apply his energies to educational possibilities out-side of the national school system, despite its nominal reforms in 1922. By the end of the 1920s, T'ao discussed his formulation of the "union of teaching, learning, and doing" as one stage leading to his theory of "life education" (sheng-huo chiao-yü).[34] This was a reversal of Dewey's famous phrase "education is life," by which Dewey meant that the subject matter of schooling was to be taken directly from daily life, so that the "little red schoolhouse" could become a microcosm of the model life which the society outside should be like. T'ao later said that he had argued for "education is life" when he returned to China in 1917, but was forced to revise the whole idea:

Seven years' experience has informed me that this road is a dead end. Only under distressing circumstances did I become aware of the validity of the union of teaching, learning, and doing. Therefore, the idea of the union of teaching, learning, and doing came as a result of my search for a new road when putting the notion of "education is life" into practice had run headlong into a wall.

The theory of "education is life" suddenly did a half-somer-sault. Those places which successfully united teaching, learn-ing, and doing never again uttered the phrase "education is life." Here schools were no longer patiently transformed into a microcosm of society.[35]

In the year 1923, T'ao increasingly committed himself to the development of a mass education movement aimed at the immediate goal of peasant literacy. He had expressed this interest in some speeches back in 1918, but did not develop it until the national reform movement proved it needed some new outlets. He first developed the idea of "relay-teaching" (*lien-huan chiao-hsueh fa*) in 1923, in which the teaching could be initiated by any literate person.[36] The father of a family, for example, would teach characters to his wife. She in turn would teach them to the daughter, and the daughter to the maid. This way literacy could spread throughout an entire household or institution.

T'ao's increasing dedication to common people's education, and his work in non-formal schooling took more of his time until, during the fall of 1923, he came to a personal realization that brought him great relief and changed his style of living. He wrote his sister in November that he had gone out and bought a common cotton tunic, cotton leggings, and a watermelon skullcap which he planned to wear so that he would not feel so estranged from the dirt farmers of China with whom he had grown up. In a sigh of relief, he said that he could feel fully Chinese again. He then proceeded to denounce the foreign aristocratic attitude his ten years of privileged education had given him: "I went through a moment of awakening, like the Yellow River breaking its dikes, and rushed back to the way of the common people."[37] The dikes T'ao had broken were, in part, the barriers of prestige he had acquired as one of the generation of returned students. He also was acknowledging and rejecting the elite status he had previously accepted as part of that small group who was given the vision of where a democratic China should be heading, and who felt they had to lead, to help the people see what popular government was like.

What was needed in 1923 to make literacy training more readily available and systematic was a literacy textbook. James Yen (Yen Yang-ch'u) had already been working on such a text for the Y.M.C.A. —something that grew from his educational work among the Chinese laborers in France during World War I.[38] He and T'ao became friends during 1923 and worked together to establish the National Association for the Promotion of Popular Education (P'ing-min chiao-yü tsu-chin hui). The Association was formed at the Second Annual

National Association for the Advancement of Education (CNAAE) meeting in August of 1923. The meeting was held at Ch'ing Hua university in Peking, and T'ao personally recommended Yen to be the director of the Popular Education Association.[39] Meanwhile T'ao himself began sponsoring programs of mass education through the CNAAE. By the end of the year, under the vigorous sponsorship of Mrs. Hsiung Hsi-ling (Hsiung Chu Chi-hui), he had "people's education" centers open in Nanking and Peking.[40] In the winter of 1923-1924, he wrote proudly to a friend that the Association for the Advancement of Education had cadre workers out in the city setting up people's reading circles (p'ing-min tu-shu ch'u). In three days these workers set up sixty-six centers on one street.[41]

The aim of these circles was to teach literacy within any natural unit that was not a school. It could be a family, an organization, or a shop. By August 1923, T'ao had published his own *Thousand Character Text* with another Deweyite teaching education at National Peking University, Chu Ching-nung.[42] The readers were a four-volume set based on 1200 common characters and were to be used in the circles, or more formal "people's schools" (p'ing-min hsueh-hsiao). At the rate of one hour per day, one should have been able to complete the four readers in four months.[43] T'ao convinced eminent acquaintances such as Liang Ch'i-ch'ao, Hu Shih, and Chiang Meng-lin to open small people's reading circles of their own. T'ao himself began teaching in prisons and looked forward to spreading the thousand character "classic" for literacy into the armies of militarists and among factory workers.[44]

By the end of 1923 T'ao's new priorities had developed into a more critical attitude toward foreign models in education. As he reported back to the Teachers College *Educational Yearbook* in that year: "China has in the past followed her teachers rather blindly but as yet no one has succeeded in offering her a satisfactory solution for her problems . . . At first she sacrificed everything old for the new. Gradually she came to a realization that the old is not necessarily bad and the new is not necessarily good. Thus our schoolmen have become much more critical than in former years."[45] By the end of the decade T'ao had zeroed in on foreign "culture" as a concept which had begun a lot of trouble in the process of borrowing from abroad. "Culture," like education, was basically a tool for life, he argued, and therefore should not be made the center of education or reform.[46] Culture is dependent upon the needs of life, T'ao pointed out, just as the telescope and electricity were invented for human use. T'ao therefore took a dim view of the abstract polemics which began in 1923 over "science versus metaphysics," succeeded by the debate over the relative values of "Eastern spiritual culture versus Western materialistic culture." His close friend Hu Shih engaged vigorously in these disputes. But to T'ao, Chinese education was in too desperate a condition to afford time for such academic wrangles.[47]

After becoming the leader of the Association for the Advancement of Education T'ao seemed to move away from the ideas of other founders of the reform movement. While T'ao had gotten Chiang Meng-lin to use the *Thousand Character Text* it was not without some personal prodding. T'ao was once at Chiang's home, and tactfully pointed out what an embarrassment it really was that the acting chancellor of the finest university in China should have a house full of illiterates.[48] T'ao offered to show how his method of mass education could work for itself if Chiang would help. Chiang followed his instructions and called together the butler and some others in the house and told them that, from now on, "all those who are illiterate in the house must study, and those who can read must teach."[49] T'ao then proceeded to give them an instant lesson by discussing a few interesting characters. They were apparently enthralled, and left the room saying they were going to tell the maid and the chauffeur. Chiang scratched his head and said to T'ao: "You really have missionary spirit."[50]

Although T'ao seemed to have distinguished himself from Hu Shih and Chiang Meng-lin in certain ways by 1924, it was not because he was in revolt against Dewey. T'ao regarded his reformulation of "education is life" as a change essential to meet Chinese conditions. Yet all the while he revealed his debt to the Deweyan ground of controversy on which he was arguing—namely, the intimate connection between education and life that originally

spurred T'ao's attack on the gap between teacher and learner. T'ao
also chose to define his more critical evaluation of foreign educational models by a rigorous application of Dewey's experimental
method: 'Their [our schoolmen's] reaction now toward new
theories and practices is no longer imitative adoption, but questioning, examination, experimentation, and selection. The logical outcome of this attitude tends to work out an education that is best
fitted for the need of New China . . . The critical and experimental
attitude is creative. It is only with such an attitude that a real
Chinese education adapted to Chinese life is possible. Such a creation has begun."[51] For T'ao these were rebellions within Deweyan
tradition but not revolt.

Still, one cannot help but feel the magnitude of the challenge
to Dewey's educational theory which T'ao's changes up to 1924
represented. Militarist political conditions had forced him to pull
his national organization further and further from the neglected
institutions of education as they existed in society. The real needs
of education in China that T'ao perceived committed him to literacy work in homes and prisons, mass-education readers, and closer
contact with the dirt farmers. These needs were not answered by
Deweyan maxims and principles that increasingly appeared aimed
at an industrialized middle-class society. The school as a microcosm
of an imitation ideal life proved no answer in China. T'ao had to
desert his own position in China's small middle and upper class.
Amid the extensive revisions of Dewey he was making, T'ao shed
his returned-student clothes, and with them the conflict of a
democratic reformer in a position separated by his "learning"
from the people.

Educational Reform, 1924-1929

From 1924 until the end of the decade, T'ao's views as a
reformer became more explicitly political in response to increased
pressures from both the militarists and the foreign powers. His
personal commitment to non-formal education, as defined by the
local conditions of Chinese villages, grew in 1922 and 1923—the
very time he was sponsoring a succession of educational authorities

from the United States. Seemingly he had to place a second hat on top of his skullcap, to accommodate to the two worlds in which he had to live. Yet he carried this out with characteristic gusto, as in the case in which he even converted the wife of Twiss, the science education expert, to study the *Thousand Character Text*. He was quite pleased when she could read a letter in Chinese he had composed. [52]

By 1924, T'ao was set on a new course of action at the village level to parallel his national-level work in the association. That year, much like 1922, witnessed a cataclysmic militarist struggle in North China. The Chihli forces which had prevailed over the Fengtien forces in 1922 were now faced with an alliance of Chang Tso-lin in the northeast and Tuan Ch'i-jui in central China, bolstered by Sun Yat-sen in the south. T'ao did not care so much about the outcome as he did about the public funds that were mercilessly drained into warlord coffers in preparation for battle. He estimated that $150,000,000 gold of public money was spent to increase and equip the armies for the war, and at the beginning of 1924 some 1,500,000 men were under arms for the battle which finally broke out in the fall.[53]

Other disastrous events for the reformers did not wait for these warlord battles to flare up. In January 1925, while returning by train from Shanghai to the university he founded, Kuo Ping-wen was thunderstruck by the news in the daily paper: the Board of Trustees of National Southeastern University had decided to terminate his contract as president. Kuo never reached Nanking that day. He got off at a local stop and returned, incensed, to Shanghai, never again to see the campus of his university.[54]

The motives behind the Ministry of Education, which controlled the board of trustees, involved political factions, as the next chapter will explain. What is critical here is that Kuo was the man who had hired T'ao and other United States returned students. His faculty and the alumni of the institution sent telegrams at the time, demanding that he be reinstated; and the event was interpreted as an ugly intrusion of politics into a first-rate institution whose president had always tried to remain independent of political affiliations.[55]

T'ao was furious and vigorously denounced what he labeled *tang-hua chiao-yü* (partyized education)—a term the Kuomintang later used willingly for their programs, despite the pejorative meaning it held for the KMT's liberal critics.[56] T'ao was the full-time director of the association when Kuo's dismissal occurred and so was not actually teaching on the Southeastern University faculty. For all in the reform movement who were associated with the event it taught a disturbing lesson. Kuo was a liberal educator who had dedicated his life to the non-partisan ideal of raising the quality of education in China. He did not see himself in a political role. But his summary expulsion from the system demonstrated the impossibility of keeping his professional work as an educator separate from politics.

Student reaction to this event combined with other irritations that resulted in another spring of demonstrations in 1925. Even before the tragic shootings which set off the May 30th Incident of 1925, students had been in the streets for weeks calling for the resignation of the Minister of Education, Chang Shih-chao. On May 7, 1925, which was National Humiliation Day commemorating the shame of the Twenty-One Demands of 1915, students were beaten and arrested when they poured out in defiance of Chang's ban on public demonstrations. This violent repression brought forth some 4,000 demonstrators two days later to demand that Chang resign.[57]

As if this crisis were not enough, on May 30, 1925, British-led police killed Chinese demonstrators in Shanghai; the next month fifty-two deaths were caused by foreign soldiers in Canton.[58] While unrelated to the early May demonstrations against the Ministry of Education, the effect of these deaths at the hands of foreign powers on Chinese soil fanned the simmering embers of nationalism in schools throughout China, causing increased irritation at militarists and foreigners simultaneously. Students from three Shanghai universities were leaders in the May 30th movement which had the support of many workers.[59] T'ao's sympathy with the demonstrations led him to argue for the legitimacy of promoting patriotism through education. At the annual meeting of the association in the summer of 1925 he was proud that, despite the depressing erosion of education in China, at least it could still respond by promoting national consciousness in a time of crisis. He said the delicate task of educators at this juncture was to establish effective patriotism without allowing reaction to harm the nation.[60]

At the 1925 meeting, T'ao expressed his frustration with the attempts of the association to be an effective leader in implementing the reformed educational system. Since 1922 his emphasis upon implementation in the association had only produced a year-long study which collected embarrassing statistics about current standards of education at all levels.[61] But the resolutions of the association recommending changes had basically remained dependent for their implementation upon the government and local areas. This was the source of the problem; the recommendations were simply not carried out.[62] The financial problem had been the greatest single difficulty during the years 1922-1925, and the lack of financing was inextricably tied to the priorities set by militarist cabinets. By 1925, T'ao's writings were reflecting the effects of the angry nationalist consciousness pervading all aspects of Chinese life. His own counsel to his colleagues in the association was to continue to fight for the fundamental principle of the reform movement: "Formal school education is a public instrument of the state, and is in a position above religious or political party considerations."[63] But his notion of what was to happen in the educational enterprise, once freed from the destructive influence of the government, was becoming itself more overtly political. He argued that schools should cultivate a "national perspective" (kuo-chia kuan), strengthen patriotism, and firm up the resolution of the people. These added elements in T'ao's educational views were responses to the renewed threat that foreign powers posed to China in the mid-1920s.[64]

In 1924 and 1925, there was vigorous debate in China over the remaining "unequal treaties" of the nineteenth century.[65] In education, the attack on these treaties combined with the anti-religious movement of 1922 to produce a widespread sentiment to "restore educational rights" from the privileged missionary schools in China. The Young China Party (shao-nien Chung-kuo hsueh-hui) spearheaded this effort as it collected some of the most fervent nationalists into its ranks in late 1923.[66] By 1924, anti-imperialist sentiment was fanned up again by controversies over the remission of Boxer indemnity funds by several countries. The Japanese indemnity was to be returned with several strings attached regarding its use, and the British were attempting similar arrangements. Reaction among educators was vocal and angry.[67] The United States did return its remaining indemnity ($12,500,000) with the stipulation that it be used uniquely for cultural and educational activities. Paul Monroe went to China in August 1924 to help set up the China Foundation for the Promotion of Education and Culture which would administer the money. Its board of trustees was composed of ten Chinese and five Americans, among them John Dewey and Paul Monroe.[68]

Another Boxer remission was important in 1924—that from the Soviet Union. Educators noticed immediately that the amount that could be used for educational purposes equalled $45,000,000, and eight major institutions had already approached the negotiator, Leo Karakhan, urging that it be used to maintain their institutions.[69] The remission was part of an even more important document, the treaty of recognition of the Soviet Union by China, signed by Wu P'ei-fu who controlled Peking, on May 31, 1924, and by Chang Tso-lin representing the anti-Chihli forces, on September 24, 1924.[70] The document was the official acceptance of the Karakhan Declaration of 1919 which had renounced all Czarist unequal treaties with China and promised return of all special rights and privileges that had been taken by force through Czarist policies.[71]

The restoration of full diplomatic relations was both a considerable achievement for Karakhan and an independent foreign policy initiative for China, although China had the precedent of one ally, England, which had recognized the U.S.S.R. in February 1924. T'ao wrote that the people were responsive to the generous renunciation of unequal treaties at a time when no democratic allies from the War were being so fair to China. As he put it:

The good feeling entertained by the Chinese toward new

> Russia is not so much for Russia's Bolshevism as for Russia's
> stand for international justice and equality, not in words but
> in action. It is yet too early to forecast the influences of this
> new friend upon our education. However, one thing we are
> pretty sure of is that contact with New Russia will make
> Chinese education less favorable for further realization of
> imperialism and capitalism.[72]

Prophetic were these words, and T'ao's own writings were to undergo a significant influence from Marxism before 1930.

The original Karakhan Declaration of 1919, which was repeated in 1920, had stirred interest among the *Hsin chiao-yü* group in
exactly what was going on in the new government of Russia which
had renounced the aggressions of the past. Chiang Meng-lin had
recognized the social message to the intelligentsia inherent in the
1917 Revolution. But he put *Hsin chiao-yü* on record in 1920 as
believing that literacy and an able citizenry would obviate revolution as it had occurred in Russia.[73] In 1925 T'ao saw "class war"
as a serious problem of developing industry, but one which did not
seem to spell revolution to him either. The educator should address
this problem by more knowledge and understanding of the whole
process of industrialization and production, he wrote, "bringing
the human element into industrialism, and cultivating a right attitude toward labor as well as capital . . ."[74] This was what Dewey
had argued in his China lectures, reflecting an extraordinary faith
that the power inherent in a scientific understanding of the world
would eliminate social conflict.

While not accepting Marxian class analysis, T'ao was clearly
impressed by the actions taken in foreign policy which made the
Soviet Union's socialist state look so different from other Western
powers. The experience of confronting two intractable sources of
power, the foreigners and the warlords, was adding political content
to T'ao's conception of education. He still argued that education
should in principle be above political party considerations. But he
was showing a willingness to use the student movement in ways
Dewey had criticized in 1920, and to add political content to school

objectives so that resistance to foreign exploitation would be part
of adequately informing new citizens of current affairs in the
schools.

The Educated Class and the People

After 1925 the continuing problems of militarist obstruction
and political intervention gradually convinced T'ao to dedicate
his energies almost exclusively to non-formal education at the
village level. His most venturesome experiment was a model school
for training teachers that he founded in a village outside of Nanking.
The Nationalist Revolution of 1927, claiming to unify China under
one government, was coincident with the founding of this school,
and was initially a source of much hope for all who felt the warlords were the greatest obstruction to democracy in China. These
hopes were short-lived for many, including T'ao. His Hsiao-chuang
Experimental Village Normal School lasted only from 1927 to 1930,
when it was closed by Kuomintang troops. But, despite its short
life, this school developed ideas that were to re-emerge after the
1949 Communist revolution as central elements in the educational
system of the People's Republic of China.

As for Dewey's educational philosophy, T'ao's shifts and reformulations became more drastic in the years leading up to 1929.
In moving below the level of institutionalized education, T'ao
dragged Dewey's theory out of the schoolroom and into society.
Under the scrutiny of the peasants, T'ao made education a living
part of village life. By 1929 T'ao's transformation of Dewey's
principles produced quite different ideas from those expounded in
the popular lecture tour a decade before.

In 1924 T'ao worked enthusiastically to formulate a concept
of literacy education, to which he also subscribed the National
Association for the Advancement of Education. His hopes for this
non-formal alternative to the school system were ambitious:
"Friends of popular education have the ambition to achieve the
miracle of eliminating illiteracy among 200 million people in ten
years."[75] Between 1924 and 1927, T'ao's commitment to the work

of "village education," or "rural education," led to the following
statement of policy by the National Association:

> Our association has a broad scope of activity, but, from now
> on, our primary responsibility is to serve our 200,400,000
> peasants through a forceful policy of rural educational reform.
> We are already committed to raise one million *yuan* [dollars]
> and amass one million comrades, to promote one million
> schools, and reform one million villages.[76]

The connection between raising the educational level of the peasant
and rural reconstruction now seemed a natural one to T'ao.

When T'ao established his own village teacher training school
in the spring of 1927, he wrote a position paper on rural education
which attacked the "bookworm" complex dominating local education. Much of the fault lay with village teachers, who themselves
needed a different preparation:

> Chinese rural education has taken the wrong path. It teaches
> people to leave the country and run to the city. It teaches
> people to eat rice, not grow it, to wear clothes but not to
> plant cotton, and to build homes rather than plant forests.
> It teaches people to admire expensive habits and look down
> on farm work. It teaches people to consume, not produce.
> It teaches farmers' children to become bookworms.[77]

To change this kind of education the new teacher needed to "cast
himself into the furnace of life to forge a new existence."[78] T'ao
was later to criticize explicitly the "learning" of returned students
that he felt also needed to be reforged.

T'ao's school was in a village not too far from Nanking called
Hsiao-chuang.[79] Teacher training at the school was integrated with
the more distant aim of rural education, village renewal. "Lived
education" prevailed as a daily life-style. The facilities were little
more than a camp ground initially, with tents as living quarters,
the maintenance and daily functions performed by the students.[80]
The potential teachers joined village peasants in their daily work,

and thereby attacked the problem of the separation of the teacher from the taught at a fundamental social level. Foreshadowing future programs in the People's Republic, T'ao claimed that rural teachers must be "peasant sensitized" (*nung-min kan-k'u hua*) in order to be effective teachers.[81] If this sensitivity to peasant problems and aspirations were present, then each village in China could, T'ao exhorted optimistically, be transformed into a completely self-governing unit as the most basic component of the Republic of China.[82]

The teachers entering T'ao's school, after it grew for a period, were given entrance examinations which included a day of farm work.[83] In the school, T'ao's principle of "the union of teaching, learning, and doing" was accepted by all as an operating procedure. Under the advantageous conditions of full internal control within the experimental environment, T'ao's generalized ideal of making living conditions into the substance of education was realizable. He lectured on the theme that "life is education," and tested what was to become his fundamental principle of education in the 1930s, *sheng-huo chiao-yü* (life-education).[84] At Hsiao-chuang his school members integrated themselves into the village community and attempted to promote democratic meetings in cases of disputes. In a dispute over well water, for example, the school arranged a public discussion to settle the problem; villagers were provided a format to share experience and knowledge, regardless of age or predetermined social status. A teenager ran the meeting, and school personnel participated from the floor to set an atmosphere in which all opinions could be considered equally.[85]

As the teachers' school expanded, a central elementary school for in-service education was established in the village. Branch schools, extending only through the compulsory four grades, grew out from the central school in a network that connected several small villages, each of about 100 families.[86] Adult classes and special sessions for working young people were available at the elementary schools.[87] Gradually other social functions were provided. The normal school established a village hospital, and a "self-defense league" for protection against bandits. The defense league had watch towers and stone defenses. It coordinated more than 240 villages in the area, and a few guns were bought. The fundamentals of military training were taught to peasants by invited army officers. Teng Yu-hsiang, the militarist, had been an admirer of T'ao's, and probably helped in getting the arms legally from the Ministry of the Interior in Nanking. But the later suppression of the school may have involved fears of Teng's support at the school.[88]

On one level, T'ao's experiment in non-elitist, non-formal education attacked a social problem common to all intellectuals who were reformers in the floundering Republic. Interest in this problem was reflected in discussions of the nature of the Chinese "intelligentsia" and social forces in history that began increasingly to appear in Chinese journals.[89] Articles on this subject proliferated following 1925 and were to burgeon into the "social history controversy" of the early 1930s. In 1927, after a year's reflection on the nature of the intelligentsia and the rising controversy, T'ao wrote an article entitled "Wei chih-shih chieh-chi" (The false intelligentsia).[90]

The background for his thinking on the subject probably included the reading of an article by his former sponsor, Chiang Meng-lin, that had been published in 1924. In a special edition of a major Peking newspaper, Chiang had raised the issue many educators felt quite personally: The "intellectual class" or intelligentsia (*chih-shih chieh-chi*) was only a form, he argued, without substance or power in the new Republic.[91] One reason their reform ideas had no effect was because intellectuals as a group were not influential. Marxist critiques of the intelligentsia as exploitative idealists were in the mid-1920s increasing and sharpening debate.[92] Another Columbia graduate, Chang Hsi-jo, wrote a major article in early 1927 to counter class-defined criticism of the intellectuals. He argued that the Russian Soviets and the British Labor Party had both found intellectuals important elements in their movements. Furthermore, he felt that China's intellectual class had an unusual tradition of concern and connection to the working class, and therefore did not need to be attacked for an exploitative attitude which was not present.[93] T'ao seemed to join the debate at this point, and began his article: "Recently tendencies have changed again, and cries to overthrow the intelligentsia have switched to cries to support the intelligentsia. We have to ask who are the intelligentsia? How have the intelligentsia been formed?"[94] His analysis was critical of the intellectual class, old and new, but not on Marxist grounds.

T'ao clearly distinguished social class identity from inborn ability. He felt the level of intellectual endowment varied only about as much as difference in height in human beings—not all that striking a difference, and certainly not a "class trait." Knowledge was also something that should never be made a class attribute, and would not be as long as it was really knowledge. T'ao proceeded to define real knowledge as that which is based on experience. In a definition substantially the same as the standard pragmatic philosophic conception of knowledge and truth, T'ao wrote a kind of pragmatic version of the Confucian text "The Great Learning," which addressed the same subject using similar metaphors. Knowledge, it said:

> is like grafting trees. One kind of tree branch can be grafted onto another kind of tree and make the foliage thicker, the flowers more beautiful, and the fruit sweeter. If we graft knowledge derived from other men's experience onto the knowledge produced from our own experience, then our knowledge will branch out widely, and our lives will be full. We must have our own experience as the root, and the knowledge from it, the branches. Then, other men's knowledge can be grafted onto this . . .[95]

In T'ao's view, difficulties arose when knowledge somehow departed from this natural process of growth based on experience.

False knowledge was to T'ao like paper currency without a gold reserve of experience behind it to give it cash value.[96] To keep passing along such knowledge as valuable required the outside support of some special power. This had been the work of the emperor in imperial China, T'ao argued, who devised the system of status built on dead knowledge to deprive the most able candidates among the people from ever attaining a position to challenge the power structure. This ingenious technique had enslaved the most brilliant and creative minds of China to exercises such as the formalistic "eight-legged essay," and rendered the intelligentsia impractical cripples.[97] T'ao developed this theme in later essays to demonstrate the debilitating effect of an educational system "which prevented those who use their hands from using their brains, and those who use their brains from using their hands. The result was nobody could do anything."[98]

Confrontation with the West in the nineteenth century had exposed the false currency of the literati. It was like "throwing eggs at a stone," T'ao argued, and the tragedy continued as the self-strengtheners held on to their counterfeit status in the late nineteenth century.[99] T'ao concluded his analysis with an indictment of the correspondingly false "foreign eight-legged essay" mentality which many who went abroad brought arrogantly back to China. Scientists were as guilty as educators, if their knowledge derived only from memorization and was untested by experience.[100]

T'ao's analysis of the intelligentsia in 1927 rested on the pragmatic definition of experimental knowledge. As Dewey put it, experience was the source of all knowledge, and was learned through a test within environmental conditions. T'ao had articulated the problem in terms of a social class defined by its possession of false knowledge. Another social class that often did possess experiential knowledge was becoming the focus of T'ao's work—the peasantry. In the debates over social history that followed the Kuomintang purge of its Marxist allies in 1927, the masses were intentionally neglected in conservative social analysis.[101] For T'ao they were gradually to assume a larger and larger role in explaining social change.

In the spring of 1927 the Northern Expedition reached Nanking, and revolutionary fervor against the hated warlords, as well as against the depredations of privileged foreigners, spilled over into the world of education. T'ao's precise reactions to the Kuomintang victory and its systematic purge of the left soon thereafter are not recorded. Yet whatever happened to push T'ao's ideas to their most radical point by 1929 may well have included his reactions to both events.

T'ao had carefully tended his new educational experiment during the two years 1927–1929 rather than joining the Kuomintang revolutionaries. But he read *San-min chu-i* (The three people's principles) avidly at the time of the revolution and recommended it as mandatory reading, along with Kropotkin, to his friends.[102] T'ao's writings became more explicitly critical of Dewey after 1927, and in 1929 he attacked Dewey's notion of "the socialization of the school."[103] Dewey's idea was to give the student, in miniature form, a sense of what society was really like. T'ao responded:

> To talk of revolutionizing someone presumes that the person is not yet a revolutionary. If that person were a revolutionary from the beginning, then what is there to "ize" (*hua*)? To say "socialize the school" is to make the same mistake.[104]

For T'ao the creation of a microcosm of society in the schoolhouse was like caging a bird and then trying to add a few dried twigs to recreate the natural world. Society itself had to provide the live lessons for learning. If this were practiced, Dewey's notions of "socialization" became a tautology because "society was the school" (*she-hui chi hsueh-hsiao*).[105]

The departures T'ao was making from Dewey's lectures of 1920 received a surprising confirmation in 1929 from none other than Dewey himself. In 1929 Dewey published his *Impressions of Soviet Russia and the Revolutionary World* in which he reported on his recent visit to the Soviet Union.[106] T'ao read Dewey's reflections on his visit with interest, and derived from them an obvious sense of justification for the increasingly drastic revisions he was making in his former teacher's ideas. Dewey had been exhilarated to find that the relationship between school and society in the Soviet Union was so integral and came to reflect on the inherent limitations of his own reformist efforts in the United States. The personal competition and desire for private profit lying just

outside the door of the school in the United States made it necessary that "in important respects school activities should be pro-
tected from social contacts and connections, instead of being
organized to create them.[107] Dewey, and followers like T'ao,
accepted the desirability of the connection between school and
society as a premise of educational reform. T'ao had been working
in a dramatically more hostile environment than Dewey's theories
confronted in the United States, and had been forced to seek alternative ways of making education have some effect in such an
environment before Dewey saw this as a problem. When T'ao read
Dewey's book in 1929, he immediately picked up Dewey's equivo-
cation about the prospects of change through "social microcosm"
education. He informed his Hsiao-chuang community that Dewey
was changing his views.[108]

Dewey had in fact come close to stating T'ao's inversion of
"life is education" in his book. Soviet education had led him to
"searchings of head and mind that are needed and wholesome."[109]
Because the whole state recognized the principle of coordinating
"the economic and industrial phase of social life" with daily life
in the classroom, the Soviet Union seemed to Dewey to be achieving overnight the unfulfilled objectives of reformers in the United
States. Dewey wrote, "The Russian educational situation is enough
to convert one to the idea that only in a society based upon the
cooperative principle can the ideals of educational reformers be
adequately carried into operation."[110] Moreover, Dewey found a
final principle at play which was dear to his heart. The educational
system was, as Dewey viewed it, flexible and experimental in a way
that could spur creativity among educators.[111] There were some
specific instances cited by Dewey that were intensely interesting
to T'ao.

Dewey recounted the story of an educator he talked with in
the Soviet Union who had been influenced by progressive education
in the United States and who experimented with new educational
techniques for several years before and after the 1917 Revolution.
His name was Stanislav Teofilovich Shatskii (1878-1934), and he
began his career with urban social work in Moscow early in the

century.[112] By 1911 he had a model experimental school operating in the summer sponsored by some philanthropic liberals. Dewey commented:

> The educator of whom I am speaking began as a liberal reformer, not a radical but a constitutional democrat. He worked in the faith and hope that the school, through giving a new type education, might peacefully and gradually produce the required transformations in other institutions. This pilgrim's progress from reforming pedagogue to convinced communist affords a symbol of the social phase of the entire Soviet educational movement.

Such a reference caught T'ao's eye, and he associated Shatskii's work precisely with the goals he was trying to accomplish at Hsiao-chuang.[113]

Shatskii's project, a few hundred miles from Moscow, included some fourteen schools "scattered through a series of villages . . . there is not in my knowledge anything comparable to it elsewhere in the world," said Dewey.[114] Clearly it had the same rural renewal aim as T'ao's experiment begun over a year before Dewey wrote. But perhaps the most interesting comparison was Shatskii's pilgrimage as described through Dewey's interview with him:

> The frustration of educational aims by economic conditions occupied a much larger place in the story of the pilgrim's progress from pedagogy to communism than did explicit and definite political and government opposition. In fact, the latter was mentioned only as an inevitable by-product of the former. There are, as he puts it, two educations, the greater and the smaller. The lesser is given by the school; the larger, and the one finally influential, is given by the actual conditions of life, especially those of the family and neighborhood. And according to his own story, this educator found that the work he was trying to do in the school even under the relatively very favorable conditions of his experimental school, was undone by the educative—or mis-educative—formation of

108

disposition and mental habit proceeding from the environment. Hence he became convinced that the social medium and the progressive school must work together, must operate in harmony reinforcing each other, if the aim of the progressive school was not to be constantly undermined and dissipated; with the growth of this conviction he became insensibly a communist. He became convinced that the central force in undoing the work of socialized reform he was trying to achieve by means of school agencies was precisely the egoistic and private ideals and methods inculcated by the institution of private property, profit, and acquisitive possession.[115]

John Dewey never had a chance to visit Hsiao-chuang. But another of T'ao's mentors at Columbia's Teachers College, William Heard Kilpatrick, did visit it in October 1929. Kilpatrick was coming from a trip to the Soviet Union where he also had seen Shatskii's schools, and he told T'ao in person that the two experimental institutions were similar in many respects. T'ao was excited to hear that "life is education" and "society is the school" were being tried by Shatskii, although T'ao had no previous knowledge of his work until he read Dewey's book and talked with Kilpatrick.[116] T'ao asked if Shatskii were a Communist Party member, and Kilpatrick indicated that he was not—apparently referring to the ten years Shatskii had experimented with his new education as a liberal reformer before 1926.[117] This interested T'ao all the more: "I then asked, if he is not a Communist Party member, how can he be an educator under a Communist government?" He answered that because he wanted to experiment with a new kind of education, the Russian government allowed him to experiment. "That point is also similar to me," T'ao said, "I am an educator under the Kuomintang government, but I am not a Kuomintang Party member."[118] The similarity was indeed accurate but T'ao did not realize the tenuous position experimental education was to maintain under the Kuomintang in the near future.

Dewey's positive comments about the Soviet system of education were not made without qualification. He could not accept those aspects of Soviet ideology that stressed "the necessity of class war and of world revolution by violence," although he did not find them a sufficient threat for the United States to withhold official recognition of the Soviet Union.[119] He also would not admit that the aims of "liberal educators" could only be carried out within an economic and social revolution on the Soviet model. Yet his praise for the Soviet educational system—"in which our professed progressive democratic ideas are most completely embodied"[120]— impressed T'ao deeply, and the effects of capitalism on educational reform soon became explicit in T'ao's analysis of his problems. "Why did Professor Dewey advocate education is life in the United States?" T'ao asked his school members rhetorically. He answered, "The United States is a capitalist country, and they experiment bit by bit, so that there are many objectives educators do not attain, and cannot put into practice, whereas in Russia these are already attained, and in practice." He concluded in 1929, that, should Dewey come to Hsiao-chuang, T'ao was sure he also would call for "life is education."[121] T'ao also began using dialectical logic to describe social change, and he was relentless, in his articles at the end of the 1920s, in his attack on various forms of educational idealism.[122]

At the risk of "teaching Confucianism on the doorstep of Confucius himself," it seemed T'ao was more than vindicated in the drastic revisions of Dewey's ideas which conditions in the 1920s had required him to make. Confirmed in his revisions, T'ao's lectures to his school at the end of the 1920s were full of hope for the prospects of "life education." The "union of teaching, learning, and doing" was programmed into the growing complex of schools, and every experienced farmer was to contribute the benefit of his knowledge for the renewal of the village.[123] In this way a small experiment in one village, T'ao argued, could become a model for villages anywhere in China. It could spread a realistic and practical education rooted in actual living conditions throughout the country.

T'ao's experiments in non-formal education pulled education below the perimeter of institutionalized power and they thereby escaped the confrontation that had led other cultural reform efforts into a dilemma. But he was only in hiding, and his alternatives were little more than pilot projects. To survive they needed sponsorship from those with political power, as Shatskii had received in the Soviet Union. T'ao was not to see this happen in his lifetime.

Chapter V

THE DENOUEMENT: EDUCATIONAL REFORM
AT THE END OF THE 1920s

By the end of the 1920s the new education reform movement
—launched with such enthusiasm in 1919—had incurred staggering
casualities. Kuo Ping-wen, the man who staffed his national
university with United States returned students and promoted
the highest standards of progressive education, was in self-exile
in New York City. Chiang Meng-lin, the prime mover behind
the reform effort, was hiding in the International Settlement in
Shanghai after his expulsion from Peking by militarist authorities.
Chiang's successor as editor of *Hsin chiao-yü*, T'ao Hsing-chih, was
also outside the sphere of the national educational system, running
his experimental normal school and working on village renewal to
expand non-formal educational alternatives.

The influence John Dewey had on these men and their reform
effort had been important. He helped define the principles of
democratic education in the initial phase of the movement that
led to the 1922 School Reform Decree. Frustration and defeat
characterized the implementation of these principles before the
Nationalist government consolidated its rule over China in 1930.
Dewey's ideas had become part of a movement, but their influence
was curtailed as the movement declined.

Upon returning from abroad, the three reform leaders had
accepted China's educational institutions as the means through
which to promote change. Kuo and Chiang were the heads of the
top two universities in China in the 1920s. T'ao had been the dean
at Kuo's institution, and then director of the Association for the
Advancement of Education, which by the time of its 1924 annual
meeting had an active membership of 2,300 educators.[1] Through
these positions they applied their energies to make the ideals of
the new education reform movement become the reality of educational practice in China. But each one was repulsed from his

immediate aims once contact was made with political power. Like some experimental guinea pigs the three were thrown back repeatedly when they made contact with the grid of political force in China's society of militarists.

The issue of power was raised on the campuses themselves by increasing student activism in the 1920s. Administrators were caught in the middle between the repressive militarists controlling the funding of their institutions and irate students. Students increasingly demanded the independence of their institutions from warlord intrigue and political favoritism, which could arbitrarily replace presidents, or more subtly, continue privilege for foreign institutions. In the year 1922 alone, there were over one hundred "student storms" (*hsueh-ch'ao*) expressing student opposition to those in power on their campuses. Chiang and Kuo were both plagued with confrontations from political activism within their student bodies, and themselves began to look like representatives of the status quo.[2]

The attitude taken by all three men was to try to turn the justifiable student anger into a responsible form of "public opinion" which would be channeled through stable political institutions in the society. Kuo and T'ao gave glowing reports to audiences in the United States about the new role of public opinion in China. Such statements may have been made to convince one relatively friendly big power that the Republic was going to make it as a new political system and deserved the confidence of foreigners. This confidence was needed to revise the unequal agreements and privileges of the nineteenth century, and to eliminate the pretense of political chaos used in the past to justify foreign incursions into China's sovereignty.[3] But what T'ao praised as the healthy "invisible force" of public opinion acting in Chinese politics in 1911 and thereafter was in reality a kind of political consciousness which directly threatened the three administrators, for it implied a politicization of educational institutions, and the consequent threat of suppression by warlords. Students were pushing their institutions to react against the undemocratic political environment in which these institutions were operating. This tension became clear in the tragic situation surrounding Kuo Ping-wen's dismissal.

Kuo Ping-wen and National Southeastern University

President Kuo had insisted that his institution be independent of political affiliation. With the rising nationalism of the 1920s and the increasing appeal of the political parties such as the Kuomintang and the Communist Party, many students came to regard this position as untenable. On the Southeastern campus itself, Kuomintang-oriented professors and students felt that Kuo's administration, in accepting money from the local militarists to run the institution, was supporting the status quo instead of being neutral.[4] Anguished personal decisions were required from the student body. Political factions among students applied pressure either to oppose Kuo or to agree with his attempted political neutrality. One group organized to demand that the Ministry of Education reinstate him. An example of the difficult judgments that took place was the case of a secret Kuomintang party organizer who was an undergraduate. His admiration for Kuo was high, even though he wanted to overthrow the militarists. In the end, he later wrote, he was unable personally to attack the respected founder of the institution and rescinded his Kuomintang party membership.[5] There was no way to remain perfectly neutral. The situation was not unlike that on many United States campuses in the 1960s, politicized by anti-Vietnam war demonstrations. Attending class at all was to break a strike called by other students. Kuo Ping-wen's personal problem had the same dimensions. Professional neutrality was proving impossible for him in the early Republic.

Kuo Ping-wen's dismissal in January 1925 was significant beyond the personal tragedy it represented for the "father" of National Southeastern University. The political attack on this sponsor of modern educational principles, and patron of the returned student group from the United States, represented the beginning of the end for the new education reform movement.

After 1925 Kuo was never again a leading figure within the educational system in China—and he spent much of the rest of his career serving China and the world of international education outside the national boundaries of his homeland.[6]

Kuo's demise at Southeastern University was due in large part to shifts in political power within China. In expanding his institution after it was granted national university status in 1921, Kuo worked unavoidably through the ruling militarists in Peking, and their deputy, the military governor of Kiangsu, who was financing his institution. These connections of Kuo and some of his institution's trustees—particularly the powerful Huang Yen-p'ei— with the Chihli clique of militarists, became a point of attack as the Kuomintang gained support in North China. Sun Yat-sen, the leader of the party, had written Kuo in the 1923-1924 academic year, commending his work and asking him openly to join the revolutionary cause.[7] But such a course would have been suicidal for Kuo as well as his institution, which was sponsored by those at civil war with Sun.

The military governor, or *tuchün*, of Kiangsu was Ch'i Hsieh-yuan, and he had been consistent in his support of Kuo's institution.[8] But, in September 1924, Ch'i broke into conflict with the *tuchün* of neighboring Chekiang. The battle was over control of Shanghai and might have ended as a local feud except that Ch'i received support from the Chihli militarists controlling Peking policy, and his opponent was backed by the old enemy of that clique, Chang Tso-lin, who headed the Fengtien forces.[9] Even before this Kiang-che war had expanded into the Second Chihli-Fengtien war, President Kuo found his finances from Ch'i cut off. Ch'i had diverted all provincial revenues to military expenditures, a condition struggling educators had met before in the early Republic.[10] Kuo was busily keeping his salaryless faculty from striking in the fall of 1924 when the conclusion of the war brought the defeat of the Chihli clique and Ch'i Hsieh-yuan with them.

General Tuan Ch'i-jui, one of the victorious forces, rushed to take Peking in late 1924 ahead of his ally, Sun Yat-sen, and the Kuomintang faction. As the new Minister of Education, General

Tuan appointed a man who he probably did not suspect was soon to become part of the Peking underground of the Kuomintang. Ma Hsu-lun (1884-   ) became the head of the propaganda department of the KMT underground. This was the important link back to events at Southeastern University, for Ma had close revolutionary ties from 1911 with dissident professors on Kuo's faculty. In particular Professor Yang Ch'üan (Yang Hsing-fo) in the Science Society clique at Southeastern was an old acquaintance of Ma's, and Yang Ch'üan had openly fought Kuo on the campus before being eliminated from the faculty in 1924. The dynamics behind Kuo's dismissal derived from new KMT influence in the north after 1924.[11]

Yang Ch'üan, the thorn in the side of Kuo's own institution, was a returned student trained at Cornell and Harvard whom Kuo had appointed. This fact needs some explanation. One might have expected loyalty from the recruited appointees, and also some agreement in views among the United States trained students at Southeastern. Two subgroups existed, however, within the United States returned students at Kuo's institution which were predisposed not to rely upon the New Culture movement and progressive education as a first priority in building the new China.

Yang Ch'üan had been the personal secretary to Sun Yat-sen in 1912, after having actively participated in the revolutionary overthrow of the Manchus. He went abroad on a government grant the following year to study science at Cornell. His revolutionary background was different from students such as Kuo Ping-wen, who had been busy studying for a B.A. at Wooster College in Ohio when the revolution took place. When Yang was appointed as the chairman of the school of commerce by Kuo in 1919, Yang had firm commitments to Sun and the goal of eliminating warlord power in the north. He was a national figure in the Chinese Science Society (K'o-hsueh she) and, as the science faculty expanded at Southeastern, some of Yang's friends who also had personal commitments to Sun were appointed. These men had direct connections with older revolutionaries in Peking and the Chekiang clique of academics such as Ma Hsu-lun.[12]

Ma and T'ang Erh-ho (1871-1940) were Chekiangese and sworn blood brothers from the days of the Shanghai underground before the 1911 Revolution. As prominent academics in Peking, they and their teacher, the eminent Chekiang scholar, Ch'en Fa-ch'en (Ch'en Chieh-shih), were instrumental in getting their fellow provincial and close acquaintance from their revolutionary circles, Ts'ai Yuan-p'ei, appointed as Chancellor of National Peking University. Another Chekiangese who was an active revolutionary in Nanking when the revolution was successful in 1911, and who was personally connected to Sun Yat-sen, was Jen Hung-chün (H. C. Zen). His younger brother had committed suicide in 1913 to oppose the assassination of an organizer of the Kuomintang.[13] Jen had worked with Yang Ch'üan at Cornell to organize the Science Society, and was trained in chemistry. Jen was appointed Vice-President of Southeastern University in 1923 after serving in the Ministry of Education in Peking. The Science Society group consolidated behind him and became a strong faction in university politics. These connections of the "science clique" with the ministry re-emerged when Kuo was fired.

Yang Ch'üan's relations with Kuo had gotten so bad that Yang was transferred from department to department at Southeastern until the college of engineering in which he was serving was abolished in 1924. This action was taken by the military governor, Ch'i Hsieh-yuan. Yang was then dismissed from the university. He went to Canton and joined Sun Yat-sen, accompanying him north as his secretary when Ch'i was thrown out of power and Kuo dismissed.[14]

In appointing men such as Yang Ch'üan and Jen Hung-chün, Kuo probably knew at least something of their support for Sun in the past, as well as of their revolutionary sympathies. The vice-president before Jen, Liu Po-ming, had also been quite sympathetic to the KMT, and probably a party member before he died in 1923. Kuo might have seen himself somewhat as Ts'ai Yuan-p'ei did in Peking—leading a university wherein all political and ideological views were freely admitted, without the university as a whole becoming characterized by any specific political affiliation. This position, however, implied its own unstated political assumptions, namely, that federal universities could exist as institutions in China free from political influence. Kuo painfully learned that his institution did indeed have a political identity, one that could engender political opposition.

In addition to returned students from the United States with previous revolutionary commitments, there was another subgroup at Southeastern University who for different reasons were not inclined to favor the New Culture movement orientation towards reform. This was a small group of ideological conservatives trained at Harvard University. They were students of literature who had studied with Irving Babbit, a classicist. As it happened, Babbit had a particular passion against representatives of scientific modernity such as Dewey. Three men, Mei Kuang-ti, Wu Mi, and Hu Hsien-su, had all returned to the faculty at Southeastern by 1921, and founded a journal in Nanking opposing language reform and the New Culture movement.[15] Hu Shih and Mei Kuang-ti, at the time they were both leaving Cornell for graduate work in 1915, took opposite sides in a literary debate on the merits of adopting the common colloquial language for scholarly and esthetic works. Harvard students such as T'ang Yueh, Wu Mi, Hu Hsien-su, and Liang Shih-ch'iu were sympathetic with Mei's conservative position in the next few years.[16] Meanwhile, at Columbia Hu Shih found sympathy for a literary revolution from many Chinese who later showed their full support of the New Culture movement. The conservative journal later founded at Southeastern, Hsueh heng (Critical review), attacked Hu Shih. The three editors all had some links to earlier expressions of cultural conservatism in the Nan she (Southern society) group of writers in 1909, or the Society for the Protection of National Studies (Kuo hsueh pao-ts'un hui) of 1905.[17] At Southeastern they never confronted Kuo as a political group, except probably in arguing for priorities in university policy.

The conservative elements in Kuo's institution also included nationalistic sensitivities expressed as an undercurrent of opposition to the generally well-received proposals of the new education reform movement. The variety of conservatism argued in Hsueh

heng was itself more traditionalistic than traditional, and accepted
a distinction between the elements of cultural tradition it wanted
to conserve, and the political form of China as a nation it was
willing to see prevail over imperial institutions. The conservative
effect of rising nationalism in the mid-1920s tended to agree in
sentiment with some of the attitudes of cultural conservatives
and allied with those views to strengthen the undercurrent
of modern conservatism among educators.

The publishing policies of the national professional journal
Chung-hua chiao-yü chieh ("Chinese Educational Circles") provides
evidence of this strain of conservative opinion. The magazine was
founded in 1913, and liberalized its views after May Fourth, as had
many older periodicals; but it remained more moderate in 1919
than Chiang Meng-lin's *Hsin chiao-yü*.[18] In fact, the new editor in
1921, Tso Shun-sheng, could not bring himself to endorse whole-
heartedly the new tide advocated by the Deweyans. Tso read all
the new education material submitted, which flourished following
Dewey's visit. He felt that the enthusiasm behind democracy,
science, and foreign educational methods and systems had overlooked altogether whatever value could be found in traditional
Chinese education. As the editor from 1921 to 1924, a period when
the new education was expanding among educators, Tso's attitude
included only a conditional acceptance of Dewey and the new
thought in education.[19]

By 1924, when Ch'en Ch'i-t'ien took over its editorship,
Chinese Educational Circles began subscribing to a new trend
among educators called "nationalistic education" (*kuo-chia chu-i
ti chiao-yü*). This trend was a reaction to the same pressures T'ao
Hsing-chih felt after 1924 deriving from disputes over foreign
privilege in China. Ch'en, like Tso Shun-sheng, had been a member
of the vocal Young China Association which spearheaded the
growing nationalistic sentiment in education.[20] The ugly May 30th,
1925 "Shanghai massacre" consolidated much support behind the
arguments this group made for considering education as a function
of the state to strengthen the state against foreign encroachment.
The movement argued that the state, rather than private individuals,

political parties, local districts, or educational associations—and most of all, rather than foreigners—should have full sovereignty over education.[21] Education thus conceived was to come under government control, and to be used as an instrument to produce citizens dedicated to national salvation in a time of crisis.[22]

Ch'en Ch'i-t'ien wrote in his *Reminiscences* that, before he took over the editorship of *Chinese Educational Circles* in the summer of 1924, he was influenced by the New Culture movement in which most people intentionally avoided practical politics. He felt this influence in 1919, and had become a graduate student at National Southeastern University to pursue the study of education not long thereafter.[23] His writings on education during these three years, he noted, were based on the principles of *min-chu chu-i* (democracy), but, when he graduated and became an editor, his views and articles shifted in emphasis, and were written according to the principles of *kuo-chia chu-i* (nationalism). Ch'en said the dominant influences in his "democratic" phase were threefold: 1) the democratic tide following World War I; 2) the New Culture tides of the May Fourth movement; 3) Dewey's educational theory.[24] These were precisely the same themes that affected the new education reform movement and *Hsin chiao-yü*.

In the two and a half years he edited *Chinese Educational Circles* (summer 1924—winter 1926), Ch'en changed his views regarding the democratic relationship between education and the government. Almost in a parody of the efforts of T'ao Hsing-chih to insist that education should be a public instrument of the state with its sovereignty separate from that of the political leaders, Ch'en insisted that education was a tool of the state. He wrote that previous talk about the "independence of education" was really concerned with the non-interference of religions, political factions, or political battles in the running of education, and should not be extended to questioning the relationship of education to the state. He claimed it was the prerogative of the state to use education as "a tool (*kung-chü*) to train citizens, promote national characteristics, and build the fortunes of the state."[25] Not only were

education and the government unalterably related, but it was clear
that one must "speak of politics (*cheng-chih*) first, and education
(*chiao-yü*) second." Here was the framework for the imperial union
of *cheng-chiao* transformed somewhat into modern nationalism,
which the reformers had been fighting to disestablish in the new
Republic.

Three Careers at a Standstill

P. W. Kuo had tried to carry out one key aspect of the new
education reform ideology. He dedicated himself to his field as a
professional educator and fought to keep education separate from
politics. His neutrality failed in 1925. One might tend to blame the
rise of intense nationalism as the unforeseen flaw in his attempt to
make his university career contribute to the new Republic. There
is some truth in this explanation. The political power plays, personal attacks from his colleagues, and pressure from activist students
were attributable to the national state of crisis which worked to
close the gap between education and politics. The radical alternatives sought by many groups including educators forced politics
into every aspect of society. The "political" character of the educational reformism Kuo was attempting, however, would have
still been there despite his nonrecognition of it. Had there not been
the resurgence of an ideological identification of state and party
with education in the mid-1920s, the reformers would still have
been frustrated in their attempt to construct a new democratic
education for China. This was more evident in the career pattern
of the Dewey student most responsible for the consolidation of
groups which began the reform effort in 1919–Chiang Meng-lin.

Chiang was not in conflict with the Kuomintang in the 1920s,[26]
but he was in despair over the ineffectiveness of the educational
reform movement. Chiang Meng-lin's exhortation to "advance
learning" (*t'i-kao hsueh-shu*) in 1922 brought no relief, and when
he next addressed the problems of educational reformers, his confused optimism had turned to bitter satire. As for intellectuals as
a group, in 1924 Chiang said they did not exist.[27] The "form"
still persisted but without organization, so that they gathered

occasionally to meet, and pass a few irrelevant, superficial, and ludicrous resolutions, and perhaps to send a few haughty telegrams. In fact, the "intellectual class" in China was a "paper tiger," he said, who the common people preposterously seemed to think could produce a "Son of Heaven" to restore peace in the midst of chaos.[28] Chiang's frustration seemed at its limit. He was finally looking at his reform program and at himself to see what had happened.

Chiang acknowledged that intellectuals and their reform efforts were largely unsuccessful and exhausted by 1924, and he attributed this ineffectiveness to the political problem of warlord rule. He saw the dilemma of his movement full blown, and articulated it in terms of the classic chicken and egg puzzle.[29] Society, and ultimately politics, can be influenced by learning, he wrote, but the opposite is also true—so which comes first the chicken or the egg? The ameliorative effect he had hoped cultural reforms would have on society was turning out in fact to be a vicious circle from which education and learning could never break out to correct the political conditions controlling them.

He did not resort to examples from the German humanities movement as he had in 1922. In despair he forced himself in 1924 to examine the premises that had gotten him into such a dilemma. He turned to *Hsin chiao-yü's* initial position regarding the educator's responsibility to engage in political "debate," but not participate in politics, and made some revisions. His conviction that the malady of Chinese politics lay well below the actions of a few vicious and corrupt men remained unshaken. "If other people want the intellectuals' help—the intellectuals answer them that first there must be social reform, or the development of learning, science, thought, etc., etc."[30] Without relinquishing this elitist reform position, he revised his views to sanction the participation of intellectuals in politics—but only to a degree. He argued that intellectuals, in their own professions as scholars, had a responsibility to study current political problems. Chiang was ready to conclude that this entailed interference and collision with politicians, and consequently that the intellectual, before he knew it, was "taking part in politics."[31] Because this connection seemed unavoidable in contemporaneous Chinese society, Chiang said such participation was worthwhile on two conditions: 1) if the involvement had the effect of renovating politics; and 2) if it did not support the status quo. But he insisted that the professional status of the intellectual—his scholarly credentials and "long-range viewpoint"—were his very qualification for taking part, and could not be limited or compromised.

As far as any solution to the chicken and egg dilemma as he posed it in 1924 was concerned, Chiang made one attempted explanation of how to get out. He argued that, despite frustrations so far, a little change either in social conditions or learning would gradually have to affect the other because they were so related— just as, "To breed good chickens, you select good chickens to lay good eggs, and select good eggs to be born as good chickens."[32] This was good Darwinism, relying on the shaping effect of environment. What had happened, however, when a few good eggs had been selected to join the "Good Man Cabinet" in the fall of 1922, or how warlord politics would ever become more tolerant to accept such leaders, Chiang did not discuss. He was not given the time to breed his way professionally out of the chicken and egg puzzle. In 1926 the ruthless suppression of free speech by a new warlord in Peking forced Chiang Meng-lin to seek refuge and later flee to Shanghai for protection.[33]

Analyzing Chiang's difficulty raises two issues which can be profitably discussed in terms of his returned student status: his elitism, and the ineffectiveness of intellectuals as a group. On the first point, it seems peculiar to see Chiang clasp his professional identity as the *sine qua non* of his hopes for reform, when progress was so minimal and held such grim prospects for the future. In explaining this view, I think that his experience as a student living in the advanced industrial society in the United States had a critical effect on the role he saw for himself as an "expert" upon returning. China's obvious backwardness required this expertise, in his view, to develop. When the Revolution of 1911 was taking place in China, Chiang had been at Berkeley for three years, and wrote the following lines to his fellow students in the United States: "Our motto is this: A government of the people, by the educated class, and for the people. To change 'by the educated class' into 'by the people' is our new political philosophy."[34] Hu Shih reflected a similar understanding of his own role in closing the gap between China's backwardness and what he saw in the West. Hu attacked the advice of a professor from Johns Hopkins who said China might do better with a constitutional monarchy than a republic with the comment that the professor's error was his failure to "understand and take into consideration the inspirations and aspirations of the intellectual class in China. The best form of government for a somewhat benighted country like China, it seems to the present writer, is one which will enable the enlightened class of people to utilize their knowledge and talents for the education and betterment of the ignorant and the indifferent."[35] Perhaps it is not surprising that a heady feeling of confidence was the natural reaction of these able students to what they saw could be accomplished if the right things were done in China.

The second point is telling, for we see Chiang and T'ao both pinpointing the problem of their "paper tiger" status as intellectuals. The returned students as part of the new intelligentsia were without a base for exercising political power. Chiang was rigorously modern in his conception of his own social role. What battered legacy of popular deference for the "intellectual class" persisted from imperial times he constantly fought to change into public opinion. He personally accepted that deferential respect only insofar as it was transformed into the authority given professional experts in any democratic society. But he was frustrated that professional opinion was only an empty "form" in the early Republic. Like Kuo Ping-wen, he insisted on living as part of a transformed intelligentsia. They both exerted what influence they could, not as ministers in militarist cabinets, but as professional educators might in a pluralistic society. The tragedy of this social role was that they were displaced persons in a society not yet democratic, and responding only superficially to their efforts to teach democracy by practicing democracy.

Chiang Meng-lin was not led to any drastic reformulations of Dewey's ideas as was T'ao. He fully subscribed to Dewey's definition of the interrelationship between democracy, education, and science. He believed in social engineering and the aim of a science of society which the experimental method, rationally applied, made possible. These ideas naturally gave a significant role to the professional and the social scientist in modern democratic society. Dewey's formulation, if anything, fostered an elitism in these reformers.

T'ao Hsing-chih was turning in the 1920s to alternatives other than reform by intellectuals through formal institutional channels. In fact he was led to challenge the definition of the intellectual himself, and had serious reservations about the value of "scholarly credentials" and "long-range viewpoints" which Chiang felt characterized the intellectual class. He finally bent his efforts below the level of obstructing political controls and worked to define education from the life of the people. He discarded his returned student assumptions about reform carried out by directions from those who had the modern knowledge. He drastically revised Dewey's educational principles and melded them with some Marxian social analysis in formulating his practical experiment in village renewal. But one issue still remained for T'ao. He could only hope that his model experiment would get the ultimate political sponsorship, as had Shatskii's in the U.S.S.R. during the 1920s.

In 1930, as the Kuomintang consolidated its internal control over Chinese politics, T'ao's school was closed by Kuomintang troops as politically threatening, and he had to flee temporarily to Japan.[36] That concluded his confrontation with power, which had grown throughout the 1920s. Kuo, Chiang, and now T'ao had all been thrown out of their work. It was clear that the reform program they had entered into provided no strategy that allowed them to deal with the power they encountered in an undemocratic political environment. Their reformism, with Deweyan principles throughout, was rather a plan geared for the improvement and more effective operation of democratic education. But starting from an institutional system which was under the arbitrary and autocratic control of militarist funding, and subject to repression, the tolerant cultural means they were using could not affect power. According to their ideas, the school should have been an initiator of change, but T'ao finally had to give up on the institution of the school altogether in order to make any progress. In accepting the institutional structure as it existed, their method of change did not work because that social environment was not subject to gradual variations which produced incremental progress. The militarists had the power to create the environment they wanted, and to determine what happened in that environment.

In the 1930s, T'ao remained disaffected with KMT educational policies. Instead of tolerance, he found another politically controlled environment after 1927. This time even the textbooks were "partyized" into doctrinaire readers on party principles. Kuo never became a KMT party member either, and remained a "refugee" from the world of education in China. Chiang flirted with an appointment as Minister of Education after 1927, but resigned after a year as a matter of principle because of the policy difficulties he encountered. Chiang fell back to his administrative position at National Peking University. The shift in political power after 1927 eliminated some of the arbitrary character of militarist administrations centralizing control over the Yangtze river provinces, but this did not establish pluralistic social conditions. The strategy of cultural subversion to change political conditions remained ineffective, as it had been in the 1920s.

PART THREE

PRAGMATIC POLITICS AND REFORM IDEOLOGY

. . . it would certainly be interesting and in all
probability revealing, to examine the non-
American refractions and criticism of pragmatism. . . In this connection it would be significant to trace the receptions of Dewey's work
in the hands of Orientals and scholars of non-
or only semi-industrialized countries, especially
those of China and India, . . .

C. Wright Mills
Sociology and Pragmatism, 1943

Chapter VI

EXPERIMENTAL POLITICS

John Dewey had not traveled away from home as had Confucius at age sixty, or as Plato to Sicily, in search of those who
would try out his political philosophy. Indeed, when he arrived in
China, political philosophy was only a recent interest of his. His
sponsors were educational organizations. But all of Dewey's
followers were trying to make republican government functional,
and the problematic relationship between educational reform and
political reform became increasingly critical in their frustrated
careers. Hu Shih had requested that Dewey address political theory
when he arrived. As Dewey began to lecture on political reform,
his analysis became the theoretical underpinning for a major faction
of Chinese liberals opposing revolutionary change.

Hu Shih convinced Dewey to develop the first systematic
application of pragmatism to social and political philosophy because
intellectuals were intensely interested in political issues when Dewey
arrived.[1] Hu knew what he was asking, for he had audited a course
Dewey began during the war years at Columbia on moral, social,
and political philosophy.[2] John Dewey was apparently intrigued
by this prospect and initially planned to publish his lectures as a
book. The sixteen-lecture series began in September 1919, and
appeared serially in Chinese as each lecture was recorded as
interpreted by Hu Shih. Hu announced that he would publish
a Chinese edition of Dewey's book to appear simultaneously
with the English edition. It was somewhat exciting for them both,
it seems, and Hu made sure the readers of the published Chinese
version of the lectures knew the significance of what they were
reading: "I hope that those who were in the audiences when these
lectures were delivered, as well as the readers of the printed version
of the lectures herewith presented, are cognizant of their rare good
fortune in sharing in Dr. Dewey's initial formal statement of his
social and political philosophy."[3] In the end Dewey decided not

to publish these lectures in English, except insofar as his monthly articles from China were incorporated in his "Popular Essays in Social and Political Philosophy" collected at the end of the 1920s. But the interpreted version of his lectures appeared in many book-length Chinese editions.[4]

The political ideas of John Dewey's followers in China were given a test which the experimentalist formulation of political change had not even undergone in the United States, although some intellectuals connected with the *New Republic* magazine in New York were just becoming interested in a pragmatic analysis of political reform. Dewey's lectures gave many liberal Chinese reformers an unusual opportunity to study and apply an extremely up-to-date and philosophically reliable formulation of the principles of modern democracy. What Dewey said in these lectures, however, was his own first-draft attempt to see how well pragmatism might be applied to politics. This point bears upon the historiography of the liberal failure in the May Fourth period.

Professor Chow's classic study, *The May Fourth Movement*, has laid the groundwork and set an admirable scholarly standard for evaluating the liberals. Professor Chow has noted that the Deweyan liberal position prevailed among many intellectuals following the initial demonstrations of the May Fourth Incident. With a clear sympathy for interpreting the May Fourth movement as, in essence, an "intellectual revolution"—a view shared by the Deweyan liberals themselves—Dr. Chow criticized the liberals for not going far enough in actually working on the social and political "problems" they attacked verbally.[5]

In his excellent study of the origins of Chinese Marxism through the person of Hu Shih's opponent on the left, Maurice Meisner has agreed with Chow that the pragmatic liberals failed to live out their issue-oriented gradualism. Meisner further indicts Dewey's problem-solving, melioristic reformism as irrelevant in the China of 1919—a society in a state of such widespread crisis that there was too little social and political stability for problem-oriented gradualism to work, no matter how hard the pragmatists tried.[6]

This analysis has been discussed in the masterful biography of Hu Shih by Jerome Grieder. Dr. Grieder presents a multi-causal analysis to locate the political limitations of Hu Shih's liberalism. Some of the limitations, he suggests, lie within the liberal creed itself, and some may be attributed to Hu Shih the individual. One weakness is indicated in the strains of elitism in Hu's personality. Overall, however, one senses most strongly in Grieder's treatment of Hu the person and the thinker, the plight of a philosophically consistent liberal whose times did not allow his voice to be heard. To become effective in the immoderate and often violent environment in which Hu lived would have required compromising the principles of his liberalism.[7]

These three studies refine and deepen understanding of the May Fourth liberals, even though there are differences of interpretation.[8] The close look at Dewey's ideological contribution to the political position of his followers in this chapter will confirm certain themes analyzed by these writers. It will seek to isolate points in Dr. Grieder's multi-causal analysis which retain their explanatory power when Hu's limitations are seen in the light of frustrations shared by his Deweyan colleagues in education. The "relevance" of Dewey's political ideas can be evaluated by carefully examining the record of what actually happened to the reform proposals of the Deweyites as they tried to practice them. Because the particular variety of reformism promoted by Dewey's China followers was also being tried by some reform-minded intellectuals in the United States during World War I, that experience is germane to an evaluation of the reform efforts in China. Political pragmatism was found inadequate at home as it was in China. Many of the frustrations of these liberals in China were not merely tied to China's peculiar cultural or political conditions, but derived from inherent limitations in Dewey's experimental political philosophy. The limitations upon the reform ideology of Dewey's followers also relate to another obstacle—sometimes down-played in evaluating China's liberals of this period—the association of American-styled liberalism with a Wilsonian peace. The understanding of World War I and its peace provisions in China was inseparable from the credibility of liberal proposals during the May Fourth period.

World War I and Internationalism in China

The leading followers of John Dewey had returned from the United States during World War I. Dewey's own fundamentally Wilsonian interpretation of the war was shared by these men, and their journals and reform aims reflected Wilsonian hopes for a new democratic era to follow the Allied defeat of autocracy. To put the Chinese Republic in tune with world democratic trends was, in fact, an explicit aim of the domestic reforms argued by Hu Shih and the Deweyan educators.[9] But the postwar international relations of the victorious Allies did not live up to the Wilsonian vision of the war years.

Like Dewey, his followers in China found a way to adjust to the disappointment of the Versailles settlement without impugning the ideals they had described so hopefully as the new democratic order. Many other intellectuals in China refused to join them. The disenchanted grew in number—taught more from the practice of Allied diplomacy at Versailles than from the carefully portrayed vision of non-imperialistic, capitalist order to follow the war, wherein all nations would be treated equally. The compromises made by Wilson at Versailles disillusioned many intellectuals in the United States and Europe; this effect was magnified many times in China. John Dewey's followers, and indeed Dewey himself, lost the convincing example of why China should listen to the experience of the United States and its Allies in looking towards the future.[10]

Throughout the 1920s, Chiang Meng-lin, Kuo Ping-wen, T'ao Hsing-chih, and Hu Shih never attacked Wilsonian assumptions about world politics, although T'ao clearly raised some serious questions after the Karakhan Treaty of 1924. They assumed, as had Wilson, that the best way to change imperialistic power politics was through a democratic alliance of the world's powers, all committed to cooperate within international institutions of government. At the time of the Versailles Conference, the fledgling revolutionary regime in Russia was not comparable in power to the capitalist Allies; Wilson did not believe the Russian regime would even last. For Chinese who had studied in the prosperous capitalist democracy of the United States it was hard to believe in 1919 that the industrial and commercial power of the capitalist Allies should be questioned by a revolutionary alternative which had not yet proven its stability. Dewey's followers in China did not respond favorably to Lenin's alternative. The claim that capitalism was the root cause of imperialism or war was less credible, coming from the untested new regime than the promise of international democracy under the supervision of the capitalist Allies. The future, according to Wilson, promised an end to the domination of the strong over the weak. It promised the guarantee of territorial integrity for weaker nations through multi-national cooperation. Underdeveloped areas such as China could imagine a halt to imperialistic encroachment, and the opportunity to build economically in an atmosphere of international cooperation.[11]

At Versailles the Big Powers agreed to transfer the German unequal treaty concession in China to Japan. This travesty of wartime ideals made a mockery of the friendly handshakes and smiles offered so fervently to the young republic during the war by the modern republics of Europe and North America. Chiang Meng-lin, along with other Deweyites who had argued for their educational and political reforms on the basis of a new era of democratic interaction, were thrown on the defensive. Dewey himself, as the visiting lecturer, was also on the spot to explain what had happened. After four months in China, he wrote to the *New Republic* that the most frequent written question he received following his talks was spurred by this disillusionment. Dewey heard it repeated over and over in different terms from his Chinese audiences; he paraphrased it as follows:

During the war we were led to believe that with the defeat of Germany there would be established a new international order based on justice to all; that might would not henceforth make right in deciding questions between nations; that weak nations would get the same treatment as powerful ones—that, indeed, the war was fought to establish the equal rights of all nations, independently of their size or armed power. Since the decision of the peace conference shows that between nations might still makes right, that the strong nation gets its own way against a weak nation, is it not necessary for China to take steps to develop military power, and for this purpose should not military training be made a regular part of its educational system?[12]

Dewey agreed with the facts of this analysis, but not with the conclusion being drawn for policy in China. He personally felt that the aims of the United States had been sold out at Versailles, and lamented the sacrifice of goals he had sought, such as "the practical reduction of armaments, the abolition of secret and oligarchic diplomacy and of special alliances, the substitution of inquiry and discussion for intrigue and threats, the founding, through the destruction of the most powerful autocracy, of a democratically ordered international government, and the consequent beginning of the end of war."[13] Dewey was sensitive to the criticism of pacifists such as Randolph Bourne in the United States, who attacked Dewey's previous justification for United States intervention.

Following Versailles, Dewey wrote from China that he still supported the tough "new liberalism" foreign policy which the *New Republic* had upheld. That policy position recommended basing international relations on national self-interest and acknowledging the policy role of intelligently-used force. Such realism, Dewey felt, had been compromised by sentimental idealism—which unbending pacifism had only abetted—when the United States entered the war. Dewey argued that the United States should have demanded that the Allies come clean regarding secret agreements, even in their crucial hour of need, when the United States entered the war. By-passing sentimentalism at that point would have avoided the confusion over peace aims, which looked democratic when the United States entered the war, but came out looking imperialistic when the peace treaty was written. For China, the lesson Dewey drew was not to fall back upon the hallucination of military strength, but to build into society those forces which were the source of stable and lasting strength—namely, industrial, economic, and scientific development.[14]

The relatively little said by Dewey and his followers in China about the war should not disguise its importance in their thinking following 1919. The urgency of China's political crisis is largely what made Dewey remain a second year. His lectures on politics were written in the context of his own reaction to the disappointments of Wilsonian diplomacy which is mentioned in them.[15] They concentrated upon the experimental underpinnings of a democratic polity. As one Russian intellectual in Peking commented, "Different people knew a different Dewey." Many were studying his philosophic lectures and his discourses on democratic education. But to the group of acquaintances Dewey met regularly at the Hotel de Pekin, he seemed consumed with interest in international politics.[16] Recovering from his disappointed expectations of peace, a "chastened" Dewey wrote to the *New Republic* in the spring of 1920 that the shocking debut of the traditionally isolationist United States into the undemocratic manipulations of Old World diplomacy should be a lesson for the United States to avoid as much contamination as possible in future commitments—until additional left-wing governments democratized foreign policy in Europe. Dewey opposed joining the League of Nations in 1920, and again in 1923, coming perilously close by the end of the 1920s to advocating the kind of pacifistic avoidance of intelligent force in world politics which he felt compelled to condemn at the time of the Versailles decision.[17]

Hsin ch'ing-nien *and* Clarté

When Hu Shih introduced the importance of Dewey's lectures on political philosophy to Chinese readers, he had them published in the pages of the prestigious journal *Hsin ch'ing-nien* (New youth). As Hu's biographer, Jerome Grieder, has pointed out, this same December 1919 issue of the magazine marked a moment of agreement by a variety of leading writers on what was basically Hu Shih's formulation of a reform ideology.[18] This agreement was

publicized in a manifesto of the journal, and included a clear statement of support for the pragmatic or experimentalist position
Dewey represented. It read in part, "We believe it is requisite for
the progress of our present society to uphold natural science and
experimentalist philosophy and to abolish superstition and fan-
tasy."[19] The manifesto opened with a Deweyan attack upon
"fixed principles" and a recognition of the need to revise tradition-
based beliefs and practices according to the demands of new social
conditions. Dewey's presence seems to have given *Hsin ch'ing-nien*
the identification with experimentalism which the *New Republic*
editors also accepted at the time Dewey left the United States.[20]
In both journals, however, the effect of the disillusioning peace
soon destroyed support for even "reformed" Wilsonianism, and for
Dewey's experimental social reform along with it.[21]

    At the time of the manifesto, the *Hsin ch'ing-nien* editors
were still adjusting to the reverberations of the political debates
following World War I. The December 1919 manifesto temporarily
closed an ideological split between liberals and leftists on the *Hsin
ch'ing-nien* editorial board which had opened in the summer. But
within a year the divisions had reopened and soon became irrepar-
able. Many intellectuals took an interest in the alternative posed
by Lenin.

    This phenomenon had echoes throughout the world as intel-
lectuals in Europe and the United States also came to grips with
the meaning of the peace. The December 1919 manifesto apparently
acquired some inspiration from another published by European
intellectuals which was translated in the same December issue of
Hsin ch'ing-nien.[22] The French writer Romain Rolland had written
that one before Versailles, as spokesman for a group of intellectuals which was largely European, but which claimed to include the
concerns of the yellow peoples of the world. Rolland condemned
the wartime abdication of political independence and intellectual
standards which, the signatories admitted, had led them into the
service of violence in their respective countries. He exhorted
intellectuals to commit themselves only to the lofty ideals of
Truth and the People, and to turn away from more selfish political

and national interests. Rolland fully supported Wilson as the spring peace negotiations approached.[23]

By the time this manifesto was published by *Hsin ch'ing-nien*, however, the results of Versailles had so jaundiced the Paris-based *Clarté* group of Rolland's successors, that summer and fall manifestoes virulently denounced Wilson.[24] The blockade against Soviet Russia by the Big Powers added to the despair of internationalists in Europe, and, as Arno Mayer has put it, "the dazed intelligentsia simply discounted the League as a combination victors' club, Holy Alliance, and capitalist directorate, all rolled into one."[25] During the years 1920-1921, the magazines *Clarté* and *Hsin ch'ing-nien* dealt with similar issues and went through a parallel radicalization. The bolshevik movement, the labor question, and the meaning of socialism concerned both journals, as the French Communist Party and the Chinese Communist Party took form in each country. Rolland and Henri Barbusse attempted to retain their independence from party affiliation, as Hu Shih did also in Peking. The journal *Clarté* evolved towards communism as the political views of its members moved away from Wilson, and by the fall of 1921 the communist minority had taken over the journal.[26] Barbusse resigned two years later. *Hsin ch'ing-nien* went through a similar rise in leftist political interest, and by 1921 a split with the liberals left it a Communist magazine in Canton.[27]

Liang Ch'i-ch'ao, Japan, and the Bolsheviks

At the same time Dewey settled in Peking to help interpret the meaning of the recent World War for his friends, a counterpart —one of the foremost intellectuals of China—settled on the outskirts of Paris to conclude a year's visit to the war-torn West. One important similarity between John Dewey and Liang Ch'i-ch'ao was that both of them had seen advantages to their respective countries' entering the war on the side of the Allies.[28] The different reactions of the two men to the failure of the peace revealed some important differences in the meaning of the war in China and in the United States. Liang was not a friend of the political left in the early Republic; in fact he was spurned by liberals such as Hu

138

Shih for working within militarist cabinets.[29] Liang's reactions to Versailles revealed no doctrinaire leftism, but rather the justifiable nationalistic indignation which was soon to lend so much fuel to the beginnings of a Marxist movement in China. The domestic Chinese implications of the Wilsonian compromise on Shantung turned out to magnify the injustice of secret diplomacy in a way that was probably hard to see at the tables of Versailles. The center of gravity of Chinese politics balanced on her shoreline, and foreign relations could greatly affect domestic political factions.

Liang's political involvement in the early Republic had been significant. He was a major leader of the Chinputang Party (Progressive Party) in 1913, and headed a factional component of constitutional monarchists with roots back to the Monarchical Constitutional Party of the Hundred Day reformers in 1898. Liang fought to oppose Yuan Shih-k'ai's attempt to become the emperor of China in 1915-1916, then assumed the leadership of the Research Clique (Yen-chiu hsi). This faction emerged as the Chinputang disbanded, and had enough followers in parliament to affect China's decision on intervention in the World War. It led sentiment toward a diplomatic break with Germany. In August 1917 China declared war on Germany and Austria.[30]

Liang's motive in working for China's entrance into the war was, as Li Chien-nung has pointed out, based on the example of the Italian statesman Cavour, who argued for Italy's participation in the Crimean War in order to enhance Italy's international position after the war.[31] Liang's ally in his promotion of intervention had been the premier, Tuan Ch'i-jui, who was leading the Peiyang clique of militarists. Tuan, unfortunately, had his own self-serving reasons for supporting the war effort, which were unknown to Liang. A declaration of war could have made it easy for General Tuan and his supporters to use "war powers" to override the majority in Parliament, who were supporters of both President Li Yuan-hung and the Kuomintang Party against General Tuan's clique. Tuan also had clandestine understandings with the Japanese. Participation in the war allowed Tuan to negotiate the Nishihara Loans, purportedly to train an army for participation in Europe, but actually to fight at home against opposing militarists. The Japanese were to organize and train the army. Japan's agreements with Tuan were tactics aimed at increasing Japanese influence in domestic Chinese politics.[32]

Immediately preceding China's entry into the war, Tuan Ch'i-jui had sent his troops into Peking and took control of the parliament he could not dominate by other means. Tuan had invaded Peking on the pretense of suppressing the restoration of the boy-emperor led by General Chang Hsun, which he had hypocritically intimated he would support. Once in power, Tuan declared war on the Central Powers.[33] At that point Liang Ch'i-ch'ao had hoped Tuan, leading the Peiyang faction, would provide the unifying force Liang believed essential in Chinese politics for national cohesion. He hoped Tuan would work in the national interest. Liang even helped Tuan negotiate a limited number of loans with Japan. But Liang resigned in November 1917, when it became apparent that the loans were being used for military operations, and not to stabilize the currency.[34] After the Versailles Conference opened discussions of peace terms in January 1919, more underhanded dealing came to light. Secret military conventions giving Japan the right to station troops in sensitive areas of China began to be made public, and Tuan was revealed as the negotiator. Barely six months before the Versailles Conference, the "gladly agree" loan had been negotiated in which Tuan's government assured the same privileges previously enjoyed by Germany in Shantung to Japan.

Liang was an observer at Versailles, and sent a telegram from Paris in late April 1919 reporting to Chinese newspapers that it was true that the Tsingtao port concession in Shantung was going to be turned over to Japan. He advised against Chinese agreement to the peace treaty. Liang's evaluation of the conference results was reported in the newspapers of China on May 2, 1919, and set the stage for the Peking demonstrations which made history two days later.[35] Liang's extreme disillusionment with Tuan's compromise of China's interests internationally was matched not long afterward at home by a separation within the Peiyang militarist faction in which Premier Tuan attacked the man who had been his president and initiated a bloody civil war.[36] The West had not only sanctioned Japanese imperialism at Versailles; it also strengthened the hand of one of the most unprincipled and self-seeking of China's militarists.

It should be noted that China's expectations from the Peace Conference at Versailles were not limited to the question of former German concessions in China. While some limited desiderata such as postponement of Boxer indemnity payments and a revision of the Chinese tariff—over which foreigners exercised determining control—were agreed to by the Allies, the broader proposal made by China regarding special privileges and spheres of influence in China was rejected by the Big Powers.[37] These included many provisions Chinese regarded as essential to their sovereignty and their recognition as equals by the West, such as the withdrawal of foreign troops and police, the reversion of postal service control to China, full tariff autonomy, and the relinquishment of special foreign concessions and settlements in China. Expectations from these proposals were dashed when the results of the Versailles Conference were published in China.[38] Liang Ch'i-ch'ao's personal attitude toward the West soured so much that his articles back to China condemning the war and the West exceeded the criticism of most disillusioned European intellectuals. The "mechanized atrocity" led Liang, in fact, to reflect critically upon ethical deficiencies he felt may have lain deep within Western society. At the end of his life he formulated a syncretism of Eastern with Western values grounded on a rejection of one characterization of the modern West: the excessive role which he perceived science was given in human affairs.[39]

Liang's internationalist call for participation in the war had failed to produce the desired results, just as John Dewey's earlier hope that a new international order could be shaped through forces harnessed by participation in the war had proved illusory. Dewey's advocates of scientific politics in China remained hopeful at the end of 1919 regarding gradual domestic progress and potential international cooperation. Liang was less sanguine.[40] Before he dedicated the final decade of his life to teaching and writing, he made at least one final public political protest of the sort the cultural reform liberals did not want *Hsin ch'ing-nien* to encourage. He actively opposed renewed Japanese attempts to settle the Shantung question bilaterally. Because China had refused to sign the Versailles Treaty, Japan proposed in January 1920 to negotiate directly with China over the issue. Liang was sensitive to the devious means Japan used to influence Chinese politics. Student groups organized against these negotiation proposals, and disruptive demonstrations took place in Peking from January 1920 until practically the first anniversary of the May Fourth Incident.[41] On that anniversary, Hu and Chiang had written their joint article to put a damper on such demonstrations.[42]

The experimentalists were also against compromise with Japan, but, from the vantage point of the social engineer, momentary political skirmishes were not equal in value to constructing social and cultural conditions which would provide a stable base for democratic politics. After Versailles, Hu and Chiang were forced to play down international politics. Instead of multi-national support for the weak who desired democracy, China had been thrown back upon the mercy of Japanese negotiators and their traitorous domestic allies. In May 1921 Hu noted in his private diary that he had recently spoken on politics from a lecture platform for the first time since his return to China in 1917.[43] His talk criticized the annual commemorations of China's humiliation from the Japanese Twenty-one Demands of 1915, such as the very meeting at which Hu spoke. Hu argued to the students of Ch'ing-hua University that the continued student attack on Japanese imperialism should be toned down in favor of attention to domestic problems. He tried to make his audience focus on the shame China had suffered since 1915 because of its travesties of the parliamentary system. Hu remarked in his diary that these views were not received with great favor.[44] Perhaps to the uncommitted the promise of becoming like the Allies had too little to recommend it.

As the Deweyites in China squirmed to adjust to domestic reaction from World War I, the new Soviet government in Moscow

made a policy initiative to Peking which attracted many disappointed intellectuals. In March 1920, it became public knowledge that
the Karakhan Declaration had offered Peking abrogation of all
former unequal treaties including several secret treaties made by
the former Tsarist government, and further offered to relinquish
any special privileges or spheres of influence it enjoyed within the
sovereign state of China. Within a month, support welled up
throughout the media in China to accept these provisions—which
many had expected from the Versailles Treaty.[45] The newspaper
of Liang Ch'i-ch'ao's old party said the Karakhan declaration
seemed in fact based on Wilsonian principles which Wilson had
been unable to carry out. Nationalistic intellectuals responded
enthusiastically to this act of international justice, and an alternative had been posed to the democracy and equality offered by
Dewey's supporters.

Back in New York, the *New Republic* liberals were also
severely challenged by the conduct of the peace. The editors,
Herbert Croly, Walter Weyl, and Walter Lippmann, who had
boasted that the *New Republic* had been partly responsible for
leading Woodrow Wilson and the intellectuals of the United States
to a commitment to join the war against Germany in 1917, all
came to desert the peace. They were disillusioned by Article Ten
of the Peace Treaty which seemed to give the spoils to the victors,
and which included punitive provisions aimed at weakening
Germany instead of rebuilding a democratic ally. They were disillusioned also with the final form of the League of Nations, which
they felt compromised the ideals behind its original intent, and
assured the dominance of a British-French-American alliance in the
post-war era. Weyl was led to the most radical conclusions, namely
that the origins and prosecution of the war should be analyzed in
class terms. He concluded that only a socialist economy committed
to economic internationalism could provide a basis for peace in the
future. Croly also reacted to his disillusionment by shifting toward
the left.[46]

John Dewey himself, like his *New Republic* cohorts who had
supported the Wilsonian intervention, was hard put to explain the

failure of a truly democratic peace to come out of the war. He could only condemn the idealistic means Wilson had relied upon, and assume all were wiser afterward and could prevent it from happening again. Hu, Chiang, and other Deweyites could do no better. The unfulfilled promises of the Allied cause contrasted sadly with the actions taken by the Soviet Union to assure the aims for which China participated in the war. It was all but impossible for the European Wilsonians to keep the faith after Versailles; in China the Wilsonian promise failed even more demonstrably. Among Dewey's immediate followers who were close to him personally in China, there was little defection from at least the goals of Wilsonianism. Among other intellectuals, however, the Allied alternative was in serious question. China lay exposed to the abuse of undemocratic power. She was too weak to prevent exploitation from abroad and had suffered it for decades; she was vulnerable to alliance with the oppressor from within. The Allied promise of a new era had, for many, proven illusory.

Testing Experimentalism as a Reform Tool

Dewey's experimentalism became a reform tool for his followers. A surprisingly detailed adaptation of Dewey's instrumentalism to political reform was made by Hu Shih during the summer debates on "Problems and Isms" after Dewey's arrival. The effectiveness of this experimentalism as a reform tool was severely tested during the two years Dewey was in China.

Hu Shih began arguing for the principles of an experimental democratic politics even before Dewey could get his lectures on that subject under way. He did so relying upon Dewey's published works in areas related to political science, and drew as well from the works of the *New Republic* writers. Hu's views were brought out in articles introducing Dewey's ideas in China, and during the summer of 1919 in a heated literary debate over methodologies of political change. His arguments for "More Study of Problems, Less Talk of Isms," were met by serious disagreement from Li Ta-chao who

defended arguments for socialism. As Hu developed his case
in the pages of *Mei-chou p'ing-lun* (The weekly critic) it is hard to
overestimate the influence of John Dewey's thought on his writing.
Hu had initiated the controversy when he found himself, somewhat against his will, editing a political journal for Ch'en Tu-hsiu,
a friend who had been imprisoned by the militarist authorities in
Peking. As a matter of principle, Hu Shih did not favor engaging
in political arguments until the intolerant, repressive atmosphere
in China changed to make political debate more likely to bring
some constructive response from those in power. He consequently
decided to argue only about the ground rules for political debate,
and published his personal prolegomena to political theory.[47]

The content of Hu's summer arguments had already appeared
in his articles written some four months before the debate. During
this time Hu wrote seven essays introducing John Dewey's thought
in China. He revised all of them, along with his lecture at Dewey's
welcoming reception in Shanghai, into a 51-page Chinese essay
which Hu included in all the editions of his collected works.[48] The
Shanghai lecture discussed Dewey's philosophy. It contained an
overview of most of the points Dewey was to develop in his philosophy lectures in China: the historical and philosophical significance
of the scientific revolution and Darwinism, the definition of experimentalism, and Dewey's descriptions of the scientific method and
pragmatic truth.[49] Three of the other articles were explications of
points in Dewey's thought, which Hu wrote by analyzing certain
works of Dewey. The last of these was an article on Dewey's
psychological analysis of the nature of thinking derived from
Dewey's book *How We Think*. Hu completed the editing of these
seven articles on July 1, 1919, and opened the "Problems and
Isms" debate in the July 20, 1919 issue of *The Weekly Critic*.[50]
This timing was more than fortuitous. The position Hu developed
in the debate, as will be shown below, was an attempt to apply
Dewey's psychological analysis of the experimental method of
thinking to political change.

As Hu Shih described the key insights of Dewey's *How We
Think* in June and July 1919, he highlighted the five steps Dewey

felt accounted for the rather simple way human beings went about thinking. Dewey lectured on these much later himself. Hu discussed how "thought" was considered by Dewey to be basically an instrument the human organism used in adapting to its environment.[51] Encountering some obstruction or difficulty in the environment begins a problem-solving process which utilizes past experience, and which tests hypothetical solutions to the difficulty. It followed from this psychology of thinking applied politically, Hu said, that any worthwhile ideas or political doctrines had to begin from concrete problems. Hu's attack on "isms" in the *Weekly Critic* applied the five steps in Dewey's analysis of thinking, one by one, to political analysis. After studying all aspects of a political problem which comes up, the exact location of the "sickness" must first be pin-pointed, Hu instructed his readers. The next step, relying on past experience and learning, is to prescribe ways of curing the disorder, and then to use imagination to test the probable results of different hypotheses. All worthwhile proposals must go through these steps to avoid the irrelevance of "bookish" ideas.[52] Hu went on to argue that every political "ism" and theory (he later admitted socialism and anarchism were his object of attack although he used Neo-Confucian schools as his examples) must be considered in solving China's problems, but that each had to be regarded as a possible solution "awaiting verification," and never as a certain belief. Regarding theories and "isms" as kinds of reference material in the process of thinking, Hu argued, allowed them to function naturally as instruments of thought, and allowed thought to be creative.[53]

This obvious debt to Dewey's book in outlining an experimental political theory had the effect of describing power relationships in society as a kind of social psychology. The injunctions tying abstractions to experience were meant by both Hu and Dewey to discount the claims of idealistic and deterministic theories, either political or philosophic, which could not stand the test of experience. The primary role given scientific thinking in political judgments had far-ranging social implications. Dewey brought this out explicitly in his lectures. Concrete experimental thinking should act as a social solvent, alleviating many social and class conflicts by providing a fuller understanding of their origins and character to the parties concerned. Open communication, and wide dissemination of ideas, were seen by Dewey as social values more important than even the institutions of democracy. To Dewey, the success of the goals of personal growth and "associated living" were determined not so much by the political forms of society as the way of thinking and interacting that took place in society.

This political outlook derived from the Darwinian-influenced "Chicago school" of social psychology at the turn of the century which Dewey helped formulate. Its influence is discernible on a generation of political theorists such as Arthur Bentley, Charles Merriam, H. D. Lasswell, and T. V. Smith, and was basically shared by Dewey's colleagues at the *New Republic*: Hu Shih had been exposed to works by these *New Republic* editors even back in New York as shall be seen below.[54] The magazine had been founded in 1914 by men who put their faith in broadly based cultural renewal as opposed to any specific political platform. One editor, Walter Lippmann, rejected immediate commitments to specific issues because he blamed the failure of the English Fabian program before World War I on short-sighted aims.[55] In its place Herbert Croly and Walter Lippmann made opinion formation and social attitudes and values their primary concern. Croly tried to practice politics somewhat as he had his first career, architecture. He saw the art of both as consisting of imposing higher standards and preferences on the "many plain people." He felt the "quality of life" determining the kind of debate which would take place was more important than institutional change and legislation which could only reflect that quality.[56]

The editors of the *New Republic* made proposals for an invigorated democratic nationalism which they saw uniting with the "little renaissance" beginning to flower in the arts in the United States before the war. They preached a cultural nationalism that would liberate the arts from vassalage either to England or to commercialism. Even Randolph Bourne, who wrote for the *New Republic* before his early reaction against the ugly violence of

World War I, saw the impact of the war acting to unify culture, as political nationality became robust.[57] Such a hope for cultural renewal was tied to a conception of politics seen as deriving from social and cultural attitudes. As one historian of the *New Republic* group put it, "What is striking . . . about Croly's later book *Progressive Democracy* (1914) and the writings of Walter Lippmann, *A Preface to Politics* (1913), *Drift and Mastery* (1914), is continued emphasis on the priority over any programmatic considerations of what Lippmann called a cultural revolution."[58]

Hu Shih used as a guideline for his own reformism a quotation from Nietzsche which sums up a chapter of Lippmann's argument in *A Preface to Politics*: "Let the value of everything be determined afresh by you."[59] That book had been required reading in Dewey's course during the war on "Moral and Political Philosophy," which Hu Shih had audited. Lippmann's *Preface to Politics* was, according to its young author, a "preliminary sketch for a theory of politics, a preface to thinking," just as Hu saw his first political writings in the summer debate of 1919.[60] In Lippmann's book he attempted an ambitious application of the insights of Georges Sorel, Sigmund Freud, Henri Bergson, and Friedrich Nietzsche to democratic politics. The brunt of the message that comes through in his book is that sanctified political creeds and philosophies of the past, for which empires were built and human lives sacrificed, had rather little to do with truth and justice. The abstract theories, moral truths, and philosophical absolutes of a given historical moment were usually themselves instruments for the much less rational impulses and desires that made up humankind. The relativization of moral and political values, and the political instrumentalism implicit in his first book, were only one step away from an experimentalist definition of the nature of democracy which Lippmann articulated in his second book, *Drift and Mastery* (1914).[61] In *Preface to Politics* (1913), Lippmann said of future reforms, "We shall feel free to choose among alternatives—to take this much of socialism, insert so much syndicalism, leave standing what of capitalism seems worth conserving. We shall be making our own house for our own needs, cities to suit ourselves, and we shall believe ourselves capable of moving mountains, as engineers do, when mountains stand in the way."[62] Hu Shih shared this optimistic outlook and faith in social engineering when he came to announce his own "preface to thinking" in the summer of 1919. Whether or not Hu identified directly with Lippmann in setting down his own ground rules for political theory, which is quite possible, he certainly agreed with Dewey and the *New Republic* group in defining democracy as a way of thinking and interacting, which implied priorities on attitudinal change over alterations in political forms.

Hu Shih was adamantly committed to non-political reformism after 1917. His strict priority on cultural renewal and avoidance of promoting specific platforms or policies sounded much like the *New Republic's* answer to Fabianism. Hu's attraction to the notion of cultural renaissance in his reform views also produced an echo from the ideas of the "cultural revolutionaries" in New York. A release from cultural vassalage, or at least tutelage, was shared by the Chinese reformers. The rejection of Japanese lessons in modern nationhood was an assumption of many journals such as *New Youth* after 1915. For the young Republic of China the stakes were somewhat higher, however, than for social engineers who were not battling relapses into monarchy. Hu's adamancy about the correct understanding of democracy in China was correspondingly more severe than that of his counterparts in New York.

Hu's specific formulation of reform owed an immediate debt to John Dewey's psychology of thinking, and represented a more thoroughgoing experimentalist interpretation of political change than had been written by the *New Republic* editors. The nature of experimental politics was being elaborated by the master himself in his Peking lecture series, and this was the basic position that Hu Shih had convinced the *Hsin ch'ing-nien* editorial staff to make a point of agreement for their manifesto in December 1919. Piecemeal and steady progress could be achieved by the steady problem-solving method, he argued, obviating the need for *en bloc* political dislocation or revolution.[63] On the heels of the summer debate in which Hu launched his political experimentalism, his friend, Chiang Meng-lin, integrated these same insights into an analysis of the politicizing convulsions taking place in China. In his psychological analysis of recent events, Chiang also relied explicitly on Dewey's instrumental definition of the nature of thinking and theories.[64] He cited Dewey to argue that social theories have to arise from concrete conditions where there is some problem or malady. After a social malady is discovered, new learning can be applied to the environment, and incorporated into society in a natural problem-solving fashion.[65]

As the year 1920 opened, the Chinese proponents of experimentalism achieved an initial endorsement from a wide spectrum of other intellectuals that experimentalism might be tried as the rationale for future political reforms. The parallels of the efforts of these trans-Pacific liberals with those in New York is striking, but there was a subtle difference in the achievement of this consensus at *Hsin ch'ing-nien*, and the relatively important influence of the voice of the *New Republic* among United States intellectuals. In the Chinese case experimentalism had to serve as a *strategy* of reform, rather than primarily as a restatement of the correct functioning of a democratic society. In trying to carry out this strategy, reform-minded experimentalists committed themselves, as had the "new educators," to a priority on cultural reform. This was consistent with their objective of building a society in which democracy could be realized in its full cultural meaning. With the new educators they shared the belief in a pluralistic society in which professionals provided an input independent of political allegiance. Acting consistently with democratic pluralism, Dewey's followers dedicated themselves after his arrival to gradual, culturally-defined reforms as a strategy of change.

Testing Pragmatic Politics

Hu and Dewey had presented a vision of what the correct social and attitudinal concept of democracy should be; but implementation was another story. In the autocratic and arbitrary political environment of militarism during the 1920s, experimental reforms had just as much trouble as progressive educational changes.

Had the "cultural revolution" Dewey was reporting back to the *New Republic* been a fully accurate portrayal of the May Fourth upheaval, that would have been different. Unfortunately the chicken and egg puzzle articulated by Chiang Meng-lin in 1924 expressed a very real dilemma faced by the experimentalists. As early as the manifesto of the summer of 1920, Hu and Chiang partially acknowledged the issue. One reason the limitations upon experimentalism were so hard to see is that Hu seemed to have an incontrovertible argument. Beginning from the actual, concrete problems as they were posed in Chinese society was a more practical and effective point of departure for reform, he argued, than utilizing any more abstract set of political assumptions. The method seemed to have the power of science itself behind it.

Conservative implications of this method appeared when it was put into operation. Hu was adamant, for example, in his "hands off" policy regarding any personal affiliation with militarist power. But his experimental reform program did necessarily begin from the existing institutions in the society, from which problems were seen to arise and could then be solved, leading to progress. Experimentalism accepted the given environment in which it could begin its chemistry of attitudinal re-orientation, social education, and egalitarian participation. This meant not a revolt against existing authority, but the acceptance of the undemocratic operation of militarist politics as the point of departure for gradual change. It was a critical flaw in experimental political theory, for problem-solving did not have the strategic power really to affect the authority structure it accepted to begin with.

In May 1920 Hu's article with Chiang Meng-lin, calling for the students to calm down and come back to the libraries and playing fields of their academic institutions, was one manifestation of their acceptance of the social order and its institutions. The students were exhorted to bring their calls for "renovation of the system" into the universities where they could benefit from the "consideration of mature people," and then initiate activity within educational institutions to contribute to social service work through popular lecturing and running night schools for the public.[66]

Events during 1920 demonstrated the absolute helplessness and ineffectiveness of educational institutions as contributors to social reform. During the summer of 1920, North China was ravaged by internecine war among the Peiyang militarists.[67] Tuan Ch'i-jui was temporarily vanquished by the Chihli faction, and national finances squandered in the process. In the spring of 1921, the eight national colleges and universities in Peking went on strike for salaries which had not been paid since the beginning of the year. Pressure built until in June the President's guard, in one of the ugliest actions taken by any militarist ruling group, beat and bayonnetted the professors and students petitioning the presidential mansion. Such was the brutal repression facing even the more flexible existing institutions.

Hu and Chiang, with another graduate of Columbia, got out of town for a weekend not long after this event in 1921. Chiang was deeply depressed. He was in despair over the different political factions trying disingenuously to befriend, buy off, or indirectly use the world of education. Chiang told his friends that the world of education in Peking was like an innocent young woman whom its enemies wanted to rape, and its supposed friends simply seduce.[68] Hu Shih, perhaps even more dismayed, described education in a prostituted position to begin with because of its financial dependence on the national budget. Hu had gone to see Dewey just days after the violence. Dewey drew a conclusion from the news which was pessimistic indeed. He said to Hu that it just seemed clear from such an event that warlords and education were simply incompatible. Hu sighed to his diary that what Dewey said was right.[69] The ramifications of such a conclusion were far-reaching, for this conclusion suggested that existing conditions could not be accepted if cultural reforms were to get started at all. In fact, the position that a certain power lay in beginning from the particular problems and social issues confronting Chinese society suffered from a kind of "misplaced concreteness." The weakness was that—like a scientific experiment—social reform by the application of scientific problem-solving presumed some controls over the environment undergoing experimentation. As a methodology applied to an uncontrolled environment, its effect was usually conservative, because it accepted the institutions as it found them and then was unable to make the systematic changes it promised.

Ch'en Tu-hsiu and Experimentalism

Ch'en Tu-hsiu, the founder and chief editor of *Hsin ch'ing-nien* (New youth), had joined Hu Shih in endorsing Dewey's experimental form of liberalism as the year 1919 concluded. His article on "The Basis for the Realization of Democracy" relied upon Dewey's summer lectures in Peking, which had been printed in the smaller political journal Ch'en edited, *The Weekly Critic.*[70] Within a year, however, Ch'en had rejected Dewey's gradualism in favor of Marxism, and soon split personally with Hu Shih over the issue. The split involved the problem of ineffectiveness in the face of power which Ch'en concluded the Deweyan liberals could not overcome.

Ch'en was representative of the intellectuals in China who had high hopes for a new era as the Armistice was signed ending World War I. In December 1918 he helped found a second journal, with some of the other dissident *Hsin Ch'ing-nien* staff, dedicated to political issues. Its statement of purpose dedicated the new journal to "Right triumphs over might." But after the disappointments at Versailles, Ch'en actively supported the student demonstrations against the government, and spent the summer of 1919 in jail. He was arrested for distributing anti-government handbills in a cafe. When Ch'en was paroled in September 1919 he moderated his views and seemed willing to underwrite the experimentalist formulation of gradual reform with Hu Shih in the fall.[71]

Ch'en's shift away from Hu's position in 1920, as has been mentioned, was related to a second arrest warrant issued against him for breaking his parole by lecturing outside of Peking in January 1920. This warrant forced him into exile in Shanghai. Ironically, it was Hu Shih's duties interpreting for John Dewey which had led Ch'en to speak illegally outside of Peking in Hu's place. This in turn led to Ch'en's final step in his break with established authority. It was not long afterwards that Ch'en became a communist and a revolutionary.[72]

From his exile in the International Settlement in Shanghai Ch'en still edited *Hsin ch'ing-nien*, and carried on a dispute with Hu Shih over whether the magazine should directly confront political issues. In this two-year debate over reform strategy Ch'en rejected the gradual experimentalism he had advocated in the fall of 1919. What he questioned was the means Hu Shih chose to carry out experimentalism—cultural reform. Piecemeal cultural renovation as the point of departure for gradually changing the reactionary politics of China had proven itself bankrupt to Ch'en.

Ch'en had risked repression before, and was more politicized than Hu when Ch'en assumed the early leadership of the New Culture movement. A magazine Ch'en was affiliated with, *The Tiger (Chia yin tsa-chih)*, had been suppressed in 1915. Li Ta-chao, incidentally, had begun his political radicalization when he worked for the successor to this paper, *The Tiger Weekly (Chia yin jih-k'an)*. That paper was also closed down by the Peiyang militarists, and Li had fled temporarily to Shanghai for refuge in 1917. When *Hsin ch'ing-nien* was begun by Ch'en under Yuan Shih-k'ai's reign, there was no possibility of constructive political criticism from a journal of academics. Hu Shih, who arrived in China from the United States in 1917, did not go through these experiences in the early Republic, and from 1917 to 1919 his rationale for supporting the priority on cultural reformism was to build essentially democratic cultural attitudes—a motivation different from the need to avoid suppression.[73]

In the spring of 1920, Ch'en Tu-hsiu and Hu began to break with one another ideologically and personally. Two years later Ch'en was still editing *Hsin ch'ing-nien* from Canton and would not agree to exclude articles on politics. At the end of correspondence on the matter, in a telling remark, Ch'en admonished his friend in the university: "I am constantly fearful lest my good friends, in their ivory tower, should let themselves be used by the politicians."[74] Ch'en drew this conclusion not because the ivory tower depended on national funding. Rather, his friends had still refused to recognize that cultural reform efforts failed to lead to political reforms, and thereby ended up simply working with the status quo, rather than changing it.

Professor Furth has correctly noted the danger of categorizing the "culturalists" in opposition to the "political activists" of the May Fourth movement.[75] The arguments of the New Culture "liberals" for non-political reformism anticipated a direct connection with democratic politics. As conceived by the experimentalists, this meant turning the direction of authority in the traditional polity upside down, so that new cultural and social patterns could build a new politics.[76] To pledge oneself not even to talk politics for twenty years while cultural reconstruction went on was Hu Shih's strategy for bringing about a new politics. But as a *strategy* of reform, it assumed that educational and cultural improvements could both avoid repression and begin the process leading gradually to desirable political consequences. It was on this point that Ch'en dissented from Hu Shih.

It may seem a paradox after one traces Ch'en's increasing resistance to cultural reform to find that in 1921 he was arguing vigorously for a justifiable separation between politics and culture. But what he meant in 1921 was that those who did not recognize the differences between the realms of cultural work and social work expected "the cultural movement to be a direct instrument to renovate politics and society."[77] When nothing happened after two or three years of cultural work, Ch'en wrote, such reformers were in the pathetic position of wondering why the nation and the society were still so unreconstructed. The answer was that the idea of falling back on the separation of culture from politics as a strategic ploy, while expecting the real connection between the two to begin political reform, was unrealistic. Ch'en's argument was made as an indictment of the ineffective strategy Hu Shih proposed. The link between cultural reform and political reform was not functional in China.

The New Republic *Magazine*

Back in New York the *New Republic* editors, who owed their own debt to Dewey-styled pragmatism, did not weather the war years any better than their Chinese counterparts. The peace treaty had brought the unanticipated intervention of power politics to frustrate their wartime ideals. But a more important lesson came from domestic events. The nationalism these editors had hoped would lead to a new union of politics and culture had proven too explosive, ugly, and unmanageable during the war to be harnessed for any social purpose.[78] Much like the situation in China, the irrational forces of the war years in the United States, which at home included a blinding passion for victory, and governmental control of word and action to the point of suppressing talk of peace, destroyed the prospect of rational change and democratic social engineering.[79] Herbert Croly's hopes for cultural nationalism—an integration of democracy and nationalism to initiate a national renaissance—were dashed by the violence and atrocity of wartime nationalism.[80]

Randolph Bourne had believed in the ideal of a national culture, but quickly denounced the *New Republic* editors when he saw them—and Dewey—endorse war.[81] Bourne had been an ardent follower of Dewey's pragmatism, and was a pacifist. When Dewey called for liberals in the United States to support Wilson's military intervention in Europe, Bourne was disgusted, and re-evaluated pragmatism as it applied politically. "We are in the war," Bourne wrote, "because an American Government practiced a philosophy of adjustment, and an instrumentalism for minor ends, instead of creating new values and setting at once a large standard to which the nations might repair."[82] He was shocked at the explosive hatred and autocratic controls in the United States and questioned whether the pragmatist's scientific environmentalism was a match for them: "Evidently the attitudes which war calls out are fiercer and more incalculable than Professor Dewey is accustomed to take into his hopeful and intelligent imagination, and the pragmatist mind, in trying to adjust itself to them, gives the air of grappling, like the pioneer who challenges the arid plains, with a power too big for it."[83] Bourne's critique was penetrating. It touched a point of critical importance concerning the ability of Deweyan experimentalism to deal with power.

Bourne's criticism was almost a lone voice of opposition at that time, but has since become a major source of revisionist

studies of the *New Republic's* liberalism. Recent critiques emphasize, with some justice, the hidden class interests and motivation
of the intellectuals writing in support of order and reason. But
most telling are points Bourne himself noted concerning the fact
that the effectiveness of pragmatism was restricted to regulated
environments such as schools, which were already under certain
environmental controls. In the Chinese case, Professor Grieder has
accurately tied Hu Shih's shift from politics to scholarship in the
mid-1920s to the restricted effectiveness of Dewey's concepts in
dealing with only controlled change.[84] When pragmatism was
applied to national politics, or to nations among nations, irrational
elements rendered the political pragmatist impotent.[85] This inherent
limitation in experimental politics was not known to Dewey and
became a painful lesson for his followers in China to learn.

America's Best

> Through John Dewey America is offering her best to China
> and she is saying to the Chinese through him: You cannot
> avoid social reform and you want social reform. Will you have
> it by the method of education, of self-discipline, of experiment
> and of method? [*sic*] Or will you have it by submitting your-
> self to the terrors of the doctrinaire or to the spurred boot
> heel of the autocrat? The question is still yours to answer.[86]

Professor C. F. Remer, the economist, wrote these lines for a
Shanghai English-language magazine after Dewey had lectured his
first year in China. He phrased the significance of Dewey's visit in
terms of what he saw the American political tradition offering
China, and that was a humane, liberal, modern political system,
somewhere between the dogmatic left and the autocratic right. The
appeal this alternative offered to a developing country Mr. Remer
apparently thought obvious.

The history of the reception of Dewey's ideas in China was
not a simple story of good versus bad. The "best" the United States
had to offer through John Dewey had severe limitations in China.

"Chastened" Wilsonianism, progressive educational reform, and the experimental political theory that his followers promoted all largely failed, in appeal and efficacy—and for good reasons.

In international relations the failure of appeal was most demonstrable. Immediately following World War I, only the Soviet Union put into practice the egalitarian policies called for in Allied wartime rhetoric. The unrealized promises of Wilsonian idealism in a world where "right" did not triumph over "might" forced Chinese intellectuals to reconsider the meaning of the war and to think about unstated aims within Allied diplomacy. Disillusionment ranged from Liang's critique of materialistic ethics in the West, to Li Ta-chao's convictions—shared by Walter Weyl back in New York—that economic interests in the capitalist democracies superseded egalitarian goals. In either case there was little support left for the proposition that Allied democratic models would lead to international justice.

The group of returned students from the United States who interpreted—literally and figuratively—what was going on in China for Dewey, already spoke in his idiom. As the British reporter once complained about rising United States influence in China, the "troublous years to come" inclined future leaders to favor the countries in which they were trained. Their interpretation of events was colored by their own interests, as has been seen. More subtly, their variety of nationalism was also distinctive. The experience of students trained in an advanced industrialized country usually gave them an acute awareness of China's backwardness in the world. They could perceive this in world diplomacy, as well as in industrial development. Their commitment to reform, which was genuine, was made with a vision of progress and development in mind. This commitment differed from that of other reformers and revolutionaries at home whose dedication came from a moral commitment to rectify social injustice within China, and who frequently perceived foreign obstacles in doing so. The impatience most United States returned students felt with conditions in China was also expressed as a lack of interest in revolutionary experiments. To them, the models of industrial progress already existed. They were too aware of China's humiliating international inferiority to be tolerant of romantic and untested proposals for social reorganization. This attitude contributed to their willingness to accept temporarily whatever social order was most feasible, so that China could get on with her internal development culturally as well as economically. Another variety of nationalism, however, was easily as prevalent in China: that which saw equal treatment internationally and full recognition of China's overall domestic affairs as goals separable from, and more important than, industrial progress.

John Dewey did not claim to know anything about China when he let himself be persuaded to teach there. In relying upon those who spoke in terms he well understood, Dewey heard some familiar echoes mixed with the native sounds of China. Until the month he left, Dewey wrote about the May Fourth upheaval as the crescendo of an intellectual and cultural revolution. This interpretation was how his followers wanted May Fourth to be, although they were actually unsuccessful in focusing the passions of the movement on psychological and attitudinal rebellion. The queer twist to this misperception by the foreign observer is that his followers wanted an attitudinal revolution in large part because that is how they had been taught true democracy was defined. John Dewey had heard echoes of his own voice in China, and seen refracted images he knew well through his followers. No doubt this made it all the harder for him to see the inapplicability of his ideas.

One other background experience which further distinguished how nationalistic reformers conceived domestic needs was previous revolutionary experience in 1911. Many of those indoctrinated in radicalism during the 1911 Revolution identified more quickly with the revolutionary overthrow of militarists, regardless of resulting disruptions in educational or economic development. Some who studied in the United States left China with an important legacy from revolutionary experience, and it distinguished them from those who left China without this experience.

"Experiment" and "method" in Mr. Remer's quotation were favorite words for Dewey in China. Unfortunately, only an illusory scientific power proved present in experimental political reform. Dewey's followers in China were testing pragmatic politics in an even more pure form than the *New Republic* liberals. The lectures on political pragmatism were an experiment themselves, and Dewey did not choose to publish them in English. In New York, just as in Peking, a major defect emerged when this science of politics was practiced in an uncontrolled environment. The intense nationalism of the war in the United States, and virulent anti-Japanese nationalism combined with the arbitrary authority of militarists in China, exposed the inability of experimentalism to function in the presence of irrational political forces, much less harness them in its service. Inherent limitations in the political ideology of Dewey's followers in China explain much of the failure of these liberals in the May Fourth period. Experimentalism proved fragile in its applicability to politics, in the United States as well as in China.

Experimentalism was fully compatible with cultural reformism. The Deweyan educational reformers discovered that there was a serious problem of effectiveness in applying American-modeled progressive principles in China. The assumption that education should remain separate from politics was one of the tenets of Dewey's followers. This principle described the democratic pluralism which was their objective, but Dewey's followers also made it into a strategy of change. *Hsin chiao-yü* argued for the autonomy of education so that reforms in the educational sector of society could be carried out by profesional standards, and contribute to social reconstruction. Professional standards were in fact raised throughout China. Dewey's ideas successfully captured the teacher training institutions. But the connection between educational improvements and democratic social reconstruction was not successfully made.

Working through existing educational institutions, which were subject to the whim of warlord governments, was one reason for this missed connection. T'ao Hsing-chih attempted to make the microcosm of the classroom influence society, as Dewey's theory proposed, but ran "headlong into a wall," as he put it. The "school is society" was unworkable in China, whether it really worked in the United States or not. T'ao was forced by political and economic obstacles such as budget control to discard the school as a source of social change. His alternative was to revise Dewey's principles radically, and to direct his efforts below the perimeter of institutional power in society. His experimental teachers' training school outside Nanking attempted to turn the local village society into the school, instead of the reverse. The democratic attitudes and rudimentary literacy he hoped to achieve were to be learned in accordance with the daily needs of the peasants, and from the social life of the village. At the village level T'ao succeeded in a full integration of education with social and political institutions in a tolerant democratic political environment. But he remained isolated in one rural area, safe only as long as he could keep out of range of the expression of political power from the government—which was only three years. To have accomplished more would have required confronting political power nationally.

Kuo Ping-wen's dismissal as President of National Southeastern University reveals a difficulty similar to the one T'ao encountered. The connection Kuo was taught between education and political affairs was far from melioristic as Dewey had described it. Despite Kuo's claims to neutrality, he was in an intensely political position, and finally suffered political ostracism for working under overthrown militarists. At the top levels of higher education in China, just as at the public school level, educational institutions had little immunity from political intervention. The ideal of political neutrality is at best a relative concept in education. The American-trained in China were unable to make it viable.

Dewey despised dualisms. Education should have been a great solvent of social conflict. Informed discussion of the origin and nature of conflicts of interest should lead to their resolution, rationally. The problems of society were conceived by Dewey to be inherently solvable. The school would continually influence society and politics to bring about needed change. But in China the links between school and society, between attitude change and political conduct, between professional non-partisanship and social betterment, were not present. Because they were not, progressive educational theory was ineffective. Dualisms persisted.

Dewey's followers added little power themselves to these limitations of doctrine. They were similar, in their "floating" social role, to the disciples of that greatest of all Chinese teachers, Confucius. By the mid-1920s Chiang Meng-lin and T'ao had recognized the weakness in their social roles. Joining the new intelligentsia of the early Republic, they had no direct ties to power in the society.[87] In retrospect, May Fourth was a time when the Deweyans attempted, momentarily, to harness the surging forces of political power which invaded academia. But the politicized students became a threat to experimental change within a year. Hu and Chiang later came to denounce the *hsueh-feng* altogether.

The greatest difficulty John Dewey's followers had in China was with something he spoke very little about—power. Deweyan experimentalism, as a way of thinking, as a way of acting politically, and as a component of democratic education, offered no strategy his followers could use to affect political power. Militarists dominated the cultural and social environment as they did the political environment. Without such a strategy, the "tragedy of the first magnitude" Dewey himself observed was the main "consequence" of his followers' pragmatic reform efforts. Their reformism was paralyzed by dilemma. The most progressive intent had become ineffective and conservative in practice. These limitations upon the appeal and effectiveness of what the humble teacher of pragmatism offered as America's best, are lessons, one senses, which he would have wanted his country to learn.

Appendix A

A TABLE OF THE PUBLISHED CHINESE SOURCES OF
JOHN DEWEY'S LECTURES DELIVERED IN CHINA,
1919-1921

1.   This table of John Dewey's lectures in China is arranged chrono-logically according to the earliest date at which each lecture was made available to the public in published form. Listed in this order, the lectures provide a rough indication of when they were actually delivered. If the exact date of delivery is known, it is listed directly under the title, along with other available facts concerning place of delivery and number of lectures in a series.

2.   Listed numerically under the earliest printed source of a lecture are all the other known sources of publication of that lecture. These include newspapers, government publications, and periodical literature from throughout China, as well as collections of Dewey's speeches in book form. All of these sources are in the Chinese language. A key to the abbreviations of titles, classified by type of publication, directly precedes the table.

Some of these sources have been acquired through the use of published indexes and other reference works, so that certain journals not available outside the People's Republic of China have, neverthe-less, been surveyed for Dewey's speeches. Those source entries which do not have page numbers were unavailable for inspection.

3.   It was common practice in the May Fourth period for periodi-cals to reprint material they wanted from other publications. Some-times mention of the original source is made, but not always. Dewey's lectures were often reprinted from major newspapers and magazines into minor periodicals, many of them short-lived. Whenever a text entered in the table indicated that it was a reprint from another source, that original source is always mentioned. If information

about the original source, such as its date of publication, is known, then it is given a separate entry in the list of sources of publication.

4.   If two Chinese texts of a given lecture are identical, the interpreter and recorder(s) of the two are necessarily the same. Therefore, if a text does not mention the interpreter or recorder, but does have an identical text in which the interpreter and recorder are known, their names have been included in the table in order to supply as much information as can be known about each text. Many of the interpreters and recorders used pen names, so a brief table converting these to their full names when known precedes the table.

5.   Entries No. 71 and 72 had no titles in the Chinese text. The English title entered is, in these two cases, that given by the editors of the East-West Center project mentioned in the preface, according to the content of the lectures.

6.   To facilitate use of the table, the method of citing periodical references had been slightly shortened following the model of Liu Chun-jo in her bibliography, *Controversies in Modern Chinese Intellectual History* (Cambridge, Harvard University Press, 1964). For example, HCK, I.6:216-224 (Oct. 15, 1919) is the shortened form of HCK, I, No. 6 (Oct. 15, 1919), 216-224.

Abbreviations Used in the Table

I. Newspapers and Official Publications

CP   *Ch'en pao* 晨報 (The morning post). A daily newspaper in Peking.

CPFK   *Ch'en pao fu-k'an* 晨報副刊 (Morning post supplement). A daily supplement to *CP*.

KMKP   *Kuo-min kung-pao* 國民公報 (Citizens' gazette). A daily newspaper in Peking.

HT   *Hsueh teng* 學燈 (Academic lamp). A major supplement to the Shanghai daily newspaper *Shih-shih hsin-pao.*

SSHP   *Shih-shih hsin-pao* 時事新報 ("The China Times"). A daily newspaper in Shanghai.

CW   *Chueh-wu* 覺悟 (Awakening). A major supplement of the Shanghai daily newspaper *Min-kuo jih-pao* 民國日報 (Republic daily).

Bulletin   *Chiao-yü pu kung-pao* 教育部公報 (Bulletin of the ministry of education). An official monthly journal of the Ministry of Education. All numbers of the Bulletin refer to the corresponding twelve months (e.g., No. 5 is May) unless otherwise indicated. Page numbers in the table refer to the appendix of the given issue of the Bulletin.

NL   Not Listed. This indicates that the information in question is not contained in the text.

II. Periodicals

CYC   *Chiao-yü ch'ao* 教育潮 (Educational tide). A monthly (and bimonthly) periodical published in Hangchow, Chekiang province.

HC   *Hsin ch'ao* 新潮 (New tide, or "The Renaissance"). A monthly published in Peking.

165

HCK   *Hsin Chung-kuo* 新中國 ("The New China").
A monthly published in Peking.

HCN   *Hsin ch'ing-nien* 新青年 (New youth, or "La
Jeunesse"). A periodical published in Peking
appearing monthly from September 1915 to
June 1923 when it became a quarterly.

HCY   *Hsin chiao-yü* 新教育 ("The New Education").
A monthly published in Shanghai.

HL   *Hsin Lung* 新隴 (New Kansu). A monthly published in Peking.

KTCYH   *Kuang-tung sheng chiao-yü hui tsa-chih* 廣東省
教育會雜誌 ("The Magazine of the
Kwang-tung Educational Association"). A monthly
published in Canton.

MCPL   *Mei-chou p'ing-lun* 每週評論 (Weekly critic
or "Weekly Review"). A weekly published in
Peking.

PMCY   *P'ing-min chiao-yü* 平民教育 (Mass education, or "Democracy and Education"). A Peking
periodical published weekly when founded
October 10, 1919, and fortnightly from November 14, 1920, when it combined with *Chiao-
yü yü she-hui* (Education and society); from
May 1922 combined with *Shih-chi chiao-yü*
(Practical education). Ceased publication after
Nos. 72–73, July 1924.

SNSH   *Shao-nien she-hui* 少年社會 (Youth and
society). A periodical published in Nanking, first
weekly, then irregularly after Vol. 1, no. 5.

TFTC   *Tung-fang tsa-chih* 東方雜誌 ("The Eastern
Miscellany"). A periodical published fortnightly
in Shanghai.

WIHCK   *Wen-i hui chi k'an* 文藝會季刊 (The literature and art quarterly). A quarterly published in
Peking.

III. Books

Five Major   *Tu-wei wu ta chiang-yen* 杜威五大演講 (Five major lectures of Dewey). Peking, Ch'en pao she 晨報社, 1920.

Three Major   *Tu-wei san ta yen-chiang* 杜威三大演講 (Three major lectures of Dewey). Interpreter Liu Po-ming 劉伯明, recorder Shen Chen-sheng 沈振聲. Shanghai, T'ai-tung t'u-shu-kuan 泰東圖書館, 1920.

Dewey and Russell   *Tu-wei Lo-su yen-chiang lu ho-k'an* 杜威羅素演講錄合刊 (Collected speeches of Dewey and Russell). Shanghai, T'ai-tung t'u-shu-kuan, 1921

Pai-hua wen-fan   *Pai-hua wen-fan* 白話文範 (Specimens of paihua style). 4 vols. Shanghai, The Commercial Press, 1920.

PMCIYCY   *P'ing-min chu-i yü chiao-yü* 平民主義與教育 ("Democracy and education"). Translator and recorder Ch'ang Tao-chih 常道直. Shanghai, The Commercial Press, 1922. This book is based on class notes from Dewey's lectures at Peking Teachers' College from the fall of 1920 to the summer of 1921. The translator took the notes in English, translated them into Chinese, with elaboration, and advises readers that it should be used as an explanatory guide to Dewey's work *Democracy and Education*.

TWCYCH   *Tu-wei chiao-yü che-hsueh* 杜威教育哲學 (The educational philosophy of Dewey). Recorder Chin Hai-kuan 金海觀. Shanghai, The Commercial Press, 1922. This book is a set of Dewey's lectures on the philosophy of education recorded by Mr. Chin Hai-kuan. This text is unavailable. It is one version of a series of lectures at Nanking Teachers' College, which differs from two other series also on the philosophy of education given in Peking.

Pen or Partial Names		Full Names	
Han Lu	涵廬	Kao I-han	高一涵
Chih Hsi	志希	Lo Chia-lun	羅家倫
Fu Lu	伏廬	Sun Fu-yuan	孫伏園
Shao-yü	紹虞	Kuo Shao-yü	郭紹虞
Chung Fan	仲帆	Chin Hai-kuan	金海觀
"Mr. C. C."	邱椿	Ch'iu Ch'un	邱椿

Title	Source of Publication	Interpreter	Recorder(s)
1. "P'ing-min chu-i, p'ing min chu-i ti chiao-yü, p'ing-min chiao-yü chu-i ti pan-fa" 平民主義, 平民主義的教育, 平民教育主義的辦法. (The relationship between democracy and education)	1) *HT*, May 8-9, 1919	Chiang Meng-lin 蔣夢麟	P'an Kung-chan 潘公展
	2) *CPFK*, May 9, 1919	"	"
	3) *CYC*, 1.2:85-93 (June, 1919). Reprinted from *SSHP*	"	"
	4) *Dewey and Russell*, 69-80	"	"
	5) *Bulletin*, 1919, No. 8, 25-31	"	"
Two lectures delivered May 3-4, 1919 to the Kiangsu Provincial Education Association, Shanghai.	6) *HCY*, I.3:326-333 (April, 1919) Dated April, but actually published in May or after		

Title	Source of Publication	Interpreter	Recorder(s)
2. "Ping-min chiao-yü chih chen-ti" 平民教育之真諦 (The real meaning of education in a democracy)	1) *CYC*, I.2:27-34 (June, 1919) 2) *CW*, July 19-23, 1919. Reprinted from *CYC*	Cheng Tsung-hai 鄭宗海	Chu Yü-k'uei 朱毓魁
A lecture delivered May 7, 1919 to the Chekiang Provincial Education Association, Hangchow.		"	"
3. Lectures given May 18, 19, 21, 24, 25, 26, 1919 at Nanking Teachers' College.	Unknown	T'ao Chih-hsing et al. 陶知行等	Unknown
4. "Mei-kuo chih min-chih ti fa-chan"	1) *MCPL*, No. 26:1-4 (June 15, 1919)	Hu Shih	Han Lu (1st & 2nd) Hu Shih (3rd)

Title	Source of Publication	Interpreter	Recorder(s)
4. (cont.) 美國之民治的發展 (The development of democracy in America) A series of three lectures given June 8, 10, and 12 or 13, 1919 in Peking.	2) *HCK*, 1.3:83-95 (July 15, 1919)	Hu Shih 胡適	Han Lu (1st & 2nd) Hu Shih (3rd) 涵廬 天風
	3) *CPFK*, June 17-20, 1919	,,	,,
	4) *HT*, June 21, 23, 27, 28, 1919	,,	,,
	5) *Bulletin*, 1919, No. 7, 1-15	,,	,,
	6) *CW*, June 20-30, 1919	,,	,,
5. "Hsien-tai chiao-yü ti ch'u-shih" 現代教育的趨勢	1) *MCPL*, No. 27:1-4 (June 22, 1919)	,,	Han Lu (1st & 3rd) T'ien Feng (2nd) 涵廬 天風

Title	Source of Publication	Interpreter	Recorder(s)
5. (cont.)			
(Trends in contemporary education)	2) *HL*, I.5 (May 20, 1921). Not complete	Hu Shih 胡適	Han Lu (1st & 3rd) T'ien Feng (2nd)
A series of three lectures given at the Peking National Academy of Fine Arts.	3) *HCY*, I.4:417–429 (May, 1919). Dated May, but actually published in late June or after.	,,	,,
	4) *HCK*, I.3:95–109 (July 15, 1919)	,,	,,
	5) *Dewey and Russell*, 26–53	,,	,,
	6) *Bulletin*, 1919, No. 9, 17–18; No. 10, 11–24	,,	,,
	7) *CW*, April 27, 1921	,,	,,
	8) *CYC*, 1.3 (Aug. 1919). Reprinted from *MCPL*	,,	,,

Title	Source of Publication	Interpreter	Recorder(s)
5. (cont.)	9) *HT*, June 30, 1919; July 1-2, 1919	Hu Shih 胡適	Han Lu (1st & 3rd) T'ien Feng (2nd)
6. "Tu-wei po-shih yü Kuei-chou chiao-yü shih-yeh ts'an-kuan t'uan t'an-hua chi-lueh 杜威博士與貴州教育實業參觀團談話紀略 (A record of Dr. Dewey's talk with the education and industry observation group from Kweichow province.)	1) *HT*, July 29, 1919	NL	NL
	2) *CW*, Aug. 27, 1919	"	"

Title	Source of Publication	Interpreter	Recorder(s)
7. "Hsueh-wen ti hsin wen-t'i" 學問的新問題 (New problems of knowledge)	1) *CW*, Aug. 14, 15, 21, 22, 1919	NL	NL
Delivered Aug. 15, 1919 at the New Learning Association, Peking.	2) *HCK*, I.5:236-240 (Sept. 15, 1919)	Hu Shih 胡適	Chih Hsi and Wu Wang 志希 毋忘
	3) *TFTC*, 16.9:205-209 (Sept. 1919)	"	"
	4) *HT*, Aug. 15, 1919	"	"
	5) *CYC*, I.4 (Sept. 1919). Reprinted from *KMKP*	"	"
	6) *Bulletin*, 1919, No. 9, 19-24	"	"
8. "Shih-yeh chiao-yü lun" 實業教育論 (Industrial education)	1) *HCK*, I.5:234-236 (Sept. 15, 1919)	NL	NL
	2) *TFTC*, 16.9:223-224 (Sept. 1919)	"	"

Title	Source of Publication	Interpreter	Recorder(s)
9. "She-hui che-hsueh yü cheng-chih che-hsueh" 社會哲學與政治哲學 (Social and political philosophy) A series of sixteen lectures in Peking, sponsored by National Peking University, the Ministry of Education, the Aspiration Society, and the New Learning Association.	1) *HT*, Sept. 24, 1919; Oct. 1, 8, 22, 1919 Nov. 5, 6, 22, 25, 30, 1919; Dec. 14, 15, 22, 23, 1919; Jan. 24, 26, 1920 (lect. 11); Feb. 3-4, 26, 27, 1920 (lect. 12, 13); Mar. 3-4, 8, 9, 1920 (lect. 14, 15); Apr. 1-2, 1920 (lect. 16)	Hu Shih 胡適 "	Wu Wang 毋忘 Fu Lu 伏廬
	2) *CW*, Sept. 24-28, 1919 Nov. 22-25, 28-30, 1919; Dec. 1, 1919; Jan. 23-26, 1920 (lect. 11); Mar. 2, 3, 7, 8, 30, 1920 (lect. 14); Apr. 1, 1920 (lect. 16)	" "	Wu Wang 毋忘 Fu Lu 伏廬
	3) *CPFK*, Feb. 16-Mar. 29, 1920	"	

Title	Source of Publication	Interpretater	Recorder(s)
9. (cont.) Note: All the published sources listed, except no. 6, are of the same text recorded by Wu Wang through lecture No. 4, and by Fu Lu (Sun Fu-yuan) from No. 4 to No. 16. Dewey's seventh lecture in the series was delivered Nov. 15, 1919.	4) *Bulletin*, 1919, No. 11 15-26 (from *KMKP*); No. 12, 11-14, 1919 1919, No. 12, 14-25; 1920, No. 1, 9-19; No. 2, 15-25; No. 3, 11-20; No. 4, 7-10; No. 5, 3-7; No. 6, 11-15.	Hu Shih	Wu Wang 毋忘
	5) *Five Major*, 1-126	,,	Wu Wang and Fu Lu 毋忘 伏廬
	6) *HCN*, 7.1:121-134 (Dec. 1, 1919); 7.2:163-182 (Jan. 1, 1920); 7.3:117-132 (Feb. 1, 1920)	,,	Kao I-han 高一涵
	7.4:1-15 (March 1, 1920). Complete only through lecture No. 12.	,,	Sun Fu-yuan (Fu Lu) 孫伏廬

Title	Source of Publication	Interpreter	Recorder(s)
9. (cont.)	7) *CP*, the daily, was publishing this series by at least lecture No. 6 (before Nov. 15, 1919). Its supplement (*CPFK*) later ran the series for over a month, and the newspaper published it in entirety as part of the book *Five Major* on Aug. 1, 1920.		
	8) *KMKP*. This daily paper published at least the first lecture in the series before it was suppressed by the government on Oct. 25, 1919.		
	9) *HCK*, I.6:207-215 (Oct. 15, 1919). Reprinted from *KMKP*	Hu Shih 胡適	Wu Wang 毋忘
	I.7:231-235 (Nov. 15, 1919)	"	NL
	I.8:193-203 (Dec. 15, 1919). Reprinted from *CP*	"	"
	II.1:165-174 (Jan. 15, 1920). Reprinted from *CP*	"	"
	II.2:199-203 (Feb. 15,	"	"

Title	Source of Publication	Interpreter	Recorder(s)
9. (cont.)	1920). Reprinted from *CP* II.4:179–192 (Apr. 15, 1920) II.6: back section, 1-5 (June 15, 1920) II.7: back section, 1-10 (July 15, 1920)	Hu Shih " "	NL " "
10. "Chiao-yü che-hsueh" 教育哲學 (The philosophy of education) A series of sixteen lectures given in Peking sponsored by National Peking University, the Ministry of	1) *HT*, Sept. 25–26, 1919 Oct. 2-4, 9, 11, 25, 31, 1919; Nov. 10, 1919; Dec. 1, 2, 7, 16, 17, 24, 26, 27, 1919; Jan. 30, 31, 1920 (lect. 12); Feb. 9, 11, 13, 1920 (lect. 13, 14); Mar. 1, 2, 5–7, 1920 (lect. 15, 16)	Hu Shih 胡適 "	Wu Wang 毋忘 Fu Lu 伏廬
	2) *CW*, Sept. 28–30, 1919; Oct. 1, 1919	"	Wu Wang 毋忘

Title	Source of Publication	Interpreter	Recorder(s)
10. (cont.) Education, the Aspiration Society, and the New Learning Association.	Oct. 2-5, 1919; Jan. 29-30, 1920 (lect. 12); Mar. 1, 1920 (lect. 15); Mar. 4-6, 1920 (lect. 16)	Hu Shih	Fu Lu 伏盧
	3) *CPFK*, Feb. 26-Aug. 23, 1920	"	"
	4) *Five Major*, 127-258	"	"
	5) *Bulletin*, 1919, No. 10, 33-36; No. 11, 27-39; No. 12, 27-40; 1920, No. 1, 21-35; No. 2, 27-32; No. 3, 21-26; No. 4, 11-16; No. 5, 9-13; No. 6, 17-27.	"	

Title	Source of Publication	Interpreter	Recorder(s)
10. (cont.)	6) HCK, I.6:216–224 (Oct. 15, 1919); I.7:235–242 (Nov. 15, 1919); I.8:203–213 (Dec. 15, 1919); II.1:174–183 (Jan. 15, 1920); II.2: 204–209 (Feb. 15, 1920); II.6: back section, 5–13 (June 15, 1920); II.7: back section, 10–19 (July 15, 1920)	Hu Shih	Sun Fu-yuan (Fu Lu) 孫伏園
	7) WIHCK, No. 2. Lectures section 1–40 (Apr. 1, 1920)	"	NL
11. "Lun-li chiang-yen chi-lueh 倫理講演紀略 (A record of lectures on ethics)	1) HT, Oct. 18, 24, 1919; 5–6, 1919; Dec. 3, 8, 21, 28, 30, 1919; Jan. 2, 1920 (lect. 11); Feb. 14, 15, 24, 1920 (lect. 12, 13); Mar. 3–5, 1920 (lect. 14)	"	"

Title	Source of Publication	Interpreter	Recorder(s)
11. (cont.) Delivered in Peking; a series of fifteen lectures.	2) *CPFK*, Oct. 15, 1919–Nov. 3, 1919; Mar. 10, 1920–Apr. 1, 1920	Hu Shih 胡 適	NL
	3) *CW*, Jan. 22, 1920 (lect. 11); Mar. 12, 22, 1920; Apr. 4, 1920	"	"
	4) *Bulletin*, 1919, No. 11, 41–45. Reprinted from *CP*; No. 12, 53, 59 (from *CP*); 1920, No. 1, 37–45 (from *CP*); No. 2, 39–47 (from *CP*); No. 3, 35–37 (from *CP*); No. 4, 29–34; No. 5, 27–33.	"	"
	5) *Five Major*, 399–472	"	"Mr. C. C." 邱 椿
	6) *HCK*, 1.7:242–247 (Nov. 15, 1919); II.1:183–191 (Jan. 15,	"	NL

Title	Source of Publication	Interpreter	Recorder(s)
11. (cont.)	1920); II.2:209–214 (Feb. 15, 1920); II.4: 193–195 (Apr. 15, 1920); II.6:13–21 (June 15, 1920)		
12. "Hsueh-sheng tzu-chih" 學生自治 (Student government) A lecture given at Peking Teachers College on the eleventh anniversary of its founding which was also the founding day of the student government organization.	1) *HCY*, II.2:163–166 (Oct. 1919) 2) *PMCY*, No. 7 (Nov. 22, 1919)	Hu Shih 胡適 ,,	Liu Ju-p'u and Shao Cheng-hsiang 劉汝甫 邵正祥 ,,

Title	Source of Publication	Interpreter	Recorder(s)
13. "P'in-ke chih yang-ch'eng wei chiao-yü chih wu shang mu-ti" 品格之養成為教育之無上目的 (Cultivation of character as the ultimate aim of education) A lecture delivered on Oct. 10, 1919 at Shansi University — given along with No. 14.	1) *HCK*, I.7:55-58 (Nov. 15, 1919) 2) *Bulletin*, 1919, No. 11, 47–49; final two paragraphs are missing. 3) *Dewey and Russell*, 86–91	Hu Shih 胡適 ,,	Teng Ch'u-min 鄧初民 ,,

Title	Source of Publication	Interpreter	Recorder(s)
14. "Hsueh-hsiao yü hsiang-li" 學校與鄉里 (School and village) A lecture delivered on Oct. 12, 1919 to normal school students at the Tenth Infantry Battalion (building) in Shansi Province—given along with No. 13.	1) *HCK*, 1.7:58-62 (Nov. 15, 1919)	Hu Shih 胡適	Teng Ch'u-min 鄧初民
15. "Ssu-hsiang chih p'ai-pieh" 思想之派別 (Types of thinking)	1) *HT*, Nov. 20, 21, 28, 29, 1919; Dec. 4, 5, 12, 13, 19, 20, 1919; Jan. 22, 25, 1920 (lect 6); Feb. 2, 6, 8, 1920 (lect. 7, 8)	" "	Shao-yü 邵虞 Fu Lu 伏廬

Title	Source of Publication	Interpreter	Recorder(s)
15. (cont.) A series of eight lectures begun on Nov. 12, 1919 at National Peking University.	2) *CW*, Nov. 20, 26, 27, 1919	Hu Shih 胡適	Shao-yü 邵羲
	Dec. 2-8, 15, 16, 1919	"	Fu Lu 伏廬
	Jan. 20, 21, 1920 (lect. 6)	"	Shao-yü 邵羲 Fu Lu 伏廬
	Jan. 31, 1920 (lect. 7)	"	Shao-yü 邵羲
	3) *Bulletin*, 1919, No. 21, 41-52; 1920, No. 1, 47-59; No. 2, 33-38; No. 3, 27-33; No. 4, 23-28; No. 5, 21-26		
	4) *Five Major*, 259-342	"	Shao-yü 邵羲
	5) *HC*, II.2:240-256 (Dec. 1919); II.3:478-495 (Feb. 1920); II.4:702-	"	Wu K'ang and Lo Chia-lun 吳康 羅家倫

Title	Source of Publication	Interpreters	Recorder(s)
15. (cont.)	719 (May, 1920); II.5: 927-945 (July, 1920)		
	6) *HCK*, II.3:165-181 (Mar. 15, 1920); II.5: 1-12 (May 15, 1920). This text is different from all the above versions, and does not contain the complete eight lectures.	Hu Shih	NL
16. "Ta-hsueh yü min-chih kuo yü-lun ti chung-yao" 大學與民治國輿論的重要	1) *CPFK*, Dec. 20, 1919	NL	,,
	2) *Bulletin*, 1920, No. 2, 49-50	Hu Shih 胡適	Kao Shang-te 高尚德
	3) *HC*, II.3:591-593 (Feb. 1920)	,,	,,

Title	Source of Publication	Interpretation	Recorder(s)
16. (cont.) (The university and public opinion in a democracy) A lecture given at National Peking University on the twenty-second anniversary of its founding.			
17. "Hsi-fang ssu-hsiang chung chih ch'üan-li kuan-nien" 西方思想中之權利觀念	1) *HT*, Jan. 27-28, 1920	Hu Shih 胡適	Wang T'ung-chao and Hsieh Ping 王統照 謝冰
	2) *CW*, Jan. 27, 1920	"	"
	3) *Bulletin*, 1920, No. 3, 39-43	"	"

Title	Source of Publication	Interpreter	Recorder(s)
17. (cont.) (The concept of "right" in western thought) Delivered Jan. 20, 1920 at the Chinese University, Peking.			
18. "Hsien-tai ti san ko che-hsueh chia" 現代的三個 哲學家 (Three philosophers of the modern period)	1) *CPFK*, Mar. 8-19, 1920; Mar. 22-27, 1920 2) *HT*, Mar. 12, 13, 16-18, 1920 (James); Mar. 9-23, 1920 (Bergson); Mar. 26-31 (Russell) 3) *CW*, Mar. 10, 15, 18, 21, 25, 28, 29, 1920	Hu Shih 胡適 " "	Fu Lu 伏廬 " NL

Title	Source of Publication	Interpreter	Recorder(s)
18. (cont.)			
A series of six lectures delivered in Peking.	4) *Bulletin*, 1920, No. 4, 17-21; No. 5, 15-20; No. 6, 29-49	Hu Shih 胡適	Fu Lu 伏廬
	5) *Five Major*, 343-398	"	"
19. "Che-hsueh shih" 哲學史 (History of philosophy)	1) *CPFK*, Apr. 9, 1920- June 29, 1920	Liu Po-ming 劉伯明	Che Fan 哲帆
	2) *HT*, Apr. 16, 23, 1920 (parts 1-2)	"	"
A series of approximately nineteen lectures, limited to Greek philosophy, delivered at Nanking Teachers' College.	Apr. 29, 30, 1920 (parts 3-4); May 3, 15, 18, 27, 18, 1920 (parts 5-8); June 24, 1920 (part 10)	"	T'ai Shuang-ch'iu and Shao Yü-lin 邰爽秋 邵毓麟

Title	Source of Publication	Interpreter	Recorder(s)
19. (cont.)	3) *Bulletin*, 1920, No. 7, 39–45 (6 parts)	Liu Po-ming 劉伯明	Chung Fan 仲帆
	1920, No. 8, 25–34	"	NL
	1920, No. 9, 35–42 (parts 15–19)	"	"
	4) *Three Major*, part II. (Apparently 10 lectures divided into 25 topics)	"	Shen Chen-sheng 沈振聲
20. "Chiao-yü che hsueh" 教育哲學 (Philosophy of education)	1) *HT*, Apr. 13, 15, 17, 20, 21, 1920 (parts 1–5)	"	Chung Fan 仲帆
	Apr. 24, 26, 1920 (parts 6–7)	"	Kuo Chi-fang and Chin Hai-kuan 郭智方 金海觀 Shih Chih-mien 施之勉
A series of twenty to thirty lectures delivered at	May 10, 1920	"	

Title	Source of Publication	Interpreter	Recorder(s)
20. (cont.) Nanking Teachers' College.	May 11, 14, 1920 (parts 9, 11)	Liu Po-ming 劉伯明	Chang Nien-tsu and Kuo Chih-fang 張念祖 郭智方 Chin Hai-kuan and
	May 19, 1920 (part 11); May 23, 1920 (part 12)	"	Ni Wen-chou 金海觀 倪文宙 and
	May 30, 1920 (part 14)	"	Kuo Chih-fang and Chin Hai-kuan 郭智方 金海觀 Chin Hai-kuan and
	July 2, 7, 1920 (parts 15, 19)	"	Ni Wen-chou 金海觀倪文宙

Title	Source of Publication	Interpreter	Recorder(s)
20. (cont.)	July 3, 12, 1920 (parts 16, 20)	Liu Po-ming 劉伯明	Ni Wen-chou and Chang Nien-tsu 倪文宙 張念祖
	July 5, 6, 14, 1920 (parts 17, 18, 21)	"	Chang Nien-tsu and Kuo Chih-fang 張念祖 郭智方
	July 15, 1920 (part 22)	"	Kuo Chih-fang and Chin Hai-kuan 郭智方 金海觀
	2) *Bulletin*, 1920, No. 7, 27-37 (ten parts)	"	Chung Fan 仲帆
	1920, No. 8, 35-40	"	Kuo Chih-fang and Chin Hai-kuan 郭智方 金海觀

Title	Source of Publication	Interpreter	Recorder(s)
20. (cont.)	1920, No. 9, 27-33	Liu Po-ming	NL
	1920, No. 10, 39-50	"	Ni Wen-chou and Chang Nien-tsu 倪文甫 張念祖
	1920, No. 11, 29-33	"	Kuo Chih-fang 郭智方
	1920, No. 12, 43-48	"	Chang Nien-tsu and Ni Wen-chou 張念祖 倪文甫
	3) *Three Major*, part I. (Apparently 22 lectures divided into 26 topics)	"	Chang Nien-tsu and Shen Chen-sheng 張念祖 沈振聲

Title	Source of Publication	Interpreter	Recorder(s)
20. (cont.)	4) *TWCYCH*	Liu Po-ming 劉伯明	Chin Hai-kuan 金海觀
21. "Hsin jen-sheng-kuan" 新人生觀 (The new conception of life)	1) *HT*, Apr. 18, 1920	"	Ts'ao Ch'u 曹匆
	HT, June 4, 1920 (separate text from above)	"	P'an Kung-chan 潘公展
	2) *SNSH*, II.3: (May 1, 1920). Incomplete text	"	Ni Wen-chou 倪文宙
	3) *CW*, June 3, 1920. This lecture was given June 1, 1920 and is a separate delivery of probably the same text as 1) and 2).	NL	NL
22. "Shih-yen lun-li hsueh" 試驗倫理學	1) *HT*, Apr. 19, 22, 25, 1920 (parts 1-3); May 21, 29,	Liu Po-ming	Hsia Ch'eng-feng and 夏承楓

Title	Source of Publication	Interpreter	Recorder(s)
22. (cont.) (Experimental logic).	1920 (parts 4-5); June 2, 9-11, 19, 1920 (parts 6-10)		Ts'ao-Ch'u 曹 芻
A series of approximately eighteen lectures delivered at Nanking Teachers' College.	2) *CPFK*, Sept. 20-Oct. 20, 1920	Liu Po-ming 劉 伯 明	Hsia Ch'eng-feng and Ts'ao-Ch'u 夏 承 楓 曹 芻
	3) *CW*, July 10-12, 1919	”	Liu Po-ming 劉 伯 明
	4) *Bulletin*, 1920, No. 11, 35-39; No. 12, 49-54; 1921; No. 1, 57-60 (parts 9-12); No. 2, 41-48 (parts 13-18)	”	Hsia Ch'eng-feng and Ts'ao-Ch'u 夏 承 楓 曹 芻
	5) *Three Major*, part III. (Apparently 10 lectures divided into 16 topics)	”	Shen Chen-sheng 沈 振 聲

	Title	Source of Publication	Interpreter	Recorder(s)
23.	"She-hui chin-hua chih piao-chun" 社會進化之標準 (Criteria for social progress)	1) *HT*, May 11, 1920 2) *CW*	Liu Po-ming 劉伯明 NL	Ch'iu I 秋倎 NL
24.	"Chiao-yü chih yao-su" 教育之要素 (Educational factors)	1) *HT*, May 12, 1920 2) *CW*	Liu Po-ming 劉伯明 NL	Ch'iu I 秋倎 NL
25.	"Chin-tai chiao-yü chih ch'u-shih" 近代教育之趨勢 (Trends in modern education)	1) *HT*, May 13, 1920 2) *CW*	Liu Po-ming 劉伯明 NL	Ch'iu I 秋倎 NL

	Title	Source of Publication	Interpreter	Recorder(s)
26.	"Chiao-yü-chia chih t'ien-chih" 教育家之天職 (The duty of educators)	1) *HT*, May 14, 1920	Liu Po-ming 劉伯明	Ch'iu I 秋佽
		2) *CW*	NL	NL
	Dewey gave lectures on this topic several times May–July, 1920 in the Shanghai-Nanking area. This text is possibly the same as No. 43 which follows.			
27.	"Chiao-yü yü she-hui" 教育與社會進化的關係 (The relationship between education and social progress)	1) *CW*, May 23, 1920	NL	NL
		2) *HT*, May 25, 1920	Liu Po-ming 劉伯明	Ch'en Ch'ang-keng and Hsu Ch'ang-nien 陳長庚 徐長年

Title	Source of Publication	Interpreter	Recorder(s)
27. (cont.) Delivered May 20, 1920 in Yangchow.			
28. "'Tzu-yu' ti chen-i" 「自由」底真義 (The real meaning of "freedom") A lecture at Yangchow.	1) *CW*, May 25, 1920	NL	NL
29. "Chih-hui tu-liang-fa ti ta-kang" 智慧度量法的大綱 (Methods for measuring intelligence— in outline)	1) *HT*, May 26, 1920	"	San Lang 三郎
	2) *CW*, May 27, 1920	"	NL

Title	Source of Publication	Interpreter	Recorder(s)
30. "Tzu-tung chih chen-i" 自動之真義 (The real meaning of independent action)	1) *HT*, May 29, 1920	Liu Po-ming 劉伯明	Ch'en Ch'ang-keng 陳長庚
31. "Chiao-yü-che ti t'ien-chih" 教育者的天職 (The duty of educators) Delivered on the 15th anniversary of the Second Teachers College (Shanghai).	1) *CW*, May 30, 1920 2) *HT*, May 31, 1920	NL Liu Po-ming 劉伯明	NL a student

	Title	Source of Publication	Interpreter	Recorder(s)
32.	"Chih-yeh chiao-yü ti ching-i" 職業教育的精義 (The essential meaning of vocational education) Delivered on Apr. 29, 1920 at the Vocational Education Association (Shanghai?).	1) *CW*, May 31, 1920	NL	NL
33.	"Chih-yeh chiao-yü yü lao-tung wen-t'i" 職業教育與勞動問題 (Vocational education and the labor problem) Delivered on Apr. 30, 1920.	1) *CW*, May 21, 1920 2) *Dewey and Russell*, 54-58	,,	,,

Title	Source of Publication	Interpreter	Recorder(s)
34. "Nan-nü t'ung-hsueh wen-t'i" 男女同學問題 (The question of co-education) Delivered May 31, 1920 at the Kiangsu Provincial Education Association, Shanghai.	1) CW, June 2, 1920	NL	NL
	2) HT, July 1, 1920	"	Keng Hsiang 耕香
35. "Chuan-men chiao-yü ti she-hui-kuan" 專門教育的社會觀 (The social conception of specialized education) Delivered at the T'ung Chi School (German sponsored) in Shanghai.	1) HT, June 3, 1920	"	NL
	2) CW, June 8, 1920	"	"

Title	Source of Publication	Interpreter	Recorder(s)
36. "Kung-min chiao-yü" 公民教育 (Education for citizenship) Delivered June 3, 1920 at P'u-tung High School (near Shanghai). 浦東中學	1) *CW*, June 4, 1920 2) *Dewey and Russell*, 63-68	NL "	NL "
37. "P'u-t'ung chiao-yü yü chih-yeh chiao-yü chih kuan-hsi" 普通教育與職業教育之關係 (The relationship between elementary	1) *CW* , June 5, 1920 2) *HT*, June 5, 1920	" "	" Feng Shu-hua 馮樹華

Title	Source of Publication	Interpreter	Recorder(s)
37. (cont.)			
education and vocational education)			
Delivered at Shanghai College (Hu Chiang Ta-hsueh). 滬江大學			
38. "She-hui chih-hua" 社會進化 (Social evolution)	1) CW, June 7, 1920	NL	NL
Delivered at the YMCA (Shanghai?).	2) HT, June 9, 1920	Liu Po-ming 劉伯明	Yao Hui-an 姚晦菴
39. "Te-mo-k'e-la-hsi ti chen-i" 德謨克拉西的真義	1) HT, June 9, 1920	"	Li Hsiao-pai 李孝白

Title	Source of Publication	Interpreter	Recorder(s)
39. (cont.) (The real meaning of democratic education) Delivered in Hangchow. 杭州	2) *CW*, June 16, 1920 3) Pai-hua wen-fan, No. 4, 87–94	NL "	NL "
40. "Kung-i ho wen-hua ti kuan-hsi" 工藝和文化底關係 (The relationship between culture and technology)	1) *HT*, June 9, 1920	Liu Po-ming 劉伯明	Chao Nai-ch'ien 趙乃謙
41. "Chiao-yü yü she-hui ti kuan-hsi" 教育與社會的關係	1) *HT*, June 9, 1920	Hsu Shou-wu 徐守五	Li Tseng-lien 李曾廉

Title	Source of Publication	Interpreter	Recorder(s)
41. (cont.)			
(The relationship between education and society)			
42. "Tsao chiu fa-tung ti hsing-chih ti chiao-yü" 造就發動的性質的教育 (Factors creating motivation in education)	1) *CW*, June 17, 1920	NL	NL
Delivered at the First Teachers College, Hangchow.			

206

	Title	Source of Publication	Interpreter	Recorder(s)
43.	"Chiao-yü-che ti tse-jen" 教育者的責任 (The responsibility of educators) Delivered at the city of Nantung, Kiangsu province.	1) *HT*, June 17, 18, 1920	Liu Po-ming 劉伯明	Lo Hung-hsuan and Fan Kai-chin 羅鴻瑄 范愷金 NL
		2) *CW*, June 19, 1920	NL	
44.	"She-hui chin-hua wen-t'i" 社會進化問題 (The problem of social progress)	1) *HT*, June 22, 1920	Liu Po-ming 劉伯明	Fei Fan-chiu 費範九
45.	"Chiao-yü ti hsin ch'u-shih yü chiao 教育的新趨勢 與教	1) *HT*, June 23, 1920	"	Shen Tzu-shan 沈子善

Title	Source of Publication	Interpreter	Recorder(s)
45. (cont.) ts'ai kai-tsu" 材改組 (New trends in education and the reorganization of teaching methods) Delivered in Süchow, Kiangsu province.	2) *CW*, June 24, 1920	NL	NL
46. "Shu-yü ti hsin ch'u-shih" 數育的新趨勢 (New trends in teaching mathematics)	1) *CW*, June 30, 1920	,,	,,

	Title	Source of Publication	Interpreter	Recorder(s)
47.	"Chiao-ts'ai ti tsu-chih" 教材的組織 (The organization of teaching materials) Delivered in Suchow.	1) *CW*, July 1, 1920	Liu Po-ming 劉伯明	Cheng Meng-chiu and Hsu Tsai-tzu 鄭蒙九 徐任孜
48.	"Chiao-yü yü shih-yeh" 教育與實業 (Education and industry) This lecture in all probability is	1) *CW*, July 2, 1920 2) *HT*, July 9, 1920	NL Cheng Hsiao-ts'ang 鄭曉滄	NL Ch'en Tan and Shen Ping-k'uei 陳旦 沈炳魁

Title	Source of Publication	Interpreter	Recorder(s)
48. (cont.) different from both No. 8 and No. 63.			
49. "Chiao-yü-che ti tse-jen" 教育者底責任	1) *CW*, July 3, 1920	Cheng Hsiao-ts'ang 鄭曉滄	Chiang Shih-chou 蔣石洲
(The responsibility of educators) Delivered in Soochow, Kiangsu province.	2) *HT*, July 9, 1920	,,	Ch'en Tan and Shen Ping-k'uei 陳旦 沈炳魁
50. "Hsiao-hsueh chiao-yü chih ch'u-shih" 小學教育之趨勢	1) *HT*, July 9, 1920	,,	

Title	Source of Publication	Interpreter	Recorder(s)
50. (cont.) (Trends in elementary education)			
51. "Chiao-yü hsing-cheng chih mu-ti" 教育行政之目的 (The aim of educational administration)	1) *CW*, July 9, 1920	Cheng Hsiao-ts'ang 鄭曉滄	NL
52. "Hsüeh-hsiao yü she-hui" 學校與社會 (School and society)	1) *HT*, July 9, 1920 2) *CW*, July 11, 1920	" NL	Ch'en Tan and Shen Ping-k'uei 陳旦 沈炳魁 NL

Title	Source of Publication	Interpreter	Recorder(s)
53. "Hsueh-sheng tzu-chih ti tsu-chih" 學生自治的組織 (The organization of student government)	1) *HT*, July 9, 1920	P'an Shen-wen 潘慎文	Ch'en Tan and Shen Ping-k'uei 陳旦 沈炳魁
	2) *Bulletin*, 1920, No. 10, 51-53	Cheng Hsiao-ts'ang 鄭曉滄	"
	3) *CPFK*, Sept. 16-19, 1920	NL	"
54. "Shih-yen chu-i" 試驗主義 (Experimentalism) Delivered at Wusih 無錫 Kiangsu province.	1) *CW*, July 16, 1920	NL	NL

Title	Source of Publication	Interpreter	Recorder(s)
55. "P'ing-min chu-i yü chiao-yü 平民主義與教育 (Democracy and education)"	1) *HT*, Nov. 5, 10, 12, 17–19, 1920 (lect. 1-6)	NL	Li Chi-min and Yang Wen-mien 李濟民 楊文冕
Classroom lectures by Dewey using *Democracy and Education* as a text, delivered from the fall of 1920 to the summer of 1921 in the department of educational research of Peking Teachers' College.	2) *PMCY*, No. 26 (Dec. 20, 1920); No. 27 (Jan. 10, 1921); No. 28 (Jan. 25, 1921); No. 29 (Feb. 20, 1921); No. 30 (Mar. 5, 1921); No. 31 (Apr. 1, 1921); No. 32 (Apr. 20, 1921); No. 33 (May 5, 1921); No. 34 (May 20, 1921); No. 35 (June 5, 1921); Nos. 41, 42 (Nov. 10, 1921)	Ch'ang Tao-chih 常道直	Ch'ang Tao-chih 常道直
	3) *PMCIYCY*	"	"

Title	Source of Publication	Interpreter	Recorder(s)
56. "Lun Chung-kuo ti mei shu" 論中國的美術 (On the Chinese fine arts) Delivered to the Fine Arts Club of Peking Teachers College.	1) *CPFK*, Mar. 7, 1921 2) *HT*, Mar. 15, 1921 3) *Bulletin*, 1921, No. 4, 47–49	Hu Shih 胡適 " "	Ts'ao P'ei-yen Wang Hui-po 曹配言 王迴波 "
57. "Ta-hsueh ti chih-ch'u" 大學的旨趣 (The aims of a university)	1) *CPFK*, Apr. 25–26, 1921	NL	NL
58. "Chiao-yü-che wei she-hui ling-shou" 教育者為社會領袖	1) *CPFK*, Apr. 30–May 2, 1921 2) *Bulletin*, 1921, No. 7, 33–35	"	"

Title	Source of Publication	Interpreter	Recorder(s)
58. (cont.)			
(Educators as leaders in society)			
Delivered at the First Teachers College of Fukien province.			
59. "Tze-tung yü tzu-chih" 自動與自治	1) *CPFK*, May 3-6, 1921	NL	NL
	2) *Bulletin*, 1921, No. 6, 41-44	"	"
(Self activity and self-government)			
Delivered at the First High School of Fukien province.			

Title	Source of Publication	Interpreter	Recorder(s)
60. "Mei-kuo chiao-yü hui chih tsu-chih chi ch'i ying-hsiang yü she-hui" 美國教育會之組織及其影響於社會 (The organization of American education associations and their influence on society) Delivered at Fukien Provincial Education Association (Foochow?).	1) *CPFK*, May 7, 1921 2) *Bulletin*, 1921, No. 10	NL "	NL "
61. "Chiao yü yü kuo-chia chih kuan-hsi" 教育與國家之關係	1) *CPFK*, May 8-9, 1921 2) *Bulletin*, 1921, No. 12, 23-25	" "	" "

Title	Source of Publication	Interpreter	Recorder(s)
61. (cont.) (The relationship between education and the state) Delivered at the Y.M.C.A. in Foochow, Fukien province.			
62. "Chiao-shou ch'ing-nien ti chiao-yü yuan-li" 教授青年底 教育原理 (Educational principles for teaching the youth) Delivered at Peking Women's Teachers' College.	1) *CPFK*, May 10–11, 1921 2) *Bulletin*, 1921, No. 8, 51–53	NL "	Fu Yin 福音 "

Title	Source of Publication	Interpreter	Recorder(s)
63. "Chiao-yü yü shih-yeh" 教育與實業 (Education and industry) Delivered at the Y.M.C.A. in Foochow, Fukien province.	1) *CPFK*, May 13-14, 1921	NL	NL
	2) *Bulletin*, 1921, No. 12, 25-28	"	"
64. "Nan-yu hsin-ying" 南遊心影 (Impressions of South China)	1) *CPFK*, June 17-19, 1921	"	Shu Lan 淑蘭
	2) *CW*, June 22, 1921	"	NL
	3) *HT*, July 3, 1921	"	Shu Lan 淑蘭
	4) *Bulletin*, 1921, No. 10	"	"

	Title	Source of Publication	Interpreter	Recorder(s)
64.	(cont.)	5) *Dewey and Russell*, 103–111	NL	Shu Lan 淑蘭
65.	"Kuo-min chiao-yü yü kuo-chia chih kuan-hsi" 國民教育與國家之關係 (The relationship between elementary education and the state) Delivered at the Y.M.C.A. in Foochow, Fukien province.	1) *CPFK*, June 20, 21, 1921	"	Wei Hsuan 味宣
		2) *HT*, July 3, 1921	"	"
		3) *Bulletin*, 1921, No. 7, 45–46	"	"
		4) *Dewey and Russell*	"	
66.	"Tzu-tung ti 自動的	1) *CPFK*, June 23, 1921	"	NL

Title	Source of Publication	Interpreter	Recorder(s)
66. (cont.)			
yen chiu" 研究	2) *HT*, July 17, 1920	NL	NL
(Spontaneity in learning)	3) *Bulletin*, 1921, No. 8, 39–40	"	"
Delivered at the Y.M.C.A. in Foochow, Fukien province.			
67. "Chiao-shih chih-yeh chih hsien-tsai chi-hui" 教師職業之現在機會	1) *CPFK*, June 24–27, 1921	Wang Cho-jan 王卓然	Shu Lan 淑蘭
	2) *CW*, June 26, 27, 1921	"	NL
	3) *HT*, July 3, 1921	"	Shu Lan 淑蘭
(Present opportunities	4) *Bulletin*, 1921, No. 8, 45–50	"	"

Title	Source of Publication	Interpreter	Recorder(s)
67. (cont.) in the teaching profession) Delivered at Peking Teachers College. The text indicates that this lecture would probably be Dewey's final public talk in Peking. The title, "Lin-pieh tseng-yen" 臨別贈言 (Farewell address) was given to the same text in sources 6) and 7).	5) *Dewey and Russell*, 92-102 6) *HT*, June 28, 1921 7) *Bulletin*, 1921, No. 7 47-51	Wang Cho-jan 王卓然 " "	Shu Lan 澍蘭 Liu Hsiao-chi 劉孝基 NL
68. "T'ien-jan huan- 天然環	1) *CPFK*, June 28-29, 1921	NL	NL

Title	Source of Publication	Interpreter	Recorder(s)
68. (cont.) ching she-hui huan-ching-yü jen-sheng chih kuan-hsi" 境社會環境與人生之關係 (The relationship of the natural and social environments with human life) Delivered at the Y.M.C.A. in Foochow, Fukien province.	2) *HT*, July 3, 1921 3) *Bulletin*, 1921, No. 8, 42–45 4) *Dewey and Russell*, 69–80	NL " "	NL " "
69. "Hsi-kuan yü ssu-hsiang" 習慣與思想 (Habit and thought)	1) *CPFK*, June 30–July 1, 1921 2) *Bulletin*, 1921, No. 10, 39–41	"	"

Title	Source of Publication	Interpreter	Recorder(s)
69. (cont.) Delivered at the Y.M.C.A. in Foochow, Fukien province.			
70. "Tung-tso tao-te chung-yao ti yuan-yin" 動作道德重要的原因 (The importance of dynamic morality) First Canton lecture, delivered at the Teachers College.	1) *KTCYH*, I.1: 116–119 (July, 1921)	NL	NL
71. (Education for Interaction)	1) *KTCYH*, I.1:120–122 (July, 1921)	"	"

223

Title	Source of Publication	Interpreter	Recorder(s)
71. (cont.) Second Canton lecture, delivered at the Kwangtung Provincial Education Association.			
72. (The Scientific Spirit and Morality) Third Canton lecture, delivered at the Kwangtung Provincial Education Association.	1) *KTCYH*, I.1:123–126 (July, 1921)	NL	NL
73. "Min-chih ti i-i" 民治的意義 (The meaning of democracy)	1) *CPFK*, July 8, 1921 2) *Bulletin*, 1921, No. 8, 54–55	" "	" "

Title	Source of Publication	Interpreter	Recorder(s)
73. (cont.) Delivered at the Fukien Shang-yu Club 尚友.			
74. "Chiao-yü-che ti kung-tso" 教育者底工作 (The work of educators)	1) *CPFK*, July 22, 23, 1921 2) *CW*, July 26, 1921	NL "	NL "
75. "She-hui chih yao-su" 社會之要素 (Social factors) Three lectures concerning society and education given as part of a series in Tsinan.			

Title	Source of Publication	Interpreter	Recorder(s)
75. (cont.)			
(1) "Chiao-yü chih she-hui ti yao-su" 教育之社會的要素	1) *CPFK*, July 24-27, 1921	Wang Cho-jan 王卓然	NL
	2) *Bulletin*, 1921, No. 9, 7-12	"	"
	3) *CW*, August 12, 1921		
(The social factor in education)	4) *Dewey and Russell*, 1-11	"	"
(2) "Hsüeh-hsiao k'o-mu yü she-hui chih kuan-hsi" 學校課目與社會之關係	1) *CPFK*, Aug. 3-7, 1921	"	"
	2) *Bulletin*, 1921, No. 11, 5-7	"	"
	3) *CW*, Aug. 18, 1921	"	"
(The relationship	4) *Dewey and Russell*, 11-19	"	"

Title	Source of Publication	Interpreter	Recorder(s)
75. (cont.) between school subjects and society)			
(3) "Hsueh-hsiao ti hsing-cheng ho tsu-chih yü she-hui chih kuan-hsi" 學校的行政和組織與社會之關係 (The relationship of school administration and organization with society)	1) *CPFK*, Aug. 8–10, 1921	Wang Cho-jan	NL
	2) *Bulletin*, 1921, No. 12, 33–36	,,	,,
	3) *CW*, Aug. 21, 1921	,,	,,
	4) *Dewey and Russell*, 19–25	,,	,,
76. "Min-pen cheng-chih chih chi-pen" 民本政治之基本	1) *Bulletin*, 1921, No. 8, 40–42	NL	,,

Title	Source of Publication	Interpreter	Recorder(s)
76. (cont.) (Essentials of democratic politics) Delivered at the Private Fukien College of Law and Administration.			
77. "Chiao-yü chih hsin-li ti yao-su" 教育心理的要素 (Psychological factors in education) The fifth lecture delivered in the Tsinan series.	1) *CPFK*, Sept. 19–21, 1921 2) *Bulletin*, 1921, No. 11, 15–20	NL "	NL "

Title	Source of Publication	Interpreter	Recorder(s)
78. "Hsueh-hsiao yü she-hui ti kuan-hsi" 學校與社會的關係 (The relationship of school and society) The sixth lecture delivered in the Tsinan series.	1) *CPFK*, Sept. 22-24, 1921 2) *Bulletin*, 1922, No. 1 (Feb.), 13-16	Wang Cho-jan 王卓然 "	NL "

Appendix B

JOHN DEWEY'S MAJOR LECTURE SERIES, PUBLISHED ARTICLES, AND PROFESSIONAL ACTIVITIES DURING HIS VISIT TO CHINA

1919:

April 30	Arrival in Shanghai.
May 3-4	First two lectures delivered, Kiangsu Education Association.
May 5	Left Shanghai for Hangchow.
May 7	Lectured in Hangchow.
May 8	Mrs. Dewey lectured in Hangchow.
May 12	Shanghai dinner with Sun Yat-sen.
May 18, 19, 21, 24, 25, 26	Lectures given at Nanking Teachers' College.
May 28	Article written in Nanking and later published as "On Two Sides of the Eastern Seas," *New Republic* (hereafter referred to as *NR*), XIX.245 (July 16, 1919), 346-348.
June 1	Deweys arrived in Peking by June 1.
June 7	Slated to speak at annual reunion of the American College Club.
June 8, 10, and 12, or 13	Delivered first public lectures in Peking, "The Development of Democracy in America," sponsored by the Hsueh-shu chiang-yen hui (The scholastic lecture society) and delivered in the auditorium of the Ministry of Education.
June 24	Article written in Peking and later published as "The Student Revolt in China," *NR*, XX.248 (August 6, 1919), 16-18.

July 8	Completed article later published as "The International Duel in China" *NR*, XX.251 (August 27, 1919), 110-112.
July 25 (approx.)	Attended an educational conference in Peking.
	Miss Lucy Dewey arrived in Peking to join the family.
July (month)	The Deweys lived temporarily in the home of John L. Childs, then foreign secretary of the International Committee of the Y.M.C.A.
July 28	Completed article later published as "Militarism in China," *NR*, XX. 253 (September 10, 1919), 167-169.
August 4 (week of)	Attended educators' meeting in Tientsin.
September 12	Completed article later published as "The American Opportunity in China," *NR*, XXI.261 (December 3, 1919), 14-17.
September 20	Address delivered at opening of school year at National Peking University. Began appointment as visiting professor.
September	One-week trip to Manchuria. Began major Peking lecture series.
October 6	Completed article later published as "Our Share in Drugging China," *NR*, XXI.264 (December 24, 1919), 114-117.
October 10-15	Lectured in Taiyuan, Shansi province, to universities and to annual meeting of the Chinese Federation of Educational Associations.
October 20	Sixtieth birthday dinner in Peking.

November	Published "Transforming the Mind of China," *Asia*, XIX.11 (November 1919), 1103-1108.
November (late)	Completed article later published as "The Sequel of the Student Revolt," *NR*, XXI.273 (February 25, 1920), 380-382.
December	Published "Chinese National Sentiment," *Asia*, XIX.12 (December 1919), 1237-1242.
1920:	
January 5	Returned from first lecture tour to Shantung Province. Completed article later published as "Shantung as Seen from Within," *NR*, XXII.274 (March 3, 1920), 12-17.
Spring-summer	Visiting Professor at Nanking Teachers' College. Delivered *Three Major* series. (Arrived in April and stayed through summer session). Toured for six weeks in Kiangsu province lecturing.
April	Published "The New Leaven in Chinese Politics," *Asia*, XX.3 (April 1920), 267-272.
May	Published ' What Holds China Back," *Asia*, XX.4 (May 1920), 373-377.
June 30	Published "China's Nightmare," *NR*, XXIII.291 (June 30, 1920), 145-147.
Fall, 1920–summer, 1921	Professor at the graduate school of Peking Teachers' College.
October 6	Published "A Political Upheaval in China," *NR*, XXIV.305 (October 6, 1920), 142-144.

October 27	Visited Changsha, Hunan, at least a week. Attended education conference; met Bertrand Russell. Visited the city of Hankow; visited Kiangsi province.
October (end of month)	Received honorary degree from National Peking University.
December 8	Published "Industrial China," *NR*, XXV.314 (December 8, 1920), 39-41.
1921:	
January 12	Published 'Is China a Nation?" *NR*, XXV.319 (January 12, 1921), 187-190.
February	Completed article later published as "Shizen kagaku ni okeru risōshugi" (Idealism in natural science), *Kaizō*, III.4 (April 1921), 198-208.
March 16	Published "The Far Eastern Deadlock," *NR*, XXVI.328 (March 16, 1921), 71-74.
March 31	Left Peking for lecture tour to Foochow, Amoy and Canton.
March	Published "Tōyō bummei wa seishinteki ni shite seiyō bummei wa busshiteki nari ya" (Is Eastern culture spiritual, and Western culture materialistic?) *Kaizō*, III.3 (March 1921), 103-114.
April 13	Published "The Consortium in China," *NR*, XXVI.332 (April 13, 1921), 178-180.
May	Fukien speeches appeared in periodicals.
May 5	Dewey in Canton. Published "Kagaku to genkon no sangyō (Science

	and the present industrial system), *Kaizō*, III.5 (May 5 1921), 103-115.
May 24	Completed article later published as "Hinterlands in China," *NR*, XXVII. 344 (July 6, 1921), 161-165.
May	Published "Old China and New," *Asia*, XXI.5 (May, 1921), 445-450, 454, 456.
By May 24	Had returned to Peking from trip to Foochow, Amoy, and Canton.
Mid-June and July	Second lecture tour to Tsinan, Shantung.
July	Published "New Culture in China," *Asia*, XXI.7 (July 1921), 581-586, 642.
July 11	Departure from China.

Appendix C

TRANSLATIONS OF JOHN DEWEY'S WORKS INTO CHINESE

Many of the translations in the following list are partial references, lacking some bibliographical information. This has been necessary because the published Chinese translations themselves are often missing a fact of publication, such as the date, and also because secondary references to books not available for inspection have been included to make this list as complete as possible. Part I of the list includes Dewey's books translated into Chinese; Part II includes articles by Dewey translated into Chinese. The list of books is organized according to the date when Dewey published the volume in English, beginning with the earliest. It has been impossible to organize the list according to the date of the Chinese translations because so many of these dates are unknown. All the Chinese translations of a given book are listed separately by a letter in parentheses under the English title of the work.

Translations of chapters in books are also listed under the English title of the book. In each of these entries it is indicated what chapter or chapters were translated and where they appear in Chinese periodicals. The Chinese periodical titles are given in romanization, characters, and English.

Part I

BOOKS BY JOHN DEWEY TRANSLATED INTO CHINESE

1. *My Pedagogic Creed*. New York, E. L. Kellogg & Co., 1897.
   a) *Wo chih chiao-yü chu-i* 我之教育主義 Tr. Cheng Tsung-hai 鄭宗海 Shanghai, Shang-wu 商務.
   b) *Wo-ti chiao-yü hsin-t'iao* 我的教育信條 Tr. Tseng Chao-sen 曾昭森 Hong Kong, Chin-pu chiao-yü ch'u-pan-she 進步教育出版社 , 1959.

2. *The School and Society*. Chicago, The University of Chicago Press, 1900.

    a) *Hsueh-hsiao yü she-hui chih chin-pu* 學校與社會之進步 (The school and social progress). Tr. Liu Chien-yang 劉建陽. *P'ing-min chiao-yü* 平民教育 ("Democracy and Education") No. 3 (Oct. 25, 1919), No. 5 (Nov. 8, 1919). This is Chapter I of *The School and Society*. It was also reprinted in *Chiao-yü ts-ung-k'an* 教育叢刊 (Education journal) Peking Teachers' College, I (Dec. 1919), 1-7.

    b) *Hsueh-hsiao ho erh-t'ung chih sheng-huo* 學校和兒童之生活 (The school and the life of the child) Tr. Liu Chien-yang 劉建陽 *P'ing-min chiao-yü* 平民教育 ("Democracy and Education") No. 7 (Nov. 22, 1919), No. 8 (Nov. 29, 1919), No. 9 (Dec. 6, 1919). This is Chapter II of *The School and Society*.

    c) *Hsueh-hsiao yü she-hui* 學校與社會. Tr. Liu Heng-ju 劉衡如 Shanghai, Chung-hua shu-chü 中華書局

3. *The Child and the Curriculum*. Chicago, University of Chicago Press, 1902.

    a) *Erh-t'ung yü chiao-ts'ai* 兒童與教材. 8th ed. Tr. Cheng Tsung-hai 鄭宗海 Shanghai, Chung-hua shu-chü 中華書局, 1930. Another edition of this translation appeared in 1947.

4. *Ethics*, written with James H. Tufts. New York, Henry Holt and Company, 1908.

    a) Tr. Yü Chia-chü 余家菊

5. *Moral Principles in Education*. Boston, Houghton Mifflin Company, 1909.

    a) *Te-yü yuan-li* 德育原理 Tr. Wen Shang-jen 文尚仁 Shanghai, Chung-hua shu-chü 中華書局

    b) Tr. Yuan Hao-wen 元好問

6. *How We Think*. Boston, D. C. Heath & Co., 1910.

    a) *Szu-wei shu* 思維術 Tr. Liu po-ming 劉伯明 Shanghai, Chung-hua shu-chü 中華書局, 1921. The third edition of this translation was published in 1933.

b) *Szu-hsiang fang-fa lun* 思想方法論 Tr. Ch'iu Chin-chang 丘瑾璋 Shanghai, Shih-chieh shu-chü 世界書局 , 1935. This translation is of Dewey's 1933 revised edition of *How We Think*.

c) *Szu-wei yü chiao-hsueh* 思維與教學 Tr. Meng Hsien-ch'eng 孟憲承 and Yü Ch'ing-t'ang 余慶棠 Shang-hai, Shang-wu 商務 , 1936. This translation is of Dewey's 1933 revised edition of *How We Think*.

7. *Interest and Effort in Education*. Boston, Houghton Mifflin Company, 1913.

a) Tr. Chang Yü-ch'ing 張裕卿.

8. *Schools of Tomorrow*. New York, E. P. Dutton & Company, 1915.

a) *Wei-lai chih hsueh-hsiao* 未來之學校 Tr. Hsu Han-hsiang 舒翰祥 *Chiao-yü pu kung-pao* 教育部公報 (Bulletin of the ministry of education) I-shu 譯述 (Translation section), *1919*, No. 5, pp. 1-5; No. 6, pp. 1-12; No. 7, pp. 1-10; No. 9, pp. 7-18; *1920*, No. 1, pp. 1-13; No. 2, pp. 15-27; No. 5, pp. 27-36; No. 7, pp. 1-13; No. 10, pp. 1-12; No. 11, pp. 17-27; *1921*, No. 1, pp. 19-30; *1922*, No. 4, pp. 1-12; No. 5, pp. 1-12; No. 6, pp. 23-33; No. 7, pp. 23-33; No. 9, pp. 15-21; No. 10, pp. 15-21.

b) *Ming-jih chih hsueh-hsiao* 明日之學校 Tr. Chu Ching-nung 朱經農 and P'an Tzu-nien 潘梓年 Shanghai, Shang-wu 商務 , 1923. Another edition appeared in 1935.

c) *Ming-jih chih hsueh-hsiao* 明日之學校 *Chueh-wu* 覺悟 (Awakening) Supplement to *Min-kuo jih-pao* 民國日報 (Republic daily). Translator is not listed, but this could be the same translation as letter b) above. Chs. 1-4, August 4, 5, 7, 8, 9, 11, 12, 15, 16, 18, 19, 21, 23, 25, 26, 28, 29, 1921; Chs. 5-9, September 1, 2, 4, 5, 6, 8, 9, 11, 12, 13, 15, 16, 18, 19, 20, 22, 23, 25, 26, 27, 29, 30, 1921; Chs. 10-11, October 2, 3, 4, 6, 7, 9, 13, 14, 16, 17, 18, 20, 1921.

9. *Democracy and Education*. New York, The Macmillan Company, 1916.

a) *Min-pen chu-i yü chiao-yü* 民本主義與教育

Tr. Tsou En-jun 鄒恩潤 5 vols. Shanghai, Shang-wu 商務 1929.
There were several editions of this translation. There were at least two editions in 1929, one in 1948, and it was re-published in two volumes by the Commercial Press in Taiwan in 1960.

b) The first four chapters of the above translation appeared first serially when Dewey was still in China: Ch. I, *Hsin Chung-kuo* 新中國 ("The New China"), II, No. 1 (Jan. 15, 1920), 61-75. Ch. II, *Hsin Chung-kuo*, II, No. 4 (April 15, 1920), 63-80. Ch. III, *Hsin Chung-kuo*, II, No. 7 (July 15, 1920), 1-15. Ch. IV, *Hsin Chung-kuo*, II, No. 8 (August 15, 1920), 1-10.

c) *Chiao-yü che-hsueh kai-lun* 教育哲學概論 Tr. Chu Wen-t'ai 朱文態 Chiao-yü pu kung-pao 教育部公報 (Bulletin of the ministry of education), I-shu (Translation section), *1920*, No. 12, pp. 19-35; *1921*, No. 9, pp. 9-28; *1923*, No. 2, pp. 11-24. This translation completes only the four first chapters of *Democracy and Education*.

d) *Chiao-yü shang chih min-chu chu-i* 教育上之民主主義 Tr. Chen Ch'ang 真常 *Chiao-yü tsa-chih* 教育雜誌 ("The Chinese Educational Review"), XI, No. 5 (May 20, 1919), 47-58; No. 6 (June 20, 1919), 59-68. This translation is only of Chapter 7 of *Democracy and Education*.

10. Reconstruction in Philosophy. New York, Henry Holt and Company, 1920.

a) *Che-hsueh chih kai-tsao* 哲學之改造 Tr. Hsu Ch'ung-ch'ing 許崇清 Shanghai, Shang-wu 商務 , 1933. There was a 1939 edition of this translation published by the Commercial Press in Changsha, and there was a 1966 edition published by the Commercial Press in Taiwan.

b) Parts of Hsu Ch'ung-ch'ing's translation first appeared in the *Kuang-tung sheng chiao-yü hui tsa-chih* 廣東省教育會雜誌 ("The journal of Kwang Tung educational association"). In I, No. 2 (February, 1930), 187-195, part of the translation appears which corresponds with pp. 7-17 of Hsu Ch'ung-ch'ing's 1933 book edition, except for minor stylistic differences. This Cantonese journal was evidently the sequel to one of the same title founded in July, 1921.

 c) *Che-hsueh ti kai-tsao* 哲學的改造 2 vols. Tr. Hu Shih 胡適 and T'ang Yueh 唐鉞 Shanghai, Shang-wu. This translation was reprinted by Wen hsing shu-tien 文星書店, Taipei, 1965.

11. *Human Nature and Conduct*. New York, Henry Holt and Company, 1922.

 a) *Jen-hsing yü hsing-wei* 人性與行為 Tr. Chou Wen-hai 鄒文海 *Hsin Szu-ch'ao* 新思潮 No. 27 (July, 1953), 23-54. Also appears in *Chou Wen-hai hsien-sheng cheng-chih k'o-hsueh wen-chi* 鄒文海先生政治科學文集 (The collected writings of Mr. Chou Wen-hai on political science). Taipei, Kuang wen shu-chü 廣文書局 1967, pp. 474-487. This is a translation of Dewey's new "Introduction" to the Modern Library edition of 1920. New York, The Modern Library, 1930.

12. *The Development of American Pragmatism*. New York, Columbia University Press, 1925.

 a) Tr. Hu Tung-yeh 胡冬野 Taipei, Hua-kuo ch'u-pan-she 華國出版社, 1950.

13. *The Sources of a Science of Education*. New York, Horace Liveright, 1929.

 a) *Chiao-yü k'o-hsueh chih ch'üan-yuan* 教育科學之泉源 Tr. Chang Tai-nien 張岱年 Peking, Jen-wen shu-tien 人文書店

 b) *Chiao-yü k'o-hsüeh chih tzu-yuan* 教育科學之資源 Tr. Ch'iu Chin-chang 丘瑾璋 Shanghai, Shang-wu 商務, 1936.

14. *Experience and Education*. New York, The Macmillan Company, 1938.

 a) *Ching-yen yü chiao-yü* 經驗與教育 Tr. Li Hsiang-hsu *et al.* 李相勖等 Kweiyang, Wen t'ung 文通

1941. This translation was reprinted in Chungking by the same publisher in 1946.

b) *Ching-yen yü chiao-yü* 經驗與教育 Tr. Li P'ei-pu 李培圃 Shanghai, Cheng-chung shu-chü 正中書局 1946.

c) *Chiao-yü yü shih-yen chu-i che-hsueh* 教育與實驗主義哲學 Tr. Hsu Ying 許瀛 Shanghai, Cheng-chung shu-chü 正中書局, 1948.

15. *Logic: The Theory of Inquiry*. New York, Henry Holt and Company, 1938.

a) *Tu-wei lun li-shih p'an-tuan* 杜威論歷史判斷 Tr. Ch'en po-chuang 陳伯莊 *Hsien-tai hsueh-shu chi-k'an* 現代學術季刊 (Contemporary philosophy and social sciences), I, No. 1 (Nov. 1956), 85-96. This text is a translation and explanation of part of Chapter 12, "Judgment as spatial-temporal distinction," from *Logic: The Theory of Inquiry*, pp. 230-239.

16. *Intelligence in the Modern World*. New York, The Modern Library, 1939.

a) *Tu-wei che-hsueh* 杜威哲學 Tr. Chao I-wei 趙一葦 2 vols. Taipei, Chiao-yü pu 教育部 (Ministry of education), 1960.

17. *Freedom and Culture*. New York, G. P. Putnam's Sons, 1939.

a) *Tzu-yu yü wen-hua* 自由與文化 Tr. Wu Chün-sheng 吳俊升 Taipei, Cheng-chung shu-chü 正中書局, 1953. Another edition was published in 1956.

b) *Tzu-yu yü wen-hua* 自由與文化 Tr. Lin I-liang 林以亮 and Lou I-che 婁貽哲 Hong Kong, Jen-sheng ch'u-pan-she 人生出版社, 1954.

18. *Education Today*. New York, G. P. Putnam's Sons, 1940.

a) Information unavailable.

Part II

ARTICLES BY JOHN DEWEY TRANSLATED INTO CHINESE

1. "Ill Advised," *American Teacher*, VI (February 1917), 31.
Dewey's opinion regarding a resolution by the American Federation
of Teachers at a recent meeting in Chicago.

    a) "Chiao-yü lien-ho hui" 教育聯合會 Tr. Hsu kan-t'ang
徐甘棠 *Hsin Chiao-yü* 新教育 ("The New Education"), II, No. 4 (December 1919), 437-439.

2. "The Aims of Science Education," A lecture given by Dewey
in Japan in 1919. It was translated into Japanese and published in
Gendai Kyoiku 現代教育 (Modern education), No. 4, by
Yoshida Kumaja 吉田熊次.

    a) 'Li-k'o chiao-yü chih mu-ti" 理科教育之目的 Trans-
lated from the Japanese by Chiang Ch'i 姜琦 *Hsin Chiao-
yü* 新教育 ("The New Education"), I, No. 5 (August,
1919), 480-485.

3. "How Reaction Helps," *New Republic*, XXIV (September 1,
1920), 21-22.

    a) "Fan-tung li tsen yang pang-mang" 反動力怎樣幫忙
Tr. Chen Ying 震瀛 *Hsin Ch'ing-nien* 新青年 (New
youth), VIII, No. 4 (December 1, 1920), 3 pp.

4. "New Culture in China," *Asia*, XXI (July, 1921), 581-586,
642.

    a) "Chung-kuo ti hsin wen-hua" 中國的新文化 Trans-
lator unknown. *Ch'en pao fu-k'an* 晨報副刊 (Supplement to *The Morning Post*), July 28–August, 1921.

5. "Culture and Professionalism in Education," *School and
Society*, XVIII (October 13, 1923), 421-424. An address at the
opening exercises of Columbia University, September 26, 1923.

    a) "Wen-hua chiao-yü yü chih-yeh chiao-yü 文化教育與
職業教育 Tr. I Tso-lin 易作霖 *Chiao-yü yü chih-
yeh* 教育與職業 (Education and vocation), No. 61
(December 3, 1924).

6. "Progressive Education and the Science of Education," *Progressive Education*, V (July, August, September, 1928), 197-204.

    a) "Chin-pu ti chiao-yü yü chiao-yü chih k'o-hsueh"進步的 教育與教育之科學　Tr. Chu Jan-li 朱然藜 *Chiao-yü tsa-chih* 教育雜誌 ("The Chinese Educational Review"), XXII, No. 12 (December 20, 1930), 27-34.

7. "What I believe," in *Living Philosophies: A Series of Intimate Credos by Twenty-two Modern Thinkers*. New York, Simon and Schuster, 1931 pp. 21-35.

    a) *Chin-jih szu ta szu-hsiang-chia hsin-yang chih tzu-shu* 今日 四大思想家信仰之自述　(Autobiographical credos of four eminent thinkers of the present age). Shanghai, Liang yu t'u-shu yin-shua kung-szu 良友 圖書印刷公司 , 1931.

ABBREVIATIONS USED IN NOTES

BDRC	*Biographical Dictionary of Republican China*, H. Boorman, ed.
CC	*Ts'ai Yuan-p'ei hsien sheng ch'üan-chi*
CE	*Characters and Events*, John Dewey
CHCYC	*Chung-hua chiao-yü chieh*
CNAAE	Chinese National Association for the Advancement of Education
CPFK	*Ch'en pao fu-k'an*
CSM	*The Chinese Students' Monthly*
CSPSR	*The Chinese Social and Political Science Review*
CYC	*Chiao-yü ch'ao*
CYKP	*Chiao-yü pu kung-pao*
CYKT	*Chung-kuo chiao-yü kai-tsao*, T'ao Hsing-chih
CYLW	*T'ao Hsing-chih hsien-sheng chiao-yü lun-wen hsuan-chi*
CYTC	*Chiao-yü tsa-chih*
HC	*Hsin ch'ao*
HCK	*Hsin Chung-kuo*
HCN	*Hsin ch'ing-nien*
HCY	*Hsin chiao-yü*
HHP	*Hsin hsueh pao*
HSWT	*Hu Shih wen-ts'un* (1921)
HSWT II	*Hu Shih wen-ts'un, ti-erh chi* (1924)
HSWT III	*Hu Shih wen-ts'un, ti-san chi* (1930)
HSWT IV	*Hu Shih wen-ts'un, ti ssu chi* (1953)
HT	*Hsueh teng*
JAS	*The Journal of Asian Studies*
KMEM	*In Memoriam: Kuo Ping-wen hsien-sheng chi-nien chi*
KTST	*Kuo-tu shih-tai chih ssu-hsiang yü chiao-yü*, Chiang Meng-lin
MCPL	*Mei-chou p'ing-lun*
MFM	*The May Fourth Movement*, Chow Tse-tsung
NR	*The New Republic*
SURVEY	*A Survey of Chinese Students in American Universities and Colleges in the Past One Hundred Years*
TFTC	*Tung-fang tsa-chih*
TWWTCY	*Tu-wei wu ta chiang-yen*, John Dewey

NOTES

Introduction

1. Mao Tse-tung, "Friendship or Aggression," August 30, 1949, in *Selected Works of Mao Tse-tung*, 4 vols. (Peking, 1969), IV, 447-448.

2. For Mao's comments on Hu Shih and other intellectuals, see "Cast away Illusions, Prepare for Struggle," August 14, 1949, p. 427.

3. For the 1951-1952 critique of Dewey's followers and of his educational principles, see *Jen-min chiao-yü* III, No. 6 (September 1951), IV, No. 1 (November 1951), and IV, No. 2 (December 1951). The campaign revives in Peking's *Kuang-ming jih pao*; see September 5, 19, and October 17, 1955 (also April 24, May 15, June 12, and July 17, 1956 issues) and simultaneously in the September and December issues of *Jen-min chiao-yü* in 1955. The book editions include: Ts'ao Fu, *Tu-wei p'i-p'an yin-lun* (Peking, 1951); Ch'en Ho-ch'in, *Pi-p'an Tu-wei fan-tung chiao-yü hsueh ti che-hsueh chi-ch'u* (Shanghai, 1956); and Ch'en Yuan-hui, *Hsien-tai tzu-ch'an chieh-chi ti shih-yung chu-i che-hsueh* (Shanghai, 1973). In the last volume, which is a revised version of a 1963 edition, reference is made on p. 72 to a 1958 printing of Dewey's *Reconstruction in Philosophy* (1920), and on p. 103 to a 1960 reprinting of *Experience and Education* (1925).

4. Hu Shih promoted Dewey in speeches and articles when he returned to Taiwan both in 1953 and at the end of his life. Educators descended from the National Southeastern University group in Nanking where Dewey's influence was strong, such as Wu Chun-sheng (Ou Tsuin-chen), also wrote to promote Dewey in Taiwan. But critics responded rapidly. The magazine *Hsueh-ts'ui* attacked Dewey's theories in Volumes II and IV. The substance of these articles was reproduced in a book by one of the major critics, Ch'iu Yu-chen, *Kuo-fu, Tu-wei, Ma-k'o-ssu* (Taipei, 1965).

Chapter I

1. Jane Dewey, ed., "Biography of John Dewey," *The Philosophy of John Dewey*, ed. Paul Schilpp (Chicago, 1939), p. 40. This biographical sketch

is, in fact, autobiographical, as is suggested in the footnote on p. 3 of the volume. This was confirmed in an interview with one of the daughters, Lucy Dewey, May 2, 1968, in Aberdeen, Maryland, when she told me her father simply was embarrassed to have his own name on the autobiographical sketch. See also John and Alice Dewey, *Letters from China and Japan* (New York, 1920), p. v; Victor Kobayashi, *John Dewey in Japanese Educational Thought* (Ann Arbor, 1964), p. 37.

2. Jane Dewey, p. 40; Kobayashi, pp. 37-38. Dewey began his graduate work at Johns Hopkins University in 1884, taught at the University of Michigan in Ann Arbor and then for a decade at the University of Chicago, 1894-1904, before moving to Columbia University at the peak of his career, where he remained until formal retirement in 1927. His lectures in Japan became his volume *Reconstruction in Philosophy* (New York, 1920). See also, George Dykhuizen, *The Life and Mind of John Dewey* (Carbondale, 1973), pp. 186-187.

3. A telegraphed invitation arrived with Dewey's students, and was signed by National Peking University, Nanking Teachers' College, and the Educational Association of Kiangsu and Chekiang provinces. In addition the Shang-chih hsueh-hui (The Aspiration Society), which promoted the introduction of Western culture into China through lecture series and translations, underwrote Dewey's first year in China. See *CYC*, I.2 (June 1919), 75. See also, Hu Shih, "Dr. Hu Shih's Personal Reminiscences, Interviewed, Compiled and Edited by Te-kong Tong with Dr. Hu's Corrections in His Own Handwriting," Oral History Project Columbia University, recorded 1958, edited by Hu Shih, 1959, p. 108. (Hereafter abbreviated as "Oral History.") See also, Chow Tse-tsung, *The May Fourth Movement* (Cambridge, Mass., 1964), pp. 187-188 (hereafter abbreviated *MFM*); for the delegation of former students, see Jane Dewey, p. 40; for permission from Columbia see, "Chi Tu-wei po-shih", *CYC* I.1 (April 1919), 102.

4. Dewey, "Mei-kuo chih min-chih ti fa-chan," *CYKP* 7 (1919), Appendix, p. 15.

5. Ibid., p. 1.

6. Ts'ai Yuan-p'ei, "Tu-wei po-shih liu-shih sheng-jih wan-ts'an hui yen-shuo tz'u," *Ts'ai Yuan-p'ei hsien-sheng ch'üan-ch'i*, hereafter abbreviated *CC* (Taipei, 1968), pp. 782-783.

7. Female children had no property rights and therefore could not care for the parents when they were old, making them more of a problem than male children to raise.

8. Interview with Lucy Dewey Brandauer, Aberdeen, Maryland, May 2, 1968.

9. Chow, *MFM*, p. 396, citing *Pei-ching ta-hsueh jih-k'an*, March 28, 1919, May 18, 1919. H. C. Hu, "The Intellectual Awakening of Young China," *The Chinese Recorder* LIV.8 (August 1923), 451. The reprinting of articles from one periodical to another was very common at this time, and the effect was to spread a good article or lecture to intellectual publications throughout the country. See, for example, the article "Tu-wei po-shih chiang-lai yu wo kuo," *HT*, March 14, 1919. See *CYC* I.1 (April 1919), 101-102; I.2 (June 1919), 85-93. See also the recorder's introduction to Dewey's first speeches in Shanghai, *HCY* I.3 (April 1919), 326; "Shih-yen chu-i ti fang-fa lun," *CPFK*, March 22-25, 1919; *MCPL*, No. 13 (March 16, 1919), 2. Until late May these magazines supposed that Dewey's initial lectures in central China would be all that he would deliver before returning from Nanking to the United States. See *Millard's Review* VIII.12 (May 17, 1919), 449.

10. Jane Dewey, p. 40.

11. Hu Shih, "John Dewey in China," *Philosophy and Culture: East and West* (Honolulu, 1962), p. 764. Hu combined the seven articles into one essay, which appeared under the title "Experimentalism" (*Shih-yen chu-i*) in his collected writings. See *HSWT*, 4th Collection, I, Chapter 2, pp. 291-342. He preferred the translation "experimentalism" rather than "pragmatism" for the phrase *shih-yen chu-i*. This was partly because his essay included international coverage of the pragmatic movement. It seems particularly appropriate for Dewey's lectures in China because of Dewey's stress on the importance of the experimental method in his lectures. Hu's articles were published in the following journals: *HCN* VI.4 (April 1919), 342-358; *HCK* I.2 (June 1919), 1-6; "Tu-wei che-hsueh ti ken-pen kuan-nien"; "Tu-wei ti chiao-yü che-hsueh," *HCY* I.3 (April 1919), 273-279, 298-308 (although dated April, this Dewey issue was not published until May or June); *CW*, June 27-30, July 1, 1919; July 6-9, 1919; July 14-19, 1919. *Chueh-wu*, a supplement to *Min-kuo jih pao*, along with *Hsueh-teng*, a supplement of *Shih-shih hsin pao*, were the major literary supplements in the central region of China.

12. John Dewey and Alice Dewey, *Letters*, p. 147. *Millard's Review*, VIII.10 (May 3, 1919), 365.

13. See P'an Kung-chan's prefatory remarks to his recording of Hu Shih, "Shih-yen chu-i," *HCY* I.2 (April 1919), 331. This talk was also published in *HT*, May 5-6, 1919, and *CYC* I.2 (June 1919), 331-335. Hu's revised version of this talk became the introductory section of his seven-part essay on "experimentalism;" see *HSWT*, 4th Coll., II, Chapter 2, pp. 291-297.

14. *Millard's Review* VIII.10 (May 3, 1919), 365. See *HCY* I.2 (March 1919), 129-139, and *HCY* I.3 (April 1919), passim.

15. *Millard's Review* VIII.12 (May 17 1919), 449, citing the *North China Daily News*, May 15, 1919.

16. Interview with Dr. Wu K'ang, Taipei, June 14, 1967. Dr. Wu was a student in the department of philosophy and was designated by Hu Shih as a recorder of the Peking series on "Types of Thinking." See Appendix A, No. 15. See also, *Millard's Review* VIII.12 (May 17, 1919), 449, citing the *North China Daily News*, May 15, 1919.

    Interview with Chang Ch'i-yun, Taipei, July 15, 1967. Mr. Chang entered Nanking Teachers' College in 1919 and heard Dewey's lectures. Kuo T'ing-i also heard these popular lectures at Nankao and attests to the eloquence of Liu Po-ming's interpretation. Interview, Academia Sinica, Taiwan, December 20, 1966. Both men were accomplished scholars in Taiwan. Kuo directed the Institute of Modern History at Academia Sinica in the 1960s.

17. Interview with Dr. Wu K'ang, Taipei, June 14, 1967. Dr. Wu was designated by Hu to record the "Types of Thinking" series in Peking which appeared in the Peking University Daily (*Pei-ching ta-hsueh jih-k'an*) after Dewey's bi-weekly lectures, and then in *Hsin ch'ao* ("The Renaissance") where they went through a final revision by the editor Lo Chia-lun.

18. See Hu Shih, "Dewey in China," *Philosophy and Culture*, p. 765. The English notes were often discarded by Dewey. Even the more elaborate typescripts he showed to recorders as a guide for their Chinese versions are no longer extant. Also, interview with Dr. Wu K'ang, Taipei, June 14, 1967. See also, "Ssu-hsiang ti p'ai-pieh," *HC* II.2 (December 1919), 240.

19. "Nan-ching kuo-shih huan-ying Tu-wei po-shih chi," *CHCYC* IX.5 (May 15, 1920), 112.

20. The best study on the movement to study abroad is Y. C. Wang, *Chinese Intellectuals and the West* (Chapel Hill, 1966). Between 1902 and 1907 alone, more than 10,000 Chinese students went to Japan to study, whereas a total of only 20,000 came to the United States up to the year 1953. See Shu Hsin-ch'eng, *Chin-tai Chung-kuo liu-hsueh shih*, 2nd ed. (Shanghai, 1929), p. 46, and *A Survey of Chinese Students in American Universities and Colleges in the Past One Hundred Years* (New York, 1954), p. 25 (hereafter abbreviated as *SURVEY*).

21. Y. C. Wang, p. 119. In 1920 the Shantung Provincial Assembly voted to decrease the number of students the provincial government sent to Japan in favor of Europe and the United States. Decimal files, Department of State, Washington, 893.42/108, Norweek Allman, Vice Consul in Charge, Tsinanfu to the Secretary of State.

22. U. S., President, 1901-1909 (Roosevelt), *Remission of a Portion of the Chinese Indemnity: Message from the President* (Washington: U.S. Government Printing Office, 1909), p. 4. See also, John Dewey and Alice Dewey, *Letters from China and Japan*, p. 243. Dewey visited the college in June of 1919 and noted that the 60 to 70 who were just graduating would leave for the United States to finish their B.A. degrees. See also, Y. C. Wang, *Chinese Intellectuals and the West*, p. 112. See also, Shu Hsin-ch'eng, *Liu-hsueh shih*, pp. 251-252, 280-281.

23. Shu Hsin-ch'eng, *Chin-tai chung-kuo liu-hsueh shih*, Table 4, pp. 229-230. See also, Y. C. Wang, *Chinese Intellectuals*, pp. 118-120.

24. "American Returned Students' Club of Nanking," *CSM* XII.8 (June 1917), 440-441. See also, "American Returned Students" Association of East China, *Chinese Students' Monthly*, No. 7 (April 1915), 462. This club was formed January 27, 1915. T'ang Shao-i, the first Premier of the Republic of China in 1912, who had been a student in the United States in 1874 with the group led by Yung Wing, was the president of the Shanghai club. See also, Decimal Files, Department of State, Washington, 893.43 C 44/1, J. Paul Jameson, Consul in Nanking to the Secretary of State, February 10, 1917. The constitution of this association was adopted on December 21, 1916.

25. Ibid.

26. Ibid.

27. Ibid., 893.43 C 442/–P. S. Heintzleman, Consul General in Canton to the Secretary of State, June 19, 1917.

28. "America in China: Issued in Commemoration of the Fifth Anniversary of the American Chamber of Commerce of China," *Millard's Review* XIII.3 (June 19, 1920), 124.

29. Decimal Files, Department of State, Washington, 893.43 Am 32, Telegram, Sammons to the Secretary of State, May 25, 1917. See also, *Millard's Review* XIII.3:195.

30. Decimal Files, Department of State, Washington, 893.42/70, Paul Reinsch, Minister in Peking to the Secretary of State, January 9, 1917 [*sic*; should be 1918].

31. Ibid., 893.42/76, Lansing to American Legation, January 11, 1918. See also ibid., 893.42/93, American Legation to the Secretary of State, May 14, 1918.

32. *The Educational Directory and Year Book of China, 1921* (Shanghai, 1921), p. 8.

33. Hollington K. Tong, "The Increase of French Influence in China," *Millard's Review* XXX.5 (July 3, 1920), 266.

34. "Americanising China," *The Daily Mail*, June 17, 1921, p. 6.

35. "Chinese Students," *The Daily Mail*, June 17, 1921, p. 6; Y. C. Wang, pp. 177-178. The percentages in these tables are, however, not absolute measures for Chinese society as the prefaces in the *Who's Who* indicate: See *Who's Who in China*, 4th ed. (Shanghai, 1931).

36. *CSM*, V.1 (November 1909), 12; XII.2 (December 1916), 107; XIII.6 (April 1918), 351; XV.3 (January 1920), 66.

37. T. L. Wang (comp.), *The Handbook of the Chinese Students in the U.S.A.* (Chicago, 1922), p. 13. See also, *SURVEY*, 40-51.

38. In 1915 of 60 Chinese at Columbia, 14 majored in political science, and 10 in education. In 1918, of 100 Chinese at Columbia, education

had the most majors with 21; political science, economics, and engineering followed with 17, 13, and 12 respectively. See *CSM* XI.2 (December 1915), 125, and *CSM* XIV.2 (December 1918), 137. Among the Tsinghua students who were back in China in 1917 and had done graduate work at Columbia, education, followed by political science, was the most popular field. See *Who's Who of American Returned Students* (Peking, 1917), Appendix. See also, *Survey*, p. 41.

39.   Kao Lin-yin, "Academic and Professional Attainment of Native Chinese Students Graduating from Teachers College, Columbia University" (unpublished Ph.D. dissertation, Teachers College, Columbia University, 1951), p. 84. See also, *CSM* XII.3 (January 1917), 170. See also, Chuang Tse-hsuan, "Ko-lun-pi-ya ta-hsueh shih-fan yuan chi Chung-kuo chiao-yu yen-chiu hui" (Teachers College, Columbia University, and the Chinese Education Club), *HCY* III.4 (April 1921), 466-476.

40.   Chuang Tse-hsuan, *HCY* III.4:475-476. In 1917 the former Minister of Education, Fan Yuan-lien, spoke as did a former dean from Peking Teachers' College, and a former editor of Chung Hua Book Company. See also *CSM* XII.3 (January 1917), 170, *CSM* XIV.3 (January 1919), 195, and *CSM* XV.3 (January 1920), 67. It is uncertain whether any publications ever appeared.

41.   R. Freeman Butts, "The Centenary of John Dewey," *Teachers College Record* LVI.3 (December 1959), 118. See "Red Letter Years at Teachers College," Second Series, No. 43 (New York, Library Consultant Service Leaflet, 1962). Both men will be discussed at length in Part Two.

42.   Y. C. Wang, pp. 147-190.

43.   See Chow Tse-tsung, *MFM*, Chapter V.

44.   Ibid., pp. 148-151, 374.

45.   John and Alice Dewey, *Letters*, pp. 226-228, 231.

46.   Jane Dewey, p. 41. John Dewey and Alice Dewey, *Letters*, p. 266. John Dewey, "The Student Revolt in China," *NR* XX.248 (August 6, 1919), 18.

47.   Hu Shih, "Intellectual China in 1919," *CSPSR* IV.4 (December 1919), 345.

48. See the varied entries in Appendix A. Note especially the sources of publication under No. 9. Chow Tse-tsung, *Research Guide to the May Fourth Movement: Intellectual Revolution in Modern China, 1915-1924* (Cambridge, Mass., 1963), p. 125.

49. See Appendix A.

50. See Chow, *MFM*, Chapters 7, 13. More will be said about the intensely political rather than intellectual character of the May Fourth movement below.

51. See Chiang Monlin, *Tides from the West* (Taipei, 1963), p. 114.

52. The editor, Ch'ang Tao-chih, was an advanced graduate student at Peking Teachers' College and published Dewey's class notes during Dewey's second year in Peking. These appeared in *P'ing-min chiao-yü* as did other articles by Ch'ang in praise of Dewey and his thought. Ch'ang later went to Columbia Teachers College to study. See Appendix A, No. 55. See also, *P'ing-min chiao-yü*, No. 29 (February 20, 1921), 20-21.

53. The journal was *Hsin hsueh pao*, founded in January 1920, and published by Chiang Ch'i in Wenchow, the city where the Yungchia School of Sung Neo-Confucianism had been located. Chiang had translated one of Dewey's Tokyo lectures into Chinese in the summer of 1919; see "Li-k'o chiao-yu chih mu-ti," *HCY* I.5 (August 1919), 480-485. In 1921 Chiang was the president of Chekiang First Normal School in Hangchow. He later attended Teachers College, Columbia University, receiving his M.A. in 1925. See *Educational Directory and Yearbook 1921*, p. 32.

54. Dewey apologizes for his lack of knowledge in articles where he makes statements about Chinese tradition.

55. See the number of these articles listed in Appendix B.

56. Interview with Lucy Brandauer, Aberdeen, Maryland, May 2, 1968. Mrs. Brandauer, who accompanied her parents to China, commented that Hu Shih was the closest of the Chinese to the family while in China, although Chiang Meng-lin was also in on most of the planning.

57. John Dewey, "New Culture in China," *Asia* XXI.7 (July 1921), 581. The friend is probably Hu Shih.

58. See Chow, *MFM*, pp. 182-196.

59. John Dewey, "The Student Revolt in China," p. 18. This article was written on June 24, 1919.

60. John Dewey and Alice Dewey, *Letters*, pp. 255-256.

61. John Dewey, 'The Sequel of the Student Revolt," *NR* XXI.273 (February 25, 1920), 380. This article was written in late November 1919.

62. Ibid., pp. 380-382.

63. Ibid., p. 387.

64. Hu Shih, "Intellectual China in 1919." This article was largely expressed first in Hu's Chinese interpretation of events of the summer, "Hsin ssu-ch'ao ti i-i," *HSWT*: 4th Coll., I, 727-736, which was written on November 1, 1919.

65. John Dewey, "Sequel of the Student Revolt," p. 387.

66. On the role of Ts'ai in the underground politics of revolution before 1911, see Mary Rankin, *Early Chinese Revolutionaries* (Cambridge, Mass., 1971). After 1912 Ts'ai attempted to use the office of Minister of Education to make the separation of education from political control a reality, but, along with other members of the first cabinet, was unable to work with Yuan Shih-k'ai. Ch'en fled to Japan after the Kuomintang's attempt to re-establish power in 1913, and edited a constitutionalist magazine until it was suppressed by Japanese authorities. See Howard Boorman, ed. *Biographical Dictionary of Republican China* (N.Y., 1967-1971), I, p. 241.

67. See Chow, *MFM*, pp. 43, 50. See also, Laurence Schneider, *Ku Chieh-kang and China's New History* (Berkeley, 1971), p. 26.

68. Hu Shih, "Wo-ti ch'i-lu," *HSWT*, 2nd Coll., II, p. 96. This essay was written in June 1922.

69. Hu Shih, "Dr. Hu Shih's Personal Reminiscences."

70. Chow, *MFM*, pp. 61-72. Jerome Grieder, *Hu Shih and the Chinese*

Renaissance (Cambridge, Mass., 1970), p. 88. See also Fu Ssu-nien's attacks on the old thought through the vernacular movement, such as "Pai-hua wen-hsueh yü hsin-li ti kai-huan," *HC* I.5 (May 1, 1919), 915-921.

71. Hu Shih, "The Chinese Renaissance," *Bulletins on Chinese Education, 1923*, II, Bulletin No. 6, 2nd ed. (Shanghai, 1923), p. 20, citing "Letter to Chang Shih-chao," *Chia-yin tsa-chih* I.10. See also *BDRC*, I, pp. 106-107.

72. See Maurice Meisner, *Li Ta-chao and the Origins of Chinese Marxism* (Cambridge, Mass., 1967), pp. 21-26, 33, 101ff.

73. Laurence Schneider, *Ku Chieh-kang*, p. 27.

74. *Peking Daily News*, May 6, 1919, p. 4. The American newspaper *Peking Daily News* openly praised the sober, calm, and moderate attitude taken at the Returned Students' Club in its editorials and strongly denounced the "paid ruffians" and irresponsible students who had burned down a house on the past Sunday. Clearly sensitive to anger that might spill over into demonstrable anti-foreign actions, the newspaper noted that any Chinese who attempted to create disorder was "nothing but a traitor to his country." See *Peking Daily News*, May 5, 1919, p. 4.

75. John Dewey, "New Culture in China."

76. Ibid., p. 583.

77. Ibid., p. 584.

78. Ibid.

79. John Dewey, "Chung-kuo ti hsin wen-hua," *CPFK*, July 28-August 1, 1921.

80. Dewey, *Letters*, pp. 226-248. See also, Hu Shih, "John Dewey in China," *Philosophy and Culture: East and West*, p. 765; H. C. Hu, "The Intellectual Awakening of Young China," p. 453.

81. C. F. Remer, "John Dewey in China," *Millard's Review* XIII.5 (July 3, 1920), 267. Professor Remer was an economist who taught at St. John's University, Shanghai, before Dewey's visit and later at Harvard and the University of Michigan. From 1919 to 1922 he was a contributing

editor of *Millard's Review* (later called the *China Weekly Review*).

82.   See Appendix A, sources of publications. Hu Shih, "Tu-wei hsien-sheng yü Chung-kuo," *HSWT*, Coll. I, I, p. 380.

83.   Robert Clopton and Tsuin-chen Ou, trs. and eds. *John Dewey: Lectures in China, 1919-1920* (Honolulu, 1973).

84.   The combined edition was entitled *Tu-wei san ta yen-chiang* recorded by Shen Chen-sheng (Shanghai, 1920). The three individual editions are available in the East Asian Library of Columbia University. John Dewey, *Tu-wei wu ta chiang-yen*, interpreted by Hu Shih, recorded by Sun Fu-yuan et al. 16th ed. (Peking, 1924). The Tōyō Bunko in Tokyo has a copy of this edition.

85.   Hu Shih asked an acquaintance from Columbia who was a native Manchurian to accompany Dewey on this trip. He was Wenpo C. Wang. Interview with Mr. Wenpo C. Wang, New York City, April 4, 1968. See also, Deweys, *Letters*, p. 299.

86.   Interview, Lucy Brandauer, Aberdeen, Maryland, May 2, 1968.

87.   See Appendix A for the sources of publication of Dewey's lectures.

88.   John Dewey, "Industrial China," *NR* XXV.314 (December 8, 1920), p. 39. See also Remer, ' John Dewey in China," p. 267.

89.   See Appendix A, Nos. 23-54. Hollington K. Tong, "A National University at Nanking," *Millard's Review* XIV.7 (October 16, 1920), 332-333.

90.   Jane Dewey, "Biography," p. 41. See also Tong, 'National University at Nanking," p. 332.

91.   See *CYKP* 1921, No. 10, 43-45, and *CYKP*, No. 12, 7-16.

92.   Bertrand Russell, *The Problem of China* (London, 1922), p. 224.

93.   Stuart Schram, *Mao Tse-tung* (London, 1970), p. 63.

94.   Russell, *Problem*, p. 224.

95. Bertrand Russell, "The Happiness of China," A letter dated October 28, 1919, to *The Nation* (London) XXVIII.15 (January 8, 1921), 505. This letter should be dated October 28, 1920, an error Bertrand Russell corrects in his *Autobiography of Bertrand Russell 1914-1944* (Boston, 1968), II, 197. See also, Chow, *MFM*, p. 192.

96. *Millard's Review* XVII.8 (July 23, 1921), 402. See also, Russell, *Autobiography 1914-1944*, pp. 195-196. See also Dykhuizen, *Life and Mind of Dewey*, pp. 198-199; Chow, *MFM*, pp. 235-237.

97. Interview with Lucy Brandauer, Aberdeen, Maryland, May 2, 1968.

98. John Dewey, "Nan yu hsin-ying," *CYKP*, 1921, No. 10, 33. See Appendix A, No. 64.

99. John and Alice Dewey, *Letters*, p. 166. Throughout the China trip, "we saw quite a lot of him." Interview with Lucy Brandauer, Aberdeen, Maryland, May 2, 1968.

100. See Ou Tsuin-chen, "Dewey's Lectures and Influence in China," in Jo Ann Boydston, ed., *Guide to the Works of John Dewey* (Carbondale, Ill., 1970), p. 352. Dewey's references to Sun's discussion appear in both of his major series of lectures on philosophy of education and ethics in Peking. See *TWWTCY*, pp. 198-447. Sun's work where he mentions the discussion with Dewey is *Hsin-li chien she* in *Sun Chung-shan chüan chi* (n.p., 1928), II, 52.

101. T. H. K. "Confucius and John Dewey: The Bankruptcy of the East and the West," *CSM*, XVI.8 (June 1921), 539. The author is probably Hollington K. Tong, an editor of *Millard's Review*. Tai Chen Hwa, "A Critical Study of the Resolutions of the Chinese Federation of Educational Associations, 1915-1926" (unpublished Ed.D. project, Teachers College, Columbia University, 1954), pp. 144-158.

102. Appendix C, No. 9.

103. See Appendix C, No. 8.

104. See Appendix C, No. 6.

105. Ibid., No. 3.

106. Interview with Hsu K'o-shih, Taipei, Taiwan, July 29, 1967.

107. Remer, "John Dewey in China," p. 267.

108. Charles Forcey, *The Crossroads of Liberalism* (New York, 1961), pp. 276-284. See also Randolph Bourne, "Twilight of the Idols," *The Seven Arts* II (October 1917), 688-702.

Chapter II

1. "Chiao-yü che-hsueh," *TWWTCY*, pp. 197-200. See Clopton and Ou, *Lectures in China*, 230ff. See also, James H. Robinson, *The New History* (New York, 1965), pp. 243, 247. This book was originally published under another title in 1912 by Macmillan.

2. Note especially "Philosophy of Education," Appendix A, No. 10. See, for example, lecture No. 8 in the series of fifteen, *TWWTCY*, pp. 178-186, or Clopton and Ou, pp. 230-237.

3. "Ssu-hsiang chih p'ai-pieh," *TWWTCY*, p. 326.

4. Ibid., p. 327.

5. "Shih-yen lun-li hsueh," Appendix A, No. 22, *CYKP*, 1920, No. 12, p. 419. John Dewey, *How We Think* (Boston, 1910).

6. "Chiao-yü che-hsueh," *TWWTCY*, p. 187. Clopton and Ou, pp. 237ff.

7. "Chiao-yü che-hsueh," *TWWTCY*, pp. 189-192. Clopton and Ou, p. 238.

8. "Chiao-yü che-hsueh," *TWWTCY*, pp. 193-196. Clopton and Ou, p. 242ff.

9. Clopton and Ou, pp. 286ff. *TWWTCY*, pp. 239-247.

10. Ibid.

11. "She-hui che-hsueh yü chen-chih che-hsueh," *TWWTCY*, p. 109. Clopton and Ou, pp. 164ff.

12. Appendix A, No. 5. The first of this three-lecture series was "Chiao-yü t'ien-jan ti chi-ch'u."

13. "Chiao-yü che-hsueh," *TWWTCY*, p. 143. Clopton and Ou, p. 199.

14. *TWWTCY,* p. 160. Clopton and Ou, p. 213. The translation is mine.

15. *TWWTCY*, p. 163. Clopton and Ou, pp. 215-216.

16. "Hsien-tai chiao-yü ti ch'u-shih," *HCY*, I.4 (May 1919), 426.

17. Material below is from Dewey's first lecture in the series "She-hui che-hsueh yü cheng-chih che-hsueh," *TWWTCY*, pp. 1-9. Clopton and Ou, pp. 51-53.

18. *TWWTCY*, pp. 8-14. Clopton and Ou, pp. 49-53.

19. *TWWTCY*, pp. 14-15, 21-22, 27. Clopton and Ou, pp. 52-53, 73, 80.

20. *TWWTCY*, pp. 46-48. Clopton and Ou, pp. 103-106.

21. *TWWTCY*, pp. 43-44, 109. See also, "Chiao-yü che-hsueh," *TWWTCY*, pp. 212-213. Clopton and Ou, pp. 101-103, 164-165, 259.

22. "She-hui che-hsueh yü cheng-chih che-hsueh," *TWWTCY*, pp. 63-65, 98-100. Clopton and Ou, pp. 122-124, 153-155.

23. *TWWTCY*, pp. 39-40. Clopton and Ou, p. 98. The translation is mine.

24. Ibid., pp. 123-124. Clopton and Ou, pp. 178-180.

25. For the reform movement use of these terms after 1915, see Chow, *MFM*, pp. 59, 293, 300, 328-333.

26. "Chiao-yü che-hsueh," *TWWTCY,* p. 203. Clopton and Ou, p. 250.

27. *TWWTCY*, p. 159. Clopton and Ou, pp. 238-239.

28. "Lun-li chiang-yen chi-lueh," *TWWTCY*, p. 471.

29. Ibid.

30. "Chiao-yü che-hsueh," *TWWTCY*, p. 256. Clopton and Ou, pp. 301-302.

31. "Lun-li chiang-yen chi-lueh," *TWWTCY*, pp. 470-471.

Chapter III

1. Hu Shih, "Tu-wei hsien-sheng yü Chung-kuo," p. 380. The article was a revision of Hu's speech on June 30, 1921, at National Peking University to send off Dewey. (Unpublished diary, Hu Shih, reel 3, see entry for July 10, 1921.)

2. Hu Shih and Chiang Meng-lin, "Wo-men tui-yü hsueh-sheng ti hsi-wang," *HCY* II.5 (January 1920), 592.

3. Hu Shih, "Tu-wei hsien sheng . . . ," p. 380.

4. The members of the League of Nations Commission were Europeans; its explicit criticism of excessive United States influence, and implicit recommendation that European education provided a more appropriate model, elicited a strong reaction from United States educators, especially those at Teachers College, Columbia University. See Ernst Neugebauer, *Anfänge pädagogischer Entwicklungshilfe unter dem Völkerbund in China 1931-1935* (Hamburg, 1971), pp. 187-225. The League critique was C. H. Becker, *et al.*, *The Reorganization of Education in China* (Paris, 1932).

5. They stretched from Shenyang (Mukden) in the north to Canton in the south, with one in the western provincial capital of Chengtu. The final three were in Wuhan, Peking, and Nanking. See P. W. Kuo, "Higher Education in China," *Bulletins on Chinese Education, 1923* (Peking, 1923), II, 8-9.

6. Nanking Higher Normal School was founded in 1914 as the successor to Chang Chih-tung's pioneering Liang-kiang Normal School, itself established in 1902 to train primary- and middle-school teachers. See Boorman, *Biographical Dictionary of Republican China*, II, 276.

7. This task was still too large to fulfill in the early Republic. The number of high schools and normal schools (i.e., schools preparing elementary school teachers) was too numerous for the five-year training program to supply so quickly. The result was that many middle-school principals were political acquaintances appointed by the provincial educational commissioner or the country magistrate (*hsien chang*), which greatly

frustrated the standards expected by professional educators. See J. P. Chu, "Normal School Education in China," *Bulletins on Chinese Education, 1923* (Peking, 1923), pp. 3, 5. See also Yin Chih-ling, *Reconstruction of Modern Educational Organizations in China* (Shanghai, 1924), p. 28.

8. Dr. Kuo was president of the new university, National Southeastern University, which shared the campus of Nanking Higher Normal School until the normal school was absorbed as the graduate school of education in 1923. The other three national universities at the time were National Peking University, Shansi University, and Peiyang University in Tientsin. P. W. Kuo, "Higher Education in China," p. 7.

9. Chu Yao-tsu, "Kuo Ping-wen hsien-sheng yü 'Nankao' 'Tung-ta' in *KMEM*, pp. 62, 65-69. In these years as dean, he actually ran the institution because the president, Chiang Ch'ien, was frequently away. John Leighton Stuart estimated that Kuo appointed as many as 50 returned students. John Leighton Stuart, *Fifty Years in China* (New York, 1954), p. 101.

10. Boorman, *BDRC* III, 244. T'ao's career will be discussed in detail below.

11. Ch'eng Ch'i-pao, "Chui-i Kuo Hung-sheng hsien-sheng," *KMEM*, p. 21. *Who's Who in China*, 3rd ed. (Shanghai, 1925), pp. 147-148. Also, interview with Ch'eng Ch'i-pao, New York City, April 7, 1968.

12. Ch'en actively promoted Dewey's ideas throughout his career until he came to renounce Dewey in 1956. See Fan Yin-nan, ed., *Tang-tai Chung-kuo ming-jen lu* (Shanghai, 1931), p. 299. *Ch'en Ho-ch'in, P'i-p'an Tu-wei fan-tung chiao-yü hsueh te ch'e-hsueh chi-ch'u* (Shanghai, 1956), passim. For the Nankao appointment, see Chu Yao-tsu, "Kuo Ping-wen hsien-sheng yü Nankao," p. 64. Chu Ping-k'uei received his Ph.D. in 1922 and became a professor of education in the same year, later taking the position of Assistant Dean. In 1925, he became the Director of the Department of Instruction. See *Who's Who in China*, 3rd ed., pp. 227-228.

13. Columbia University, *Commencement Number*, 1919 (New York, 1917), pp. 21-39. The Cheng article appears in *HCY* I.2 (March 1919), 129-139. See Appendix A for interpreting. Cheng Tsung-hai, "Tu-wei po-shih chih-hsueh ti ching-shen chi ch'i chiao-yü hsueh-shuo ti ying-hsiang," *CHCYC* XVIII.5 (May 1930), 33 pp. The significance of *Hsin chiao-yü* will be discussed later.

14. Lu was heavily influenced by Dewey; interview with Ch'eng Ch'i-pao, New York, April 7, 1968. On Chu, see *Ching-hua t'ung-hsueh lu* (Peking, 1933), p. 33. See also, Chu Chin, "Chiao-yü yü she-hui," *HCY* I.3 (Dewey issue, April 1919), pp. 227-231.

15. For publication, see *HCY* "Dewey Issue," I.3 ("Tu-wei chih lun-li hsueh," pp. 169-273). See translated appendix and Appendix A. Liu Po-ming did his Ph.D. at Northwestern University. See Kuo's article upon his premature death in 1924. Kuo Ping-wen, "Liu Po-ming hsien-sheng shih-lueh," *Hsueh-heng* 26 (February 1924), Appendix 1-4. Kuo himself did not lecture and publish on Dewey but actively promoted Dewey's followers and to the end of his career believed in the continued applicability of Dewey's educational theory. See, Wu Chun-sheng, "Yeh shih Kuo Hung-sheng hsien-sheng chiao tse chui-ssu tu," *KMEM*, p. 11. See also, Ch'eng Ch'i-pao, "Chui-i Kuo Hung-sheng hsien-sheng," *KMEM*, p. 22. Wu Chun-sheng (Ou Tsuin-chen) went to the University of Paris after graduation from Southeastern and published his doctoral dissertation on *La Doctrine Pedagogique de John Dewey* (Paris, 1932).

16. The term *p'ing-min* came in the next few years to mean "mass education." See *WSSCCK*, I, p. 348. The other journal was *Chiao-yü ts'ung-k'an* (Educational journal), I (December 1919), whose opening issues carried three articles on Dewey and began translation of *School and Society*. Peikao became a teachers' college in 1924.

17. See Appendix A, p. 332.

18. Chu Ching-nung, a graduate of Teachers College, was also a professor of education at National Peking University. See *Who's Who in China*, 3rd ed. supplement, p. 50. Chu was appointed when he returned to China in 1920. He co-published a serial translation of Dewey's *Schools of Tomorrow* as he assumed his post. See Appendix C, No. 8.

19. Ts'ai Yuan-p'ei, "Tui-yü chiao-yü fang-chen chih i-chien," *CYTC*, No. 11 (February 1912), reprinted in the translation in Ssu-yu Teng and John Fairbank, eds., *China's Response to the West* (New York, 1963), p. 235.

20. On societies pledged not to serve the government, see Chow, *MFM*, p. 51; Ts'ai Yuan-p'ei, "Chiao-yü tu-li i," *HCY* IV.3 (March 1922); *CC*, pp. 523-525. See also *BDRC* III, 295-296.

21. Huang Yen-p'ei, an officer in the Kiangsu Education Association and

a founder of the vocational education movement, will be discussed briefly below. See Jen Shih-hsien, *Chung-kuo chiao-yü ssu-hsiang shih* (Taipei, 1964), pp. 339-354. Ch'en Ch'i-t'ien, *Tsui-chin san-shih nien Chung-kuo chiao-yü* (Taipei, 1962), pp. 176-184. This is a reprint of the 1930 edition. The five groups are listed on the frontispiece of *HCY* I (February 1919).

22.   Tsinan Institute had been a middle school which in 1917 was promoted to include a normal school and a commercial school. It had ties through personnel to Nankao. Li Shou-yung, "Kuo-li chi-nan ta-hsueh" in Chang Ch'i-yun, ed., *Chung-hua min-kuo ta-hsueh chih* (Taipei, 1953), p. 131.

23.   Chiang Meng-lin, *Tides from the West*, p. 114.

24.   In February 1911, the Kiangsu Public Education Society in Shanghai called a meeting of the societies from other provinces, and recommenda-tions were submitted to the Hsueh Pu (First Ministry of Education, established in 1905), *CCNL*, pp. 32-33. For the origin of the *chiao-yü hui*, see H. S. Brunnert and V. V. Hagelstrom, *Present Day Political Organization of China*, rev. Noth Kolessoff, tr. A. Beltchenko and E. E. Moran (Shanghai, 1912), p. 409.

25.   Tai Chen Hwa, "Critical Study of the Resolutions of the Chinese Federation of Educational Associations," pp. 3-6. Ministry officials attended these meetings, *CCNL*, p. 58. The precedent for annual con-ferences was the Deliberative Convention on Higher Education; see Brunnert and Hagelstrom, p. 135.

26.   Calculated from *CCNL*; see topical index in back, p. 2.

27.   Saito Akio, *Chūgoku gendai kyōiku-shi* (Tokyo, 1962), p. 79. See also, Chow, "Anti-Confucian Movement . . . ," pp. 291-292. Yuan had re-sisted the proposal of the Confucian Society to establish Confucianism as a national religion, but the Confucian classics Ts'ai had abolished from the curriculum were reinstituted in 1915. K'ang Yu-wei had been the Confucian advisor when the short-lived restoration of the Manchu boy emperor was attempted in 1917.

28.   See Chow Tse-tung, *The May Fourth Movement*, pp. 85, 76. See also Chiang Meng-lin, "Shih-chieh ta chan hou wo kuo chiao-yü chih chu yao tien," *CYTC* X (October 1918), Discussion Section, pp. 131-132.

29. Cyrus Peake, *Nationalism and Education in Modern China* (New York, 1932), pp. 80-81.

30. See *HCY* I (February 1919), 2-3. See also, Peake, p. 79.

31. Ting Chih-p'in, ed., *Chung-kuo ch'i-shih-nien lai chiao-yü chi-shih* (Shanghai, 1935), p. 81. See also, Shu Hsin-ch'eng, ed., *Chin-tai Chung-kuo chiao-yü shih liao* (Shanghai, 1928), II, 114. The new school system will be discussed below.

32. See Chow, *MFM*, pp. 223, 44-45. Hu, in 1920, split with the original editor of *Hsin ch'ing-nien*, Ch'en Tu-hsiu, over the politicization of the journal. See Jerome Grieder, *Hu Shih and the Chinese Renaissance*, pp. 184-187.

33. *HCY* I.1 (February 1919), 1.

34. Chiang Meng-lin, "Shih-chieh ta chan hou wo kuo chiao-yü chih chu yao tien," *CYTC* X.10 (October 1918), reprinted in *KTST*, pp. 142-143.

35. Chiang Meng-lin, "Ho-p'ing yü chiao yü, *KTST*, pp. 58-59.

36. See also, Chow, "The Anti-Confucian Movement . . . ," pp. 292ff. See also, Liu Chun-jo, *Controversies in Modern Chinese Intellectual History* (Cambridge, Mass., 1964), pp. 100-115. Also Chiang Meng-lin, "Ko-jen chih chia-chih yü chiao-yü chih kuan-hsi," *CYTC* X.4 (April 1919), reprinted in *KTST*, p. 53. Chiang Meng-lin, "Ko-hsing chu-i yü ko-jen chu-i," *CYTC* XI.2 (February 1919), reprinted in *KTST*, p. 26.

37. Ibid., p. 27. See also, Chiang, "Ko-jen chih chia-chih . . . ," p. 53.

38. Chiang, "Shih-chieh ta chan hon . . . ," *KTST*, pp. 143-147.

39. Chiang Meng-lin, *Tides from the West*, pp. 123-124. See also, Albert Borowitz, "Chiang Monlin: Theory and Practice of Chinese Education, 1917-1930," *Papers on China*, VIII, February 1954 (Cambridge, Mass., 1954), pp. 107-135, reprinted in Chiang Meng-lin, *Chinese Culture and Education: A Historical and Cooperative Study* (Taipei, 1963), Appendix, pp. 24-25. See also, Chiang, "Pei-ching ta-hsueh k'ai-hsueh yen-shu tz'u," reprinted in *KTST*, pp. 194-195. Delivered September 11, 1920.

40. Appendix A, No. 12. See Chiang Meng-lin, *KT*, pp. 79-83. Both speeches were reproduced in *HCY* II.2 (October 1919). See Chiang Meng-lin, "Chiao-yü ssu-hsiang ti ken-pen kai-ko," a lecture at a Shanghai normal school, reprinted in *KTST*, p. 78. See also, Chiang Meng-lin, "Shen-ma shih chiao-yü te ch'u-ch'an-p'in?" *HCY* II.3 (November 1919), reprinted in *KTST*, p. 72.

41. Wang Mou-tsu, "Chung-hua chiao-yü kai-chin she yuan-ch'i chi chang-ch'eng," *HCY* V (October 1922), 343.

42. C. W. Luh, "China's New System of Education," *Bulletins on Chinese Education 1923* II.8 (Shanghai, 1923), 1-2, 16-17. A translation of the provisions of the law and commentary on the seven new aims is printed in this article.

43. See Luh, p. 7. The flexibility of secondary education was a key issue distinguishing progressive opinion from more conservative views among educators.

44. Ibid., pp. 1-2, 16-17. Monroe's advice, on the heels of Dewey's visit, was earnestly requested at the 1921 Canton meeting of educators where the basic text of the reform proposals was formulated. See Paul Monroe, "A Report on Education in China: For American Educational Authorities" (New York, 1922), third series, Bulletin No. 4 (October 20, 1922), p. 32. Dewey had addressed the same convention of educators in 1919 when the initial reform proposal was drafted. See also Ou Tsuin-chen, "Dewey's Lectures and Influence in China," in Jo Ann Boydston, ed., *Guide to the Works of John Dewey*, pp. 357ff. See also Barry Keenan, "Educational Reform and Politics in Early Republican China," *JAS* (February 1974), 227.

45. See Chiang Meng-lin, *Tides from the West*, p. 117.

46. Chu Yao-tsu, *KMEM*, p. 68.

47. *BDRC* II, 211.

48. Ch'en Ch'i-t'ien, *Tsui-chin san-shih-nien* . . . , pp. 176-184.

49. Marie-Claire Bergère, "La Bourgeoisie Chinoise et Les Problèmes du Dèveloppement Économique (1917-1923)," *Revue d'Histoire Moderne et Contemporaine* XVI (Avril-Juin 1969), 266.

Along with subtle resistance accompanying the democratic lessons
of 1918, there were also important economic changes in China during
the war which tended to create future support for the new education.
The war years were unprecedented in the prosperous growth of China's
national industries, partly because they were relieved of European competition. Although in political collapse, China from 1917 to 1923 experienced a significant economic expansion. Such a boost swelled the
ranks of earlier business entrepreneurs, and these men began to take
their place nationally as a small and rising middle class. The rising
business class was predisposed to favor political change based on national development through industrialization. That is, they favored
political democracy and free enterprise capitalism, for which they
found models among the Allied countries. During the war and immediately
thereafter, these forces supported boycotts in their own interest, as well
as custom tariff autonomy and international economic cooperation. The
new education reform group of 1919 accepted their relationship within
this growing middle class and tried to use private sources for educational
reform. By 1924 economic chaos hurt the support reformers had received from business. See also, T'ao Hsing-chih, "China," *Educational
Yearbook 1934* (New York, 1925), p. 99.

50.   See Charlotte Furth's excellent study of *Ting Wen-chiang* (Cambridge,
      Mass., 1970), esp. pp. 156-161. See also Yu-sheng Lin, "Radical
      Iconoclasm in the May Fourth Period and the Future of Chinese Lib-
      eralism," *Reflections on the May Fourth Movement: A Symposium,*
      Benjamin Schwartz, ed. (Cambridge, Mass., 1972), pp. 23-59.

51.   John Dewey, "New Culture in China," *Asia* XXI.7 (July 1921), 584.

52.   Chiang Meng-lin, "Introduction: Chinese Culture and Education as
      Seen Fifty Years Later," *Chinese Culture and Education*, pp. 1, 6, 8.
      See Edward Rice, "The Campaign to Criticize Lin Piao and Confucius,"
      Pacific Community VI.1 (October 1974), 94-107.

53.   Chu Chin, "Chiao-yü yü she-hui," *HCY* I (April 1919), 228.

54.   See Lawrence Schneider, *Ku Chieh-kang and China's New History*,
      pp. 5-6, 11.

55.   Chiang Meng-lin, "Chiao-yü yü cheng-chih," *HCY* I (February 1919),
      1-2.

56. Ibid.

57. See *HCY* II (October 1919), 118-121 and Dewey's speech in the same issue, pp. 163-166. Note also follow-up articles in *HCY* II (November 1919), 248-264.

58. Chiang specifically praised Shansi province for its combination of compulsory education and progress in local self-government. Chiang Meng-lin, "Chiao-yü yü ti-fang tzu-chih," *HCY* II (March 1919), 26-27. Chiang Meng-lin, "Chiao-yü yü cheng-chih," p. 2.

59. Hu Shih, "Oral History," pp. 193-199.

60. Chiang Meng-lin, "She-hui yun-tung ti chiao-yü," *HCY* II (December 1919), 404.

61. Ibid.

62. Ibid. Although the issue is dated December 1919, it appeared late and Chiang signed the beginning of his article February 1920. See *KTST*, p. 91.

63. Ibid.

64. Ibid., p. 401.

65. Chiang Meng-lin, "Chiao-chou wen-t'i yü chiao-yü ch'üan," *HCY* I (May 1919), reprinted in *KTST*, pp. 221-222. See also, Chiang Meng-lin, "Chiao-yü pu hsin ching-shen chih li-yung," *HCY* I (May 1919), reprinted in *KTST*, p. 222.

66. Ibid. In July 1919 Chiang became acting chancellor and professor of education at National Peking University. The arrangement was worked out with Ts'ai Yuan-p'ei, his old teacher from childhood schools in the Shaohsing area of Chekiang, who resigned. Chiang became a dean when Ts'ai returned in September 1919. Chiang was acting chancellor from 1923-1926 after Ts'ai had again resigned in protest over the "Good Man" government. See Chiang, *Tides from the West*, p. 117.

67. Chiang Meng-lin, "Kai-pien jen-sheng ti t'ai-tu," *HCY* I (June 1919), 447-450. Chiang Meng-lin, "Hsueh-ch'ao hou ch'ing-nien hsin-li ti

t'ai-tu chi li-tao fang-fa," *HCY* II (October 1919), 24. Hu Shih, "Hsin ssu-ch'ao ti i-i," *Hsin ch'ing-nien*, VII (December 1919), 5-12; signed November 1, 1919.

68.　Chiang Meng-lin, "Kai-pien jen-sheng ti t'ai-tu," p. 450.

69.　Chiang Meng-lin, "Hsin chiu yü t'iao-ho," *Shih-shih hsin pao*, October 10, 1919, reprinted in *KTST*, pp. 19-20.

70.　Hu Shih and Chiang Meng-lin, "Wo-men tui-yü hsueh-sheng ti hsi-wang," *KTST*, pp. 592-597.

71.　Ibid., p. 592.

72.　Chiang Meng-lin, "Hsueh-feng yü t'i-kao hsueh-shu," *Ch'en pao fu-k'an*, Fourth Anniversary Issue, December 2, 1922, reprinted in *KTST*, p. 97.

73.　Chiang Meng-lin, "Chih-shih chieh-chi ti tse-jen wen-t'i," *Ch'en pao*, Sixth Anniversary Issue, November 1924, reprinted in *KTST*, p. 48. On Hu's disillusionment, see Grieder, *Hu Shih*, pp. 176-177, especially the Oral History source.

74.　Chow, *MFM*, pp. 125-126.

75.　Hu Shih, "Oral History," p. 189.

76.　See Benjamin Schwartz, *Chinese Communism and the Rise of Mao* (New York, 1967), pp. 19-22.

77.　Hu Shih, "Oral History," pp. 189-191. He had gone to lecture in Hu Shih's place, because Hu was too busy interpreting for John Dewey and could not accept the invitation.

78.　Ibid., p. 192. See also, Jerome Grieder, *Hu Shih*, p. 184 n23.

79.　Saito Akio, p. 97.

80.　Ibid., pp. 91-92. See also, Kao Yin-tsu, ed., *Chung-hua min-kuo ta shih chi* (Taipei, 1957), p. 65.

81.　Chow, *MFM*, p. 261.

82. Ibid. See also, Monlin Chiang, *Tides from the West*, pp. 133-134.

83. Hu Shih, Chiang Meng-lin, et al., "Cheng tsu-yu hsuan-yen," *TFTC* XVII.6 (August 25, 1920), 133-134.

84. Chiang Meng-lin, *Tides from the West*, pp. 112-115.

85. Chow, *MFM*, p. 247.

86. Ibid., pp. 226-227.

87. John Dewey, "Industrial China," p. 39.

88. Ibid., p. 40.

89. Chow, *MFM*, p. 261.

90. "Chiao-yü tu-li yün-tung," *CYTC* XIV (March 1922), "news," p. 4.

91. See Grieder, *Hu Shih*, p. 204. Chow, *MFM*, pp. 241-242. Ts'ai Yuan-p'ei, "Wei Lo Wen-kan tsao fei-fa tai-pu an tz'u-chih ch'eng," *Ts'ai Yuan-p'ei hsien-sheng ch'üan-chi*, pp. 1114-1115.

92. Chiang Meng-lin, "Hsueh-feng yü t'i-kao hsueh-shu," p. 92.

93. Ibid., p. 97.

94. Ibid., p. 99.

95. John Dewey, "American and Chinese Education," *New Republic* XXX.378 (March 1, 1922), 16.

96. Chow, *MFM*, pp. 323-325. See also, Ka-che Yip, "The Anti-Christian Movement in China" (unpublished Ph.D. dissertation, Columbia University, 1970), passim.

Chapter IV

1. Chiang was sent as a representative of the National Federation of Education Associations and the National Chambers of Commerce, two groups who were holding joint conferences in 1921. See *CCNL*, p. 93.

2. Paul Reinsch, *An American Diplomat in China* (New York, 1922), p. 377.

3. T'ao chose never to complete this degree, although he received permission not to return for an oral examination when his thesis was sent from China. See Don-chean Chu, *Patterns of Education for the Developing Nations* (Tainan, 1966), p. 6, citing Official Document Registrar's Office, Teachers College, Columbia University.

4. T'ao Hsing-chih, "Chiao-hsueh tso ho-i" in T'ao Hsing-chih, *T'ao Hsing-chih chiao-yü lun-wen hsuan-chi*, Fang Yü-yen, ed. (Peking, 1949), p. 14. (Hereafter abbreviated *CYLW*.) See below, p. 103.

5. T'ao Hsing-chih, "Shih-yen chu-i yü chiao-yü," *HCY* I (February 1919), reprinted in T'ao Hsing-chih, *Chung-kuo chiao-yü kai-tsao* (Shanghai, 1928), pp. 1-7. (Hereafter abbreviated *CYKT*.)

6. T'ao published "Chieh-shao Tu-wei hsien-sheng ti hsueh-shuo," *HCK* I.3 (July 15, 1919), 271-272. See also, Tai Po-t'ao, *T'ao Hsing-chih ti sheng-p'ing chi ch'i hsueh-shuo* (Peking, 1949), p. 31. He interpreted Dewey's lectures.

7. T'ao Hsing-chih, "Chiao-hsueh-tso ho-i," pp. 13-14. See also, P'an K'ai-p'ei, *T'ao Hsing chih chiao-yü ssu-hsiang ti p'i-p'an* (Peking, 1952), p. 50, citing T'ao, "Sheng-huo chi chiao-yü" in T'ao, *Chiao-hsueh-tso ho-i t'ao-lun chi* (n.p., n.d.). The material P'an cites is probably prefatory remarks by T'ao in this edition of some collected speeches. See also, Appendix A, No. 3.

8. T'ao Hsing-chih, "Sheng-huo chi chiao-yü" in *T'ao, Wei chih-shih chieh-chi* (Peking, 1950), pp. 20-27.

9. T'ao, *CYKT*, Preface.

10. T'ao Hsing-chih, *Chih-hsing shu hsin* (Shanghai, 1929), p. 56. Both Hu and T'ao were from Anhwei province, as was Ch'en Tu-hsiu.

11. Ibid.

12. Monroe had already given informal educational counsel on his two-week trip in 1913; see Paul Monroe, "Address to the Kiangsu Educational Association," *CSM* IX.2 (December 10, 1913), 126-130. See Wang

Mou-tsu "Meng-lu po-shih chih lai Hua yü shih-chi chiao-yü tiao-ch'a she chih yuan-ch'i," *Chiao-yu ts-ung-k'an* II.8 (October 1921), 1-2.

13. *CCNL*, pp. 93-94.

14. Paul Monroe, *A Report on Education in China: For American Educational Authorities*, p. 32. Monroe's lectures in Chinese (translated) and advice were published in Ch'en Pao-ch'uan, T'ao Hsing-chih, Hu Shih, eds., *Meng-lu ti Chung-kuo chiao-yü t'ao-lun* (Shanghai, 1922).

15. *CCNL*, p. 95.

16. "Chinese National Association for the Advancement of Education: Its Objects, Organization and Activities," p. 10. See also William McCall, "Scientific Measurement and Related Studies in Chinese Education," in *Bulletins on Chinese Education*, 1923, 19pp. McCall's book *How to Experiment in Education* (New York, 1923), was translated into Chinese as: *Chiao-yü shih-yen fa*, tr. Hsueh Hung-chih (Shanghai, 1925). McCall's volume, *How to Measure in Education*, was also translated, but the date of translation is unknown; see *Chin pai nien lai Chung i Hsi shu mu-lu* (Taipei, 1958), p. 105.

17. George R. Twiss, *Science and Education in China* (Shanghai, 1925), pp. 1-2. Twiss was a younger man apparently in the doctoral dissertation stage of his studies.

18. Ibid., pp. 4-5.

19. Ibid., p. 8 and passim.

20. See Tai Chen Hwa, p. 149. Kilpatrick was an eminent professor at Teachers College, Columbia University, who had taught T'ao. His "project method" was a teaching method in which students individually or in groups decided upon assignments or projects to gather and integrate data, carrying out the project independently of a teacher. The Dalton Plan was adopted in Dalton, Massachusetts, in 1920, and organized the school's curriculum around "jobs." The monthly assignments or "jobs" were completed individually by students with workbooks and instruction sheets provided for each discipline. Group cooperation and individual planning on work schedules were encouraged.

21.   *CCNL*, pp. 123-138. Kilpatrick had his lectures published in Chinese, and both had books translated into Chinese: William Kilpatrick, *K'o-po-chueh-chiang-yen chi*, tr. Liao Chü-nung, n.p., n.d.; Helen Parkhurst, *Education on the Dalton Plan* (New York, 1922). *Tao-erh-tun chih chiao-yü*, tr. Tseng Tso-chung and Chao T'ing-wei (Shanghai, 1924). There was a second edition in 1927; William Kilpatrick, *Education for a Changing Civilization* (New York, 1926). There were two Chinese translations, the later one was dated 1939. See *Chin pai nien lai Chung i Hsi shu mu-lu*, p. 102.

22.   T'ao Hsing-chih, "Tui-yü ts'an-yü kuo-chi chiao-yü yun-tung ti i-ch'ien," *HCY* IV.3 (March 1920), p. 522.

23.   Ibid.

24.   John Dewey, "The Need for Schools in China" (excerpted from the *Educational Review* of the China Christian Educational Association), *CSM* XVI.8 (June 1921), 591. Paul Monroe, "Remarks," in *Record of the Testimonial Dinner to Charles K. Edmunds* (New York, 1922), p. 8.

25.   Tao Hsing-chih, "Chiao-hsueh-tso ho-i," p. 14.

26.   Ibid.

27.   Ibid., p. 15.

28.   Ibid., p. 14.

29.   Chao Pu-hsia Frederick, "Education for a Democratic China" (unpublished Ed.D. dissertation, Teachers College, Columbia University, 1946), p. 300, citing T'ao Hsing-chih letter to the China Aid Council, December 10, 1945 (New York City).

30.   The first annual meeting in the summer of 1922 was keynoted by speeches from Ts'ai Yuan-p'ei and Liang Ch'i-ch'ao, was attended by over 300 educators, and published some 400 pages of proceedings. *HCY* V.3 (October 1922), entire issue.

31.   Douglas Spelman, "Ts'ai Yuan-p'ei, 1868-1923," unpublished Ph.D. dissertation, Harvard University, 1974, p. 190.

32.   *CCNL*, pp. 102, 107.

33. *CYTC* XV.12, p. 2. See also *CCNL*, p. 102.

34. T'ao Hsing-chih, "Sheng-huo chi chiao-yü," pp. 20-21.

35. P'an K'ai-p'ei, *T'ao Hsing-chih chiao-yü ssu-hsiang ti p'i-p'an*, pp. 50-51, citing T'ao Hsing-chih, "Sheng-huo chi chiao-yü" in T'ao Hsing-chih, *Chiao-hsueh-tso ho-i t'ao lun chi*. The quotation is probably from introductory material by T'ao as other editors of the essay do not reproduce it.

36. T'ao, *Letters*, pp. 17ff, 105.

37. Ibid., p. 55. See also Kuhn, "T'ao Hsing-chih," p. 170.

38. Yen Yang-ch'u (1893-   ), born in Szechwan and raised a Christian, went to Hong Kong University and Yale University before doing social work in France under the Y.M.C.A. during World War I. His commitment to literacy education began while writing letters home for the Chinese labor battalions recruited by the British from Shantung province. Yen published his "Thousand Character" literacy text in February 1922 with the Y.M.C.A. press in Shanghai. See Peake, *Nationalism and Education*, p. 160.

39. T'ao, "China," *Educational Yearbook*, p. 142. T'ao, *Letters*, pp. 19-20. For the origins and development of the Mass Education Movement, see, Charles Hayford, "Rural Reconstruction in China: Y. C. James Yen and the Mass Education Movement," unpublished Ph.D. dissertation, Harvard University, 1973, passim.

40. She was the aunt of Chu Ching-nung, a Deweyite who taught at Peita, and edited literacy texts with T'ao. She was also the wife of Hsiung Hsi-ling, Premier 1913-1914; see Boorman, I, 443; II, 108.

41. T'ao, *Letters*, p. 83.

42. Peake, Appendix I, p. 159.

43. T'ao, W. Tchishin, "China," *Educational Yearbook*, 1924, p. 142.

44. T'ao, *Letters*, pp. 32, 63.

45. T'ao, "China," p. 103.

46. T'ao, "Sheng-huo chi chiao-yü," p. 24.

47. T'ao, "Wei chih shih . . . ," p. 8. T'ao, "Sheng-hui kung-chü chu-i chih
     chiao-yü," *CYKT*, pp. 154-156.

48. T'ao, *Letters*, p. 63.

49. Ibid.

50. Ibid., p. 64.

51. T'ao, "China," p. 103.

52. T'ao, *Letters*, pp. 80-83.

53. T'ao, "China," p. 94. See also, James Sheridan, *Chinese Warlord: The
     Career of Feng Yu-hsiang* (Stanford, 1966), pp. 130-133.

54. Ch'eng Ch'i-pao, "Liu-shih nien chiao-yü sheng-ya," *CCWH* XXIII.2
     (August 1, 1973), 9.

55. *CYTC* XVII.2 (February 1925), News section, 8-9. See also, *CCNL*,
     p. 118. Chao Pu-hsia, "Education for a democratic China," pp. 125-130.

56. Peake, p. 96; Chao, p. 131. One is tempted not to use the general term
     "liberal" at all for fear of imprecision. As used here it means educational
     reformers who believed in the separation of education from the state.

57. *CCNL*, pp. 121-122. Chang was the constitutionalist who founded *The
     Tiger* magazine back in 1917. He accepted positions in Tuan Ch'i-jui's
     cabinet in 1925 to try and achieve his goals through power.

58. The demonstrations in Shanghai had been in sympathy with a strike
     to improve labor conditions in a Japanese cotton mill. The Canton
     demonstrations were in reaction to the Shanghai "massacre." See
     P. W. Kuo, "International Aspects of the China Situation," speech at
     Johns Hopkins University, September 1925, *KMEM*, p. 22.

59. *CYTC* XVII.7 (July 1925), News, 1. The three universities were Chiao-
     tung University, T'ung-chi University, and Futan University.

60. T'ao Hsing-chih, "Nien-hui kan yan," *HCY* XI.2 (September 1925), 147.

61. The survey was carried out from May 1922 to April 1923. See Chinese National Association for the Advancement of Education, *Bulletin on Chinese Education 1923*, final section.

62. T'ao, "Nien-hui kan yan," p. 148.

63. T'ao, "Chung-kuo chiao-yü chih shang-chio," *HCY* XI.2 (September 1925), 204.

64. Ibid. Foreign pressure, protecting its own interests, was a constant. In 1923, militarists even reduced their warfare for fear of foreign intervention. See Sheridan, pp. 130-131.

65. T'ao, "China," p. 94.

66. *Chiao-yü ta tz'u-shu*, pp. 403-404. See also, Chow, *MFM*, p. 251.

67. T'ao, "China," p. 95. *CYTC* XVII.6 (June 1925), News, 6. The Association got into the controversy in 1926. *CYTC* XIX.7 (July 1926), News, 3.

68. T'ao, "China," p. 96. See also, The China Foundation for the Promotion of Education and Culture, *First Report* (Peking, 1926), p. 1. The United States had a good name in this matter as it was alone in remitting much of its indemnity in 1908 when Tsinghua College was established. The new foundation granted $850,000 for the 1926-1927 fiscal year to Chinese universities and scholarly organizations to be used mostly for promoting science teaching as Monroe and Twiss had advocated.

69. T'ao, "China," p. 96. Allen Whiting, *Soviet Policies in China, 1917-1924* (Stanford, 1968), p. 215.

70. Whiting, pp. 228-231.

71. Ibid., pp. 269-275.

72. T'ao, "China," p. 95.

73. Chiang Meng-lin, "She-hui yun-tung yü chiao-yü"; see *KTST*, p. 91.

74. T'ao, "China," p. 99. See also, T'ao, "Chung-kuo chiao-yü cheng-ts'e," p. 204.

75. T'ao, "China," p. 143.

76. T'ao Hsing-chih, "Chung-hua chiao-yü kai-chin she kai-tsao chüan-kuo hsiang-ts'un chiao-yü hsuan-hsin shu," *CYKT*, pp. 129-130.

77. T'ao, "Chung-kuo hsiang-ts'un chiao-yü chih ken-pen kai-tsao," *CYKT*, 131.

78. Philip Kuhn, "T'ao Hsing-chih, 1891-1946: An Educational Reformer," Papers on China, 13 (Cambridge, Center for East Asian Studies, Harvard University, December 1959), p. 182.

79. Originally called "little village." T'ao exchanged an homophonous word for little, *hsiao*, and changed the village name to mean "dawn village."

80. Kuhn, p. 176, citing K'ung Yun-hsiung, *Chung-kuo chin-jih chih nung-ts'un yun-tung*, 2nd ed. (Nanking, 1935), p. 281.

81. T'ao, "Wo-men ti hsin-t'iao," *CYKT*, pp. 113-114. This creed was written and co-endorsed for a joint meeting of the administrative staffs of several elementary schools in the Yangtse delta. It was signed December 21, 1926. See also, Hu Chang-tu, *Chinese Education Under Communism* (New York, 1962), introductory essay.

82. T'ao, "Wo-men ti hsin-t'iao," *CYKT*, p. 114.

83. Kuhn, p. 177, citing T'ao, "Chung-kuo hsiang-ts'un chiao-yü chih ken-pen kai-tsao," *CHCYC* XVI.10 (April 1927), 3.

84. T'ao, "Sheng-huo chi chiao-yü," pp. 20-27. This speech was to Hsiao-chuang students in the winter of 1929. See Chu Don-chean, Chapters 6-7.

85. Ibid., pp. 24-25.

86. Chu Don-chean, *Patterns of Education*, p. 117.

87. Ibid.

88. Kuhn, p. 177, citing Tai Po-t'ao, pp. 41-48.

89. The Northern Expedition and the subsequent KMT purge of the Marxists was a strong impetus to the social history debates which were

grounded in a more historicist sense of the underlying role of social forces than had existed at the time of the New Culture movement. See Arif Dirlik, "Mirror to Revolution: Early Marxist Images of Chinese History," *JAS* XXXIII.2 (February 1974), 219-221. See also, Laurence Schneider, *Ku Chieh-kang and China's New History*, pp. 85-121.

90. T'ao, "Wei chih-shih chieh-chi," in *CYKT*, pp. 189-209.

91. Chiang Meng-lin, "Chih-shih chieh-chi ti tse-jen wen-t'i."

92. See Laurence Schneider, *Ku*, pp. 108-115.

93. Chang Hsi-jo, "Chung-kuo chin-jih chih so-wei chih-shih chieh-chi," *Hsien-tai p'ing-lun*, Second anniversary issue (January 1927), pp. 88-92.

94. T'ao, "Wei chih-shih chieh-chi" in *Wei Chih-shih chieh-chi*, p. 1.

95. Ibid., pp. 2-3. See also, William James, "Pragmatism's Conception of Truth," in his *Essays in Pragmatism* (New York, 1957), pp. 159-176.

96. Ibid., pp. 4-5. Cash value is another image used by William James.

97. Ibid., pp. 5-9.

98. T'ao Hsing-chih, "Chiao-hsueh-tso ho-i hsia chih chiao-k'o shu," *CYLW*, p. 37. This essay was originally published in October 1931.

99. Ibid., p. 7.

100. Ibid., p. 8.

101. See Dirlik, p. 196.

102. Chao Pu-hsia, pp. 131-132.

103. See John Dewey, "Hsien-tai chiao-yü ti ch'u-shih," *HCY* I.4 (May 1919), 426-429.

104. T'ao, "Sheng-huo chi chiao-yü," p. 21.

105. Ibid.

106. John Dewey, *Impressions of Soviet Russia and the Revolutionary World; Mexico-China-Turkey 1929* (New York, 1964). The Soviet articles appeared serially in the *New Republic* beginning in November 1928 and were published as a book with other essays by the *New Republic* in 1929.

107. Ibid., p. 88.

108. T'ao, "Sheng-huo chi chiao-yü," p. 22.

109. Dewey, *Impressions*, pp. 99-100.

110. Ibid., p. 89.

111. Ibid., p. 108.

112. Ibid., pp. 75-77.

113. T'ao, "Sheng-huo chi chiao-yü," p. 22. Shatskii did not become a communist until a decade after 1917, and had the freedom to experiment all that time as a liberal reformer, which impressed Dewey.

114. Dewey, *Impressions*, p. 107.

115. Ibid., p. 80.

116. T'ao, "Sheng-huo chi chiao-yü," p. 22. On relationship to Kilpatrick, see T'ao Hsing-chih chi-nien chi wei-yuan-wei, *T'ao Hsing-chih chi-nien chi* (n.p., 1949), p. 653. See also, Chu Don-chean, who has the best description of Hsiao-chuang pedagogically. He cites Kilpatrick's private diary for his impressions of Hsiao-chuang.

117. T'ao, "Sheng-huo chi chiao-yü," p. 22. Dewey and Kilpatrick were apparently in agreement that liberals should try to make their contributions to educational change even under governments they did not fully support. See *Impressions*, p. 78.

118. T'ao, "Sheng-huo chi chiao-yü," p. 22.

119. Dewey, *Impressions*, p. 111. The United States recognized the Soviet Union only in 1933.

120. Ibid., pp. 99-100.

121. T'ao, "Sheng-huo chi chiao-yü," p. 22.

122. T'ao, "Sheng-huo chi chiao-yü," pp. 20-26. He described the stages of social progression of the notion of "life is education" in terms of a dialectical development which culminated in a reversion to the most primitive level of society when all education came from the social environment; see p. 22. He attacked Dewey's volume *Schools of Tomorrow* as idealistic, as well as the use of the concept of "culture"; see pp. 26-27.

123. T'ao, "Sheng-huo chi chiao-yü," p. 26.

Chapter V

1. *Chiao-yü ta tz'u shu* (Shanghai, 1930), p. 92.

2. I am indebted to Professor Ka-che Yip of the University of Maryland, Baltimore County campus, for this information. See Ch'ang Tao-chih, *Hsueh hsiao feng-ch'ao yen-chiu* (Shanghai, 1925), and Yang Chungming, "Min-kuo shih-i-nien chih hsueh-ch'ao," *HCY* IV.8 (August 1923), 1-4. These protest demonstrations took place at universities, secondary institutions including normal schools, and even primary schools. See also, Monlin Chiang, *Tides from the West*, pp. 129-135. A discussion of Kuo's particular situation follows.

3. T'ao, "China," *Educational Yearbook*, 1924, p. 96. For Kuo's view, see "China and the United States," Harris Foundation Lectures, 1925, in *KMEM*, pp. 64ff. The argument is so similar to T'ao's in his article "China" in the 1924 *Educational Yearbook* that it strongly suggests that T'ao gave Kuo the article for reference when he left the country to give the Harris lectures in Chicago. After the May 30th Incident, it seems T'ao may have been willing to vary his views on the student movement somewhat, and to recognize the educative value of political demonstrations. See Chao Pu-hsia, pp. 13ff.

4. Chao Pu-hsia, pp. 125-130.

5. Chao renounced his membership rather than attack his institution

and its president as most KMT leaders advocated. See Chao Pu-hsia, pp. 125-130.

6. Kuo left the country to lecture in Chicago in 1925, and remained in the United States as head of the China Institute in America, which he organized. In the 1930s he held a post as Vice-Minister of Finance in the Kuomintang government but was in England for most of his tenure of office. He then worked for the United Nations Relief and Rehabilitation Administration, and retired in Washington, D.C. See *BDRC* II, 276-278.

7. Chao, pp. 129-130.

8. See *BDRC* II, 277.

9. See Sheridan, *Chinese Warlord*, pp. 130-133.

10. Ibid., p. 131. See "Tung-nan ta-hsueh," *CYTC* XVII.2 (February 1925), News, 9. In 1920 a governor in Anhwei province had dissolved the schools for a year to use the money for his army. See John Dewey, "Industrial China," pp. 39-40.

11. See Chao Pu-hsia, p. 126; Ma Hsu-lun, *Wo tsai liu-shih sui i-ch'ien* (Shanghai, 1947), pp. 84-86. This connection will be developed in the following pages. See *BDRC* IV.5-6 and Yang Hsing-fo, "Yü Tung-ta t'ung-hsueh lun chun-fa yü chiao-yü shu," *Yang Hsing-fo wen-ts'un* (Shanghai, 1929), p. 318. See Ma Hsu-lun, pp. 84-86.

12. See *BDRC* IV,5; III, 228-230; II, 465-468 and Ma Hsu-lun, *Wo tsai liu-shih sui i-ch'ien*, p. 88. Ch'eng Ch'i-pao interview, March 27, 1974, in New York City confirmed that Ma was a friend of the Science Society group.

13. *BDRC* III.229; II, 465-468. Many of these men surface again together in national politics at the time the "Good Man Cabinet" of Wang Ch'ung-hui was formed in 1922. See also, *BDRC* II, 222.

14. *BDRC* IV, 5.

15. The journal was *Hsueh heng* ("The Critical Review"). See Chow, *MFM*, p. 282. See also Li Chi, "Wo tsai Mei-kuo ti ta-hsueh sheng-huo," *Ta-hsueh-sheng ti hsiu-yang*, 4 vols. (Taipei, 1962), I, 52.

16. Hu Shih, "Oral History," pp. 134-139. See also, Y. C. Wang, *Chinese Intellectuals and the West*, p. 401.

17. I am indebted to Professor Laurence Schneider for this information. See his *Ku Chieh-kang*, p. 42, and Liu Ya-tzu, *Nan-she chi-lueh* (Shanghai, 1940), membership appendix.

18. Chow Tse-tsung, *Research Guide*, p. 124.

19. Tso Shun-sheng, *Chin san-shih nien chien-wen tsa-chi* (Hong Kong, 1954), p. 23. One of the very few anti-Dewey articles published in this period appeared under Tso's editorship. Lin Chao-yin, "Tu Tu-wei 'P'ing-min chu-i yu chiao-yü' hou chih chi ko i-wen," *Chung-hua chiao-yü chieh*, XII.4 (April 1923), 1-6.

20. The following monograph was published by two members of the Young China Association, who soon became founding members of the nationalistic Young China Party: Yu Chia-chü and Li Huang, *Kuo-chia chu-i ti chiao-yü*, circulated in 1923, and published by 1925 in book form by Chung Hua Book Company, Shanghai. See Ch'en Ch'i-t'ien, *Tsui-chin san-shih nien Chung-kuo chiao-yü shih*, p. 195. See also, Chow Tse-tsung, *MFM*, pp. 251-253.

21. Ch'en Ch'i-t'ien, *Tsui-chin san shih nien Chung-kuo chiao-yü shih*, pp. 195-198.

22. Ibid., p. 198.

23. See also, Ch'en Ch'i-t'ien, *Chi yuan hui-i lu* (Taipei, 1964), p. 97.

24. Ibid.

25. Ch'en Ch'i-t'ien, "Chiao-yü yü Cheng-chih," *CHCYC*, XV.7 (January 1926), 4.

26. Chiang had been close to Sun and his movement since he edited Sun's revolutionary newspaper in San Francisco in 1909. See Chiang, *Tides from the West*, p. 80. See also, Ma Hsu-lun, *Wo tsai liu-shih sui*, p. 86, for the 1920s.

27. Chiang Meng-lin, "Chih-shih chieh-chi ti tse-jen wen-t'i," p. 44.

28.   Ibid.

29.   Ibid., pp. 46-47. This is a traditional Chinese puzzle as well as a Western puzzle.

30.   Ibid., p. 46.

31.   Ibid., p. 47.

32.   Ibid.

33.   *BDRC* I, 124, 348.

34.   Chiang Monlin, "Chinese Political Philosophy," *CSM* VII.7 (May 10, 1912), 613.

35.   Hu Shih, "A Philosopher of Chinese Reactionism," *CSM* XI.1 (November 1915), 19.

36.   T'ao's friendly relationship with Feng Yu-hsiang and personal rebuff of a visit by Chiang Kai-shek to his school were also factors in the problem; see Tai Po-t'ao, pp. 41-44. Censorship laws were instituted by the KMT in 1930. See *BDRC* III, 245-246.

Chapter VI

1.   Clopton and Ou, *John Dewey: Lectures in China*, pp. 43-44, citing Hu Shih, "Introductory Note," as it appears in *HCN* VII.1 (December 1, 1919), 135-136. Hu acknowledges the pioneering work being written in this field by Graham Wallas and Walter Lippmann.

2.   A syllabus and notes from the 1917-1918 version of this course exist. See Boydston, *Guide to the Works of John Dewey*, p. 149. When Hu sat in on the course, it was entitled "Moral and Political Philosophy." See Hu Shih transcript, Registrar's Office, Columbia University. I am indebted to Dr. Irene Eber for this information.

3.   Clopton and Ou, *John Dewey: Lectures in China*, p. 44.

4.   John Dewey, *Characters and Events: Popular Essays in Social and Political Philosophy*, ed. Joseph Ratner, 2 vols. (New York, 1929). See Appendix A, No. 9.

5. See Chow's discussion of Dewey's appeal and the role of the liberal faction, *MFM*, pp. 176, 215-228.

6. Meisner, *Li Ta-chao and the Origins of Chinese Marxism*, pp. 105ff.

7. Grieder, *Hu Shih and the Chinese Renaissance*, Chapter 10.

8. See also the two helpful biographies of men directly related to Dewey's followers, Charlotte Furth, *Ting Wen-chiang: Science and China's New Culture*; and Laurence Schneider, *Ku Chieh-kang and China's New History: Nationalism and the Quest for Alternative Traditions*.

9. Hu Shih long before 1919 had subscribed to Dewey's argument distinguishing the intelligent use of force from violence in justifying the allied prosecution of the war, and anticipating a new era of "right over might" in international relations. Chiang's articles before Versailles were literally filled with Wilsonian idealism. See Grieder, *Hu Shih*, pp. 59-63, and Chiang, *KTST*, Section 6.

10. For Dewey's advocacy of the Wilsonian interpretation of the war, see John Farrell, "John Dewey and World War I: Armageddon Tests a Liberal's Faith," *Perspectives in American History* IX (1975), 303.

11. N. Gordon Levin, *Woodrow Wilson and World Politics: America's Response to War and Revolution* (New York, 1968), Chapter 1.

12. John Dewey, "The Discrediting of Idealism," *NR* XX (October 1919), 285-287, reprinted in *CE* II, 629.

13. Ibid., p. 630.

14. Ibid., pp. 629-635. For the "new liberalism" in foreign policy, see Charles Forcey, *The Crossroads of Liberalism* (New York, 1961), Chapter VII.

15. Clopton and Ou, p. 161.

16. Marc Kasanin, *China in the Twenties* (Moscow, 1973), p. 110.

17. Farrell, pp. 325ff.

18. Grieder, *Hu Shih*, p. 185.

19. Ibid., p. 183, citing "Hsin ch'ing-nien tsa-chih hsuan-yen," *HCN* VII.1
     (December 1919), 1-4.

20. Forcey, *Crossroads of Liberalism*, pp. 20-21, 118, 163. Chow, *MFM*,
     p. 176. Ch'en Tu-hsiu, "Hsin ch'ing-nien tsa-chih hsuan-yen," *Tu-hsiu
     wen-ts'un*, 2 vols. (Hong Kong, 1965), I, 365.

21. The reactions of the *New Republic* editors will be discussed compara-
     tively in a following section.

22. Chow, p. 176. For a copy of the manifesto see Arno J. Mayer, *Politics
     and Diplomacy of Peacemaking* (New York, 1967), p. 887. A less ade-
     quate translation of the whole document appears in *The Nation* (Lon-
     don) XXVI.2 (October 11, 1919), 35-37.

23. Mayer, p. 886. Nicole Racine, "The Clarté Movement in France, 1919-
     21," *The Journal of Contemporary History* II.2 (April 1967), 200-201.

24. Mayer, p. 891.

25. Racine, p. 202.

26. Racine, pp. 202-208.

27. Chow, p. 250. Meisner, *Li Ta-chao*, pp. 104-114. Grieder, *Hu Shih*,
     pp. 184-187. Details of the political split will be discussed below.

28. Liang Ch'i-ch'ao (1873-1929). Generally regarded as the foremost in-
     tellectual of the first two decades of the twentieth century in China, he
     led the radical 100 Days Reform with his teacher K'ang Yu-wei in 1898,
     and organized a constitutional monarchist party following the 1911 Revo-
     lution. He led the Research Clique faction generally associated with the
     Chinputang (progressive) Party until he retired from politics about
     1920. His essays reared a generation in revolt against the dynastic
     system.

29. Grieder, *Hu Shih*, p. 189.

30. Chow, *MFM*, p. 76n. See also, Li Chien-nung, *The Political History of
     China 1840-1928* (Stanford, 1956), pp. 363-384.

31. Li Chien-nung, *Political History*, p. 365.

32. Madeleine Chi, *China Diplomacy, 1914-1918* (Cambridge, Mass., 1970), p. 123. See also, Li, *Political History,* pp. 365, 383.

33. Chi, *China Diplomacy,* p. 128.

34. Li Chien-nung, *Political History,* pp. 381-383. See also Philip Huang, *Liang Ch'i-ch'ao and Modern Chinese Liberalism* (Seattle, 1972), pp. 141ff.

35. Chow, *MFM,* pp. 79, 87-92.

36. Li Chien-nung, pp. 378-384.

37. Chi, *China Diplomacy,* pp. 130-137. See also, Chow, *MFM,* p. 89.

38. See Chow, *MFM,* pp. 89-94.

39. See Grieder's excellent chapter contrasting the thought of Liang and of Hu Shih in the 1920s, *Hu Shih,* Chapter V. See also, Philip Huang, *Liang Ch'i-ch'ao,* Chapter VII.

40. Chow, *MFM,* pp. 174-175.

41. Chow, *MFM,* pp. 262ff. See Li Chien-nung, *Political History,* p. 381, for the collapse of Liang's aspirations to be a political force.

42. Hu Shih and Chiang Meng-lin, "Wo-men tui-yü hsueh-sheng ti hsi-wang."

43. *The Weekly Critic* articles of the summer of 1919 were not public speeches.

44. Hu Shih, Unpublished Diary, entry for May 9, 1921.

45. Chow, *MFM,* p. 213.

46. Forcey, *Crossroads of Liberalism,* pp. 242, 273-274, 285, 289, 290.

47. Grieder, *Hu Shih,* pp. 180-182.

48. "Shih-yen chu-i," *HSWT* IV, i, 291-341. Note date, p. 341.

49. Hu Shih, "Shih-yen chu-i," *HCY,* I.3 (April 1919), 331-335.

50. John Dewey, *How We Think* (Boston, 1910). Hu's last essay was initially published in Chinese as "Tu-wei lun ssu-hsiang," *HCK* I.2 (June 1919), 1-6. *HSWT* IV, i, 341, 346. See also, Grieder, pp. 181-182, and Chow, *MFM*, p. 218.

51. Hu Shih, "Shih-yen chu-i," *HSWT*, IV, i, 323. See also, Chapter IV above.

52. Hu Shih "Wen-t'i yü chu-i," *HSWT*, IV, i, 345-346. This article appeared originally in *MCPL*, July 20, 1919.

53. Ibid., p. 346. See also, Grieder, *Hu Shih*, p. 182.

54. Herbert Schneider, *A History of American Philosophy*, 2nd ed. (New York, 1963), p. 488; Bernard Crick, *The American Science of Politics* (Berkeley, 1959), passim; Darnell Rucker, *The Chicago Pragmatists* (Minneapolis, 1969), passim. See also, Paul F. Bourke, "The Pluralist Reading of James Madison's Tenth Federalist," *Perspective in American History*, IX (1975), 271-299.

55. Paul F. Bourke, "The Status of Politics 1909-1919: *The New Republic*, Randolph Bourne and Van Wyck Brooks," *Journal of American Studies* VIII.2 (August 1974), 176n11.

56. Ibid., p. 179.

57. Forcey, *Crossroads of Liberalism*, pp. 198-205.

58. Bourke, p. 179.

59. Walter Lippmann, *A Preface to Politics* (London, 1913), p. 245. See also Jerome Grieder, *Hu Shih*, p. 110.

60. Lippmann, *Preface to Politics*, Introduction, p. vi.

61. (New York, 1914), pp. 275-276. See also Forcey, *Crossroads of Liberalism*, pp. 118, 163-169.

62. Lippmann, *Preface to Politics*, p. 244.

63. See Hu Shih, "Hsin ssu-ch'ao ti i-i," *HSWT* I, 730. See also Hu's restatement in English of several main points from this essay in Hu Shih, "Intellectual China in 1919," p. 354.

64.   Chiang Meng-lin, "Hsin-chiu yü t'iao-ho," *KTST*, pp. 17-20, 10/1919
      SSHP. See also Chiang Meng-lin, "Hsin wen-hua ti nu-ch'ao" in *KTST*,
      p. 30.

65.   Hu Shih's personal interpretation of the 'New Thought Tides" in De-
      cember 1919 elaborated Chiang's interpretation of three months earlier.
      It is in this article that Hu evoked Nietzsche's statement regarding the
      transvaluation of all values—to encourage the *esprit critique* he felt was
      arising from the student movement. Hu's elaborate development of the
      problem-solving method of reform in this article was in the service of
      such a "critical attitude," which he wanted applied steadily and con-
      structively to rebuild Chinese civilization. In January 1920, Chiang in
      turn referred to Hu's treatment—and recited Nietzsche's statement as
      well—to bolster his original interpretation of the new thought currents,
      which had come under conservative attack. This cat and mouse support,
      from the summer of 1919 through January 1920, revealed that the two
      Dewey students were of one mind in their conviction that experimental-
      ism should underlie the reconstruction of the new China. See Hu Shih,
      "Hsin ssu-ch'ao ti i-i," pp. 727-729, 736. See also, Chiang Meng-lin,
      "Ho-wei hsin ssu-hsiang," *TFTC* XVII.2 (January 25, 1920), 117-120,
      reprinted in *KTST*, p. 21. He was responding to a critique in *TFTC* of
      Chiang's "Hsin-chiu yü t'iao-ho" published in *SSHP* in October 1919.

66.   Hu Shih and Chiang Meng-lin, "Wo-men tui-yü," *KTST*, pp. 83-90.

67.   Li, *Political History*, pp. 393ff.

68.   See Grieder, *Hu Shih*, p. 186n23. See also Chow, *MFM*, p. 261.

69.   See Unpublished Diary, entries for June 6, 1921 and June 10, 1921.

70.   Chow, *MFM*, p. 231. See also Appendix A, No. 4, and Schwartz,
      Chinese Communism, pp. 19-20.

71.   See Grieder, *Hu Shih*, p. 181, for a translation of *The Weekly Critic*
      manifesto of December 1918. Ibid., p. 181n, and Hu Shih, *Oral History*,
      pp. 189-190, for the account of Ch'en's imprisonment.

72.   See above, p. 74. See also J. Grieder, *Hu Shih*, pp. 183-188, and
      Chow, *MFM*, pp. 248-249.

73.   Chow, *MFM*, p. 43. Meisner, *Li Ta-chao*, p. 33. See also Grieder, *Hu
      Shih*, p. 176.

74.   Jerome Grieder, *Hu Shih*, p. 192, citing, Ch'en Tu-hsiu letter to Hu
      Shih, February 15, 1921, in Chang Chang-lu, ed., *Chung-kuo hsien-tai
      ch'u-pan shih-liao* (Peking, 1954-1959), I, 13.

75.   Charlotte Furth, "May Fourth in History," in Benjamin Schwartz, ed.,
      Reflections on the May Fourth Movement (Cambridge, Mass., 1972),
      p. 66.

76.   See Jerome Grieder, "The Question of 'Politics' in the May Fourth Era,"
      in ibid., pp. 97-99.

77.   Ch'en Tu-hsiu "Wen-hua yun-tung yü she-hui yun-tung," *Tu-hsiu wen-
      ts'un*, II, 117, originally published on May 1, 1921.

78.   Forcey, *Crossroads of Liberalism*, Chapter VIII.

79.   Christopher Lasch, *The New Radicalism in America 1889-1963* (New
      York, 1963), pp. 203-204.

80.   Forcey, Chapter VIII.

81.   Ibid., pp. 279-281.

82.   Randolph Bourne, "Twilight of Idols " *The Seven Arts* II (October
      1917), reprinted in Bourne, *War and the Intellectuals*, p. 62.

83.   Ibid., p. 54.

84.   Grieder, *Hu Shih*, p. 342.

85.   See Lasch, pp. 206-207. Other new left critiques are Forcey's pre-
      cursing study, *Crossroads of Liberalism*, and Clarence Karier, "Liberal-
      ism and the Quest for Orderly Change," *History of Education Quarterly*
      XII.1 (Spring 1972), 57-80. Related studies include John Farrell (see
      p. 45n10) in *Perspectives in American History*, IX (1975), 299-343,
      and Daniel Levine, "Randolph Bourne, John Dewey and the 'Legacy of
      Liberalism,'" *Antioch Review* XXIX.2 (Summer 1969), 234-245.

86. Remer, "John Dewey in China," pp. 266-268.

87. For a perceptive analysis of the sociological ambivalence of other New Culture movement liberals, see Laurence Schneider, *Ku Chieh-kang*, Chapter III.

BIBLIOGRAPHY

Academia Sinica, Taiwan. Hu Shih Archives, Williams Letters.

"American Returned Students' Association of East China," *The Chinese Students' Monthly*, X.7 (April 1915), 462-463.

"American Returned Students' Club of Nanking," *The Chinese Students' Monthly*, XII.8 (June 1917), 440-441.

"Americanising China," *The Daily Mail* (London), June 17, 1921, p. 6.

Arnold, Julean. "The Chinese American-Returned Student," *Millard's Review* XV.11 (February 12, 1921), 594-596.

Bastid, Marianne. *Aspects de la Réforme de l'Enseignement en Chine au Début du 20ᵉ Siècle, d'Apres des Écrits de Zhang Jian.* Paris, Mouton & Co., 1971.

Beach, Harlan P. "American Colleges in China," *The Chinese Students' Monthly*, VI. 3 (January 10, 1911), 250-258.

Becker, C. H., et al. *The Reorganization of Education in China.* Paris, League of Nations Institute of Intellectual Cooperation, 1932.

Bergère, Marie-Claire. "La Bourgeoisie Chinoise et Les Problèmes du Développement Économique (1917-1923)," *Révue d'Histoire Moderne et Contemporaire* XVI (Avril-Juin 1969), 246-267.

———"Le Mouvement du 4 Mai 1919 en Chine: La Conjoncture Économique et le Rôle de la Bourgeoisie Nationale," *Révue Historique* (Avril-Juin 1969), 309-326.

Berry, Thomas. "Dewey's Influence in China," *John Dewey: His Thought and Influence*, ed. John Blewett. New York, Fordham University Press, 1960.

Boorman, Howard L., ed. *Biographical Dictionary of Republican China.* 4 vols. New York, Columbia University Press, 1967-1971.

Borowitz, Albert. "Chiang Monlin: Theory and Practice of Chinese Education, 1917-1930." Papers on China, VIII. Cambridge, Committee on International and Regional Studies, Harvard University, February 1954.

Bourke, Paul F. "The Status of Politics 1909-1919: *The New Republic*, Randolph Bourne and Van Wyck Brooks," *Journal of American Studies* VIII.2 (August 1974), 171-203.

–––"The Pluralist Reading of James Madison's Tenth Federalist," *Perspectives in American History* IX (1975), 271-299.

Bourne, Randolph. "Twlight of Idols," *The Seven Arts* II (October 1917). Reprinted in Bourne, *War and the Intellectuals.*

–––*War and the Intellectuals: Essays by Randolph S. Bourne 1915-1919.* Ed. Carl Resek. New York, Harper Torchbooks, 1964.

Boydston, Jo Ann, ed. *Guide to the Works of John Dewey.* Carbondale, University of Southern Illinois Press, 1970.

Brandauer, Lucy Dewey. Interview May 2, 1968, Aberdeen, Maryland.

Brière, O. *Fifty Years of Chinese Philosophy 1898-1950.* Tr. Laurence G. Thompson. London, George Allen & Unwin, Ltd., 1956.

Brunnert, H. S. and V. V. Hagelstrom. *Present Day Political Organization of China.* Rev. N. Th. Kolessoh. Tr. A. Beltchenko and E. E. Moran. Shanghai, Kelly & Walsh, 1912.

Butts, R. Freeman. "The Centenary of John Dewey," *Teachers College Record* LVI.3 (December 1959), 117-120.

Caute, David. *Communism and the French Intellectuals 1914-1960.* New York, The Macmillan Co., 1964.

Chan Lien. "Chinese Communism Versus Pragmatism," *Journal of Asian Studies* XXVIII.3 (May 1968), 551-570.

Chan Wing-tsit. "Hu Shih and Chinese Philosophy," *Philosophy of East and West* VI.1 (April 1956), 3-12.

Chang Chi-yun 張其昀 et al., ed. *Chung-hua min-kuo ta-hsueh chih* 中華民國大學誌 (Annals of colleges in the Chinese republic). 2 vols. Taipei, Chung-hua wen-hua ch'u-pan shih-yeh wei-yuan-hui, 1954.

Chang Ching-lu 張靜廬, ed. *Chung-kuo hsien-tai ch'u-pan shih liao* 中國現代出版史料 (Materials on the history of contemporary Chinese publishing). 4 vols. Shanghai, Chung-hua shu-chü, 1954-1957.

Chang Chun 章羣, ed. *Min-kuo hsueh-shu lun-wen so yin* 民國學術論文索引 (Articles in learned periodicals published since 1912). Taipei, Chung-hua wen-hua ch'u-pan shih-yeh wei-yuan-hui, 1954.

Chang Chun 張準. "Wu-shih nien lai Chung-kuo chih k'o-hsueh" 五十年來中國之科學 (Chinese science in the last fifty years), in *Tsui chin wu-shih nien* 最近五十年 (The last fifty years). Shanghai, Shen pao kuan, 1923.

Chang Hao. *Liang Ch'i-ch'ao and Intellectual Transition in China, 1890-1907.* Cambridge, Harvard University Press, 1971.

Chang Hsi-jo 張奚若. "Chung-kuo chin-jih so-wei chih-shih chieh-chi" 中國今日之所謂智識階級 (The so-called intelligentsia in present-day China), *Hsien-tai p'ing-lun* 現代評論 (Contemporary review), Second anniversary issue (January 1927), pp. 88-92.

Ch'ang Tao-chih 常道直. "Tu-wei chiao-shou lun liu-hsueh wen-t'i" 杜威教授論留學問題 (Professor Dewey discusses the problem of study abroad), *Chiao-yü tsa-chih* XVII.7 (July 1925), 1-3.

Chao Pu-hsia, Frederick. "Education for a Democratic China."

Unpublished Ed.D. dissertation, Teachers College, Columbia University, 1946.

CHCYC. See *Chung-hua chiao-yü chieh.*

Chen pao fu-k'an 晨報副刊 (Morning post supplement). February 1919-1927.

Ch'en Ch'i-t'ien 陳啓天. *Tsui-chin san-shih nien Chung-kuo chiao-yü shih* 最近三十年中國教育史 (History of Chinese education in the last thirty years). Taipei, Wen hsing shu-tien, 1962.

―――*Chi yuan hui-i lu* 寄園回憶錄 (Reminiscences from the Chi garden). Taipei, Commercial Press, 1965.

Ch'en Ho-ch'in 陳鶴琴 *P'i-p'an Tu-wei fan-tung chiao-yü hsueh ti che-hsueh chi-ch'u* 批判杜威反動教育學的哲學基礎 (A criticism of the philosophic foundations of Dewey's reactionary educational thought). Shanghai, Hsin chih-shih ch'u-pan she, 1956.

Ch'en Tu-hsiu 陳獨秀. "Pen-chih tsui-an chih ta-pien shu" 本誌罪案之答辯書 (Our answers to the charges against the magazine) *Hsin ch'ing-nien* VI.1 (January 15, 1919), 10-11.

―――"T'an cheng-chih" 談政治 (Talking politics), *Hsin ch'ing-nien* VIII.1 (September 1, 1920); *Tu-hsiu wen-ts'un,* ii, 541-556.

―――"Wen-hua yun-tung yü she-hui yün-tung" 文化運動與社會運動 (Cultural movements and social movements), dated May 1, 1921; *Tu hsiu wen-ts'un,* II, 114-117.

―――"T'ao-lun wu-cheng-fu chu-i ti hsin" 討論無政府主義的信 (Letter discussing anarchism), in *She-hui chu-i t'ao-lun chi* 社會主義討論集 (Collected essays on socialism). Canton, Ch'ing-nien she, 1922.

―――"Ching-kao ch'ing-nien" 敬告青年 (Call to youth), *Hsu ch'ing-nien* I.1 (September 15, 1925), 1-2.

———*Tu-hsiu wen-ts'un* (Collected essays of Tu-hsiu). 2 vols. Hong Kong, Yuan-tung t'u-shu kung-ssu, 1965.

Ch'en Yuan-hui 陳元暉. *Hsien-tai tzu-ch'an chieh-chi ti shih-yung-chu-i che-hsueh* 現代資產階級的實用主義哲學 (The pragmatic philosophy of the modern capitalist class). Shanghai, Jen-min ch'u-pan she, 1973.

Cheng Tsung-hai 鄭宗海."Tu-wei po-shih chih chiao-yü chu-i" 杜威博士之敎育主義 (The educational principles of Mr. Dewey), *Hsin chiao-yü* I.2 (March 1919), 129-139.

———"Tu-wei po-shih chih-hsueh ti ching-shen chi ch'i chiao-yü hsueh shuo ti ying-hsiang" 杜威博士治學的精神及其敎育學說的影響 (Dr. Dewey's spirit of teaching and the influence of his educational theories), *Chung-hua chiao-yü chieh* XVIII.5 (May 1930).

Ch'eng Ch'i-pao 陳其保. "Twenty-five years of Modern Education in China," *The Chinese Social and Political Science Review* XII.3 (July 1928), 451-471.

———"Liu-shih nien chiao-yü sheng-ya" 六十年敎育生涯 (Sixty years in the education profession), *Chuan-chi wen-hsueh* (Biographical literature) XXIII.2, 135 (August 1, 1973), 5-11.

———Interview, April 7, 1968, New York City.

———"Chui-i Kuo Hing-sheng hsien-sheng" 追憶郭鴻聲先生 (Recollections of Mr. Kuo Hung-sheng) in *In Memoriam Kuo Ping-wen hsien-sheng chi-nien chi.*

Chi, Madeleine. *China Diplomacy, 1914-1918.* Cambridge, Harvard University Press, 1970.

"Chi Tu-wei po-shih" 記杜威博士 (A sketch of Dr. Dewey), *Chiao-yü ch'ao* I.1 (April 1919), 101-102.

Chiang Meng-lin 蔣夢麟. "Western and Eastern Philosophical Ideals," *The Chinese Students' Monthly* V.8 (June 1910), 558-560.

———"Chinese Political Philosophy," *The Chinese Students' Monthly* VII.7 (May 10, 1912), 612-614.

———*A Study in Chinese Principles of Education*. Shanghai, The Commercial Press, 1918.

———"Chiao-yü yü cheng-chih" 教育與政治 (Education and politics), *Hsin chiao-yü* I.1 (February 1919), 1-2.

———"Ko-hsing chu-i yü ko-jen chu-i" 個性主義與個人主義 (Individuality and individualism), *Chiao-yü tsa-chi* XI.2 (February 1919). *Kuo-tu shih-tai chih ssu-hsiang yü chiao-yü*, pp. 116-119.

———"Chiao-yü yü ti-fang tzu-chih" 教育與地方自治 (Education and local self-government). *Hsin chiao-yü* II (March 1919), 26-27.

———"Tu-wei chih lun-li hsueh" 杜威之倫理學 (Dewey's ethics), *Hsin chiao-yü* I.3 (April 1919), 255-262.

———"Hsin-chiu yü t'iao-ho" 新舊與調和 (The compromise of the new and the old), *Shih-shih hsin-pao* ("The China Times," October 1919); *Kuo-tu shih-tai chih ssu-hsiang yü chiao-yü*, pp. 17-20.

———"She-hui yun-tung ti chiao-yü" 社會運動的教育 (Social action education), *Hsin chiao-yü* II.4 (December 1919); *Kuo-tu shih-tai chih ssu-hsiang yü chiao yü*, pp. 91-96.

———"Kai-pien jen-sheng ti t'ai-tu" 改變人生的態度 (Changing one's attitude toward life), *Hsin chiao-yü* I.4 (June 1919), 447-450.

———"Hsueh-feng yü t'i-kao hsueh-shu" 學風與提高學術 (Academic winds and advancing learning), *Ch'en pao fu-k'an* (December 2, 1922), Fourth anniversary issue; *Kuo-tu shih-tu chi ssu-hsiang yü chiao yü*, pp. 97-99.

———"Chih-shih chieh-chi ti tse-jen wen-t'i" 智識階級的責任問題 (The question of the responsibility of the intellectual class), *Ch'en pao* (The morning post). Sixth anniversary issue (November 1924), *Kuo-tu shih-tai chih ssu-hsiang yü chiao-yü*, pp. 44-48.

———*Kuo-tu shih-tai chih ssu-hsiang yü chiao-yü* 過渡時代之思想與教育 (Thought and education in a transitional period). Taipei, Shih-chieh shu-chü, 1962.

———*Chinese Culture and Education: A Historical and Comparative Survey*. Taipei, The World Book Co., Ltd., 1963.

———*Tides from the West*. Taipei, The World Book Co., Ltd., 1963.

Chiao-yü ch'ao 教育潮 (The educational tide). April 1919–January 1921, monthly.

Chiao-yü pu 教育部編, ed. *Ti-i Chung-kuo chiao-yü nien-chien* 第一次中國教育年鑑 (The first educational yearbook of China). Shanghai, Kai ming shu-chü, 1934.

Chiao-yü pu kung-pao 教育部公報 (Bulletin of the ministry of education), 1919-1922.

Chiao-yü ta tz'u shu 教育大辭書 (The encyclopedia of education). Shanghai, The Commercial Press, 1930.

Chiao-yü tsa-chih 教育雜誌 ("The Chinese Educational Review"), 1917-1927.

Chiao-yü tsa chih she 教育雜誌社 *Chiao-yü tsa chih so yin* 教育雜誌索引 (Index to "The Chinese Educational Review"). Shanghai, The Commercial Press, 1936.

Chin Hai-kuan 金海觀 "Hsiang-ts'un chiao-yü lun-wen so-yin" 鄉村教育論文索引 (Index of articles on rural education), *Chung-hua chiao-yü chieh* XVI.10 (April 1924).

Chin pai nien lai Chung i Hsi shu mu-lu 近百年來中譯西書目錄 (A bibliography of Western books translated into Chinese in the last hundred years). Taipei, Chung-hua wen-hua ch'u-pan shih-yeh wei-yuan-hui, 1958.

China Foundation for the Promotion of Education and Culture. *First Report*. Peking, March 1, 1926.

The China Press (Shanghai). January-June, 1919.

296

Chinese National Association for the Advancement of Education. *Bulletins on Chinese Education, 1923*. Shanghai, The Commercial Press, 1923.

———*Bulletin No. 20*, Vol. II, 1923. Peking, Chinese National Association for the Advancement of Education, 1923.

The Chinese Students' Monthly. V–XVI (1909–1921).

Ch'ing-hua t'ung-hsueh lu 清華同學錄 (Student directory of Tsinghua). Peking, Tsinghua University, 1933.

Ch'iu Yu-chen 邱有珍 *Kuo-fu, Tu-wei, Ma-k'o-ssu* 國父, 杜威, 馬克斯 (The father of the nation, Dewey, and Marx). Taipei, Yu-shih shu-tien, 1965.

Chou Yu-chin 周由僅 "Yueh-han Tu-wei po-shih chiao-yü shih-yeh chi" 約翰杜威博士教育事業記(The educational career of Dr. John Dewey), *Tung-fang tsa-chih* XVI.6 (June 1919), 40–44.

Chow Tse-tsung. "The Anti-Confucian Movement in Early Republican China," in *The Confucian Persuasion*. Ed. Arthur Wright. Stanford, Stanford University Press, 1960.

———*The May Fourth Movement: Intellectual Revolution in Modern China, 1915–1924*. Cambridge, Harvard University Press, 1960.

———*Research Guide to the May Fourth Movement: Intellectual Revolution in Modern China, 1915–1924*. Cambridge, Harvard University Press, 1963.

Chu Chin 朱進 "Chiao-yü yü she-hui" 教育與社會 (Education and society). *Hsin chiao-yü* I.2 (April, 1919), 227–231.

Chu Ching-nung 朱經農 et al. *Chiao-yü ta tzu-shu* 教育大辭書 (Encyclopedia of education). Shanghai, The Commercial Press, 1930.

Chu Don-chean. *Patterns of Education for the Developing Nations: Tao's Work in China, 1917–1946*. Tainan, Kao-chang Printing Company, 1966.

Chu, J. P. "Normal School Education in China," *Bulletins on Chinese Education, 1923*. Peking, Chinese National Association for the Advancement of Education, 1923.

Chu Yao-tsu 朱耀祖. "Kuo Ping-wen hsieu-sheng yü 'Nankao' 'Tung-ta'" 郭秉文先生與「南高」東大」(Mr. Kuo Ping-wen and 'Nankao' 'Southeastern'), *In Memoriam. Kuo Ping-wen hsien-sheng chi-nien chi*, pp. 62-70.

Ch'u 楚 "Tu-wei hsien-sheng t'ao-hsien" 杜威先生討嫌 (The objectionable Mr. Dewey), *Hsiang Chiang p'ing-lun* 湘江評論 (Hsiang River review), I.2 (July 21, 1919).

Ch'üan kuo Chung-wen ch'i-kan lien-ho mu-lu 全國中文期刊聯合目錄 (National union list of Chinese periodicals). Peking, Pei-ching t'u-shu-kuan, 1961.

Chuang Tse-hsuan 莊澤宣. "Ko-lun-pi-ya ta-hsueh shih-fan yuan chi Chung-kuo chiao-yü yen-chiu hui" 哥倫比亞大學師範院及中國教育研究會 (Teachers College, Columbia University, and the Chinese Education Club), *Hsin chiao-yü* III.4 (April 1921), 466-476.

Chueh-wu 覺悟 (Awakening, a supplement to *Min-kuo jih pao* 民國日報 [Republic daily]) June 16, 1919-January 1926.

Chung-hua chiao-yü chieh 中華教育界 (Chinese educational circles) 1915-1926, monthly.

Chung-kuo shih-hsueh so-yin 中國史學索引 (Index to articles on Chinese history). 2 vols. Peking, Ko-hsueh ch'u-pan she, 1957.

Clopton, Robert W. "John Dewey in China," *Educational Perspectives*, IV.1 (March 1965), 15-17, 35-36.

Clopton, Robert and Tsuin-chen Ou, trs. and eds. *John Dewey: Lectures in China, 1919-1920*. Honolulu, University of Hawaii Press, 1973.

Columbia University. Archives, Special Collections, John Dewey
  Collection.
———*University Bibliography 1909-1931*. 4 vols. New York,
  Columbia University Press, annual.
CPFK. See *Ch'en pao fu-k'an*.
Cremin, Lawrence, A. *A History of Teachers College*. New York,
  Teachers College, Columbia University, 1954.
Crick, Bernard. *The American Science of Politics*. Berkeley, Uni-
  versity of California Press, 1959.
CYC. See *Chiao-yü ch'ao*.
CYKT. See T'ao Hsing-chih, *Chung-kuo chiao-yü kai-tsao*.
CYLW. See T'ao Hsing-chih, *T'ao Hsing-chih chiao-yü lun-wen
  hsuan-chi*.
CYTC. See *Chiao-yü tsa-chih*.
Cywar, Alan. "John Dewey in World War I: Patriotism and Inter-
  national Progressivism," *American Quarterly* XXI.3 (Fall
  1969), 578-594.
———"John Dewey: Toward Domestic Reconstruction, 1915-1920,"
  Journal of the History of Ideas XXX.3 (July-September 1969),
  385-400.

Decimal Files, Department of State, Washington, "Internal Affairs,"
  1905-1930.
de Francis, John. *Nationalism and Language Reform in China*.
  Princeton, Princeton University Press, 1950.
Dewey, Jane M., ed. "Biography of John Dewey," *The Philosophy
  of John Dewey*. Ed. Paul Schilpp. Chicago, Northwestern Uni-
  versity Press, 1939.
Dewey, John. *How We Think*. Boston, D. C. Heath and Co., 1910.
———"America in the World." An address delivered at Smith
  College on February 22, 1918. Printed as "America in the

World," *The Nation* 106 (14 March 1918). Reprinted in *Characters and Events*, ed., Joseph Ratner; 2 vols. (New York, 1929).

——— "On Two Sides of the Eastern Seas," *New Republic* XIX.245 (July 16, 1919), 346-348.

——— "The Student Revolt in China," *New Republic* XX.248 (August 6, 1919), 16-18.

——— "The International Duel in China," *New Republic* XX.251 (August 27, 1919), 110-112.

——— "Militarism in China," *New Republic* XX.253 (September 10, 1919), 167-169.

——— "Transforming the Mind of China," *Asia* XIX.11 (November 1919), 1103-1108.

——— "Chinese National Sentiment," *Asia* XIX.12 (December 1919), 1237-1242.

——— "The American Opportunity in China," *New Republic* XXI.261 (December 3, 1919), 14-17.

——— "Our Share in Drugging China," *New Republic* XXI.264 (December 24, 1919), 114-117.

——— *Tu-wei Fu-chien chiang-yen lu* 杜威福建講演錄 (Dewey's recorded lectures in Fukien). Fukien, Board of Education, 1920.

——— "The Sequel of the Student Revolt," *New Republic* XXI.273 (February 25, 1920), 380-382.

——— "Shantung as Seen from Within," *New Republic* XXII.274 (March 3, 1920), 12-17.

——— "Address, Annual Meeting of the Chihli-Shansi Christian Educational Association," *Educational Review* XII.2 (April 1920), 104-111.

——— "The New Leaven in Chinese Politics," *Asia* XX.3 (April 1920), 267-272.

———"What Holds China Back," *Asia* XX.4 (May 1920), 373-377.

———"China's Nightmare," *New Republic* XXII.291 (June 30, 1920), 145-147.

———"A Political Upheaval in China," *New Republic* XXIV.305 (October 6, 1920), 142-144.

———"Bolshevism in China." Service Report. From H. A. December 2, 1920. Received in Military Intelligence, Division of War Department, Washington, D.C. January 8, 1921. Records of the War Department. General and Special Staffs MID 7657-I-154.

———"Industrial China," *New Republic* XXV.314 (December 8, 1920), 39-41.

———*China, Japan and the U.S.A.: Present-Day Conditions in the Far East and Their Bearing on the Washington Conference.* New York, Republic Publishing Co., 1921.

———*Tu-wei chiao-yü che hsueh* 杜威教育哲學 (The educational philosophy of Dewey). Interpreted by Liu Po-ming 劉伯明 recorded by Chin Hai-kuan 金海觀, Kuo Chih-fang 郭智方, Chang Nien-tsu 張念祖 and Ni Wen-yu 倪文宙. Shanghai, The Commercial Press, 1931.

———*Tu-wei san ta yen-chiang* 杜威三大演講 (Dewey's three major lectures). Interpreted by Liu Po-ming 劉伯明. Recorded by Shen Chen-sheng 沈振聲. Shanghai, T'ai-tung t'u-shu-kuan, 1921.

———"Is China a Nation?" *New Republic* XXV.319 (January 12, 1921), 187-190.

———"The Far Eastern Deadlock," *New Republic* XXVI.328 (March 16, 1921), 71-74.

———"The Consortium in China," *New Republic* XXVI.332 (April 13, 1921), 178-180.

———"Old China and New," *Asia* XXI.5 (May 1921), 445-450, 454, 456.

———"New Culture in China," *Asia* XXI.7 (July 1921), 581-586, 642.

―――"Hinterlands in China," *New Republic* XXVII.344 (July 6, 1921), 161-165.

―――"Divided China," *New Republic* XXVII.346 (July 20, 1921), 212-215; *New Republic* XXVII.347 (July 27, 1921), 235-237.

―――"Chung-kuo ti hsin wen-hua" 中國的新文化 (New culture in China). Translator unknown. *Ch'en pao fu-k'an*, July 28-August 1, 1921.

―――"Shantung Again," *New Republic* XXVIII.336 (September 28, 1921), 123-126.

―――"The Tenth Anniversary of the Republic of China," *The China Review* I.4 (October 1921), 171.

―――"Federalism in China," *New Republic* XXVIII.358 (October 12, 1921), 176-178.

―――*P'ing-min chu-i yü chiao-yü* 平民主義與教育 (Democracy and education). Ed. and tr. Ch'ang Tao-chih. 常道直 Shanghai, The Commercial Press, 1922.

―――"As the Chinese Think," *Asia* XXII.1 (January 1922), 7-10, 78-79.

―――"America and Chinese Education," *New Republic* XXX.378 (March 1, 1922), 15-17.

―――*Tu-wei wu ta chiang-yen* 杜威五大演講 (Dewey's five major lectures). Interpreted by Hu shih. 胡適 Recorded by Sun fu-yuan 孫伏園 et al. 16th ed. Peking, Ch'en pao she, 1924.

―――*Characters and Events: Popular Essays in Social and Political Philosophy*. Ed. Joseph Ratner. 2 vols. New York, Henry Holt and Company, 1929.

―――*Impressions of Soviet Russia and the Revolutionary World: Mexico, China, Turkey, 1929*. Introduction and Notes by William Brickman. New York, Teachers College, Columbia University, 1964.

―――*Reconstruction in Philosophy*. Boston, The Beacon Press, 1966.

———and Alice Dewey. *Letters from China and Japan.* New York, E. P. Dutton and Company, 1920.

———and Bertrand Russell. *Tu-wei Lo-su yen-chiang lu ho-k'an* 杜威羅素演講錄合刊 (Collected speeches of Dewey and Russell). Edited by Chang Ching-lu 張靜廬 Shanghai, T'ai tung t'u-shu-kuan, 1921.

Dirlik, Arif. "Mirror to Revolution: Early Marxist Images of Chinese History," *Journal of Asiatic Studies* XXXIII.2 (February 1974), 219-221.

Djung Lu-dsai. *A History of Democratic Education in Modern China.* Shanghai, The Commercial Press, 1934.

Duggan, Stephen. *A critique of the report of the League of Nations Mission of Educational Experts to China.* New York, Institute of International Education, 1933.

Dykhuizen, George. *The Life and Mind of John Dewey.* Carbondale, Southern Illinois University Press, 1973.

Eber, Irene. "Hu Shih (1891-1962): A Sketch of His Life." Unpublished Ph.D. dissertation, Claremont Graduate School, 1965.

Educational Directory and Yearbook of China, 1918-1922. Shanghai, Edward Evans & Sons, Ltd., annual.

Fan Chi-ch'ang 樊際昌 . Interview, May 4, 1967, Taipei.

Fan Yin-nan 樊蔭南 ed. *Tang-tai Chung-kuo ming-jen lu* 當代中國名人錄 (Contemporary who's who of China). Shanghai, Liang-yu t'u-shu-kuan, 1931.

Farrell, John C. "John Dewey and World War I: Armageddon Tests a Liberal's Faith," *Perspectives in American History* IX (1975), 299-343.

Farrell, Thomas. "Pragmatism and the War, 1917-1918. A Search for John Dewey's Public." Unpublished Ph.D. dissertation, University of Wisconsin, 1974.

Forcey, Charles. *The Crossroads of Liberalism: Croly, Weyl, Lipp-mann, and the Progressive Era*. New York, Oxford University Press, 1961.

Fu Ssu-nien 傅斯年. "Pai-hua wen-hsueh yü hsin-li ti kai-huan" 白話文學與心理的改換 (Vernacular literature and psychological change), *Hsin ch'ao* I.5 (May 1, 1919), 915-921.

Furth, Charlotte. *Ting-Wen-chiang: Science and China's New Culture*. Cambridge, Harvard University Press, 1970.

———"May Fourth in History," *Reflections on the May Fourth Movement*. Ed. Benjamin Schwartz. Cambridge, East Asian Research Center, Harvard University, 1972.

Gasster, Michael. *Chinese Intellectuals and the Revolution of 1911*. Seattle, University of Washington Press, 1969.

Geiger, George R. "Dewey's Social and Political Philosophy," in *The Philosophy of John Dewey*. Ed. Paul Schilpp. Chicago, Northwestern University, 1939.

Goldman, Eric. *Rendezvous with Destiny*. New York, Vintage Books, 1956.

Grieder, Jerome. *Hu Shih and the Chinese Renaissance*. Cambridge, Harvard University Press, 1970.

———"The Question of 'Politics' in the May Fourth Era," in Benjamin Schwartz, ed. *Reflections on the May Fourth Movement: A Symposium*. Cambridge, East Asian Research Center, Harvard University, 1972.

Han Lih Wu. "Professor Dewey's Second Visit to China," *The China Weekly Review*, LVI (April 4, 1931), 176-177.

Hayford, Charles. "Rural Reconstruction in China: Y. C. James Yen and the Mass Education Movement." Ph.D. dissertation, Harvard University, 1973.

HC. See *Hsin ch'ao*.

HCN. See *Hsin ch'ing-nien*.

HCK. See *Hsin Chung-kuo*.

HCY. See *Hsin chiao-yü*.

Heng-ju 衡如 "Tu-wei lun che-hsueh kai-tsao" 杜威論哲學 改造 (Dewey on reconstruction in philosophy), *Tung-fang tsa-chih* XVIII.8 (April 25, 1921), 37-50.

Hervouet, V. *Catelogue des Périodiques Chinois dans les Bibliotheques d'Europe.* Paris, Montou & Co., La Haye (Hague), 1958.

HHP. See *Hsin hsueh pao*.

Hofstadter, Richard. *Social Darwinism in American Thought.* Boston, The Beacon Press, 1962.

Hoh Yam-tong. "The Boxer Indemnity Remissions and Education in China." Unpublished Ph.D. dissertation, Teachers College, Columbia University, 1933.

Houn, Franklin. *Central Government of China, 1912-1923.* Madison, University of Wisconsin Press, 1957.

Hsiao, Theodore. *A History of Modern Education in China.* Shanghai, The Commercial Press, 1935.

Hsin ch'ao 新潮 ("The Renaissance"). 1919-1922, monthly.

Hsin chiao-yü 新教育 ("The New Education"). February 1919-October 1925, monthly.

Hsin ch'ing-nien 新青年 (New youth). September 1915-July 1926, monthly.

Hsin Chung-kuo 新中國 ("The New China"). 1919-1920, monthly.

Hsin hsueh pao 新學報 (New learning). 1920-1921, semiannual.

Hsu Kao-yuan 徐高阮, Interview, June 22, 1967, Academia Sinica, Nankang, Taiwan.

Hsu Wen-ch'iang 許文鏘. "Tu-wei chiao-yü ti kuan-nien" 杜威教育的觀念 (Dewey's conception of education) *Hsin hsueh pao* I.1 (January 1920), 9-17.

Hsueh-teng 學燈 (Academic lamp, supplement to *Shih-shih hsin*

pao 時事新報 ["The China Times"]). March 1918–
December 1925.

HSWT. See Hu Shih, *Hu Shih wen-ts'un* (1921, 1924, 1930, and
1953).

HT. See *Hsueh-teng*.

Hu Chang-tu, ed. "Bibliographical Notes." *Chinese Education
Under Communism*. New York, Teachers College, Columbia
University, 1962.

Hu, H. D. "The Intellectual Awakening of Young China," *The
Chinese Recorder* LIV.8 (August 1923), 447-455.

Hu P'u-an 胡樸安 *Erh-shih-nien hsueh-shu yü cheng-chih chih
kuan-hsi* 二十年學術與政治之關係 (The relation-
ship between learning and politics in the past twenty years),
Tung-fang tsa-chih XXI.1 (January 10, 1924), 20th anniversary issue, 1-3.

Hu Shih 胡適 . "A Philosopher of Chinese Reactionism,"
Chinese Students' Monthly XI.1 (November 1915), 16-19.

———"Shih-yen chu-i" 實驗主義 (Experimentalism), *Hu Shih
wen-ts'un* IV.i, 291-341.

———"Shih-yen chu-i" 實驗主義 (Experimentalism), *Hsin
chiao-yü* I.3 (April 1919), 331-335.

———"Shih-yen chu-i" 實驗主義 (Experimentalism), *Hsin
ch'ing-nien* VI.4 (April 1919), 342-358.

———"Tu-wei che-hsueh ken-pen kuan-nien" 杜威哲學根本
觀念 (Dewey's basic philosophic viewpoint), *Hsin chiao-yü*
I.3 (April 1919), 273-278.

———"Tu-wei ti chiao-yü che-hsueh" 杜威的教育哲學
(The educational philosophy of John Dewey), *Hsin chiao-yü*
I.3 (April 1919), 298-303.

———"Tu-wei lun ssu-hsiang" 杜威論思想 (Dewey on thinking), *Hsin Chung-kuo* I.2 (June 1919), 1-6.

———"Wen-t'i yü chu-i" 問題與主義 (Problems and isms),

Mei-chou p'ing-lun (Weekly critic, July 20, 1919); *Hu Shih wen-ts'un* IV.ii, 345-346.

———"Hsin ssu-ch'ao ti i-i" 新思潮的意義 (The meaning of the new thought tide), *Hsin ch'ing-nien* VII (December 1919), 5-12.

———"Intellectual China in 1919," *The Chinese Social and Political Science Review* IV.4 (December 1919), 345-355.

———et al. "Wo-men tui-yü hsueh-sheng ti hsi-wang" 我們對於學生的希望(Our hopes for the students), *Hsin Chiao-yü* II.5 (January 1920); *Kuo-tu shih tai chih ssu-hsiang yü chiao-yü*, 83-90.

Hu Shih et al. "Cheng tzu-yu hsuan-yen" 爭自由宣言 (Manifesto of struggle for freedom), *Tung-fang tsa-chih* XVII.6 (August 25, 1920), 133-134.

———Unpublished Diaries, 1921-1935. Microfilm in the archives of the Oral History Project, Columbia University. 6 reels.

———*Hu Shih wen-ts'un* 胡適文存 (Collected essays of Hu Shih). 4 vols. Shanghai, Ya-tung t'u-shu kuan, 1921; Collection II, 4 vols., 1924; Collection III, 4 vols., 1930; combined ed. with Collection IV, 4 vols., Taipei, 1953.

———"Tu-wei hsien-sheng yü Chung-kuo" 杜威先生與中國 (Professor Dewey and China), *Tung-fang tsa-chih* XVIII.13 (July 10, 1921); *Hu shih wen-ts'un* IV.ii, 380-382.

———*The Development of the Logical Method in Ancient China*. Shanghai, The Oriental Book Company, 1922.

———"Wo-ti ch'i-lu" 我的岐路 (My crossroads), *Hu Shih wen-ts'un* II.iii, 91-108.

———"Wu-shih nien lai chih shih-chieh che-hsueh" 五十年來之世界哲學 (Philosophy the last fifty years), *Hu Shih wen-ts'un* II.ii, 217-304.

———"Yü Kao I-han teng ssu-wei hsin" 與高一涵等四位的信 (A letter to Kao I-han and three others), *Hu Shih wen-ts'un* II.iii, 141-144.

Hu Shih. "The Chinese Renaissance." *Bulletins on Chinese Education, 1923* II.6. 2nd ed. Shanghai, The Commercial Press, 1925.

———"Hu Shih," in *Living Philosophies*. Ed. Albert Einstein, et al. New York, Simon and Schuster, 1931.

———"What I Believe: Living Philosophies XVI," *Forum* 85.1 (January 1931), 38-43; 2 (February 1931), 114-122.

———*The Chinese Renaissance: The Haskell Lectures, 1933*. Chicago, University of Chicago Press, 1934.

———"My Credo and Its Evolution," *The People's Tribune* VI (February 16, 1934), 219-237.

———"Living Philosophies, Revised," in *I Believe: The Personal Philosophies of Certain Eminent Men and Women of Our Time*. Ed. Clifton Fadiman. New York, Simon and Schuster, 1939.

———"The Political Philosophy of Instrumentalism," in *The Philosopher of the Common Man: Essays in Honor of John Dewey to Celebrate His Eightieth Birthday*. New York, G. P. Putnam's Sons, 1940.

———"Chieh-shao wo tzu-chi ti ssu-hsiang" 介紹我自己的思想. (Introducing my own thought), *Hu Shih wen-ts'un* IV.iv, 608-624.

———*Hu Shih yen lun chi* 胡適言論集 (Collected lectures of Hu Shih). Taipei, Hua-kuo ch'u-pan she, 1953.

———"Dr. Hu Shih's Personal Reminiscences: Interviewed, Compiled, and Edited by Te-kong Tong with Dr. Hu's corrections in his own handwriting." Oral History Project, Columbia University. Tapes recorded, 1958, ed. Hu Shih, 1959.

———*Hu Shih liu-hsueh jih chi* 胡適留學日記 (Hu Shih's diary while studying abroad). 4 vols. Taipei, The Commercial Press, 1959.

———"Science Is Spiritual Achievement—A New Concept." An Address delivered by Dr. Hu Shih before the Science Education Conference in Taipei, November 6, 1961, in *Symposium on Chinese Culture*. Ed. Ch'eng Ch'i-pao. New York, 1964.

308

———"John Dewey in China," in *Philosophy and Culture: East and West*. Honolulu, University of Hawaii Press, 1962.

——— et al. *Hu Shih yü Chung-hsi wen-hua* 胡適與中西文化 (Hu Shih and Eastern and Western civilization). Taipei, Shui-niu ch'u pan she, 1967.

———*Ssu-shih tzu-shu* 四十自述 (Autobiography at forty). Taipei, Yuan-tung t'u-shu-kuan, 1967.

Hu Shih ssu-hsiang p'i-p'an 胡適思想批評 (A critique of Hu Shih's thought). Peking, Sheng-huo, tu-shu, hsin-chih, 1955.

Huang, Philip. *Liang Ch'i-ch'ao and Modern Chinese Liberalism*. Seattle, University of Washington Press, 1972.

Hummel, Arthur, ed. *Eminent Chinese of the Ch'ing Period*. Washington, D.C., United States Government Printing Office, 1943-1944.

I Chieh 易价 "Kuo-li Pei-p'ing shih-fan ta-hsueh" 國立北平師範大學 (National Peking Teachers College), in Chang Ch'i-yun, ed., *Chung-hua min-kuo ta-hsueh chih*.

Irick, Robert L. *American-Chinese Relations, 1784-1941: A Survey of Chinese Language Materials at Harvard*. Cambridge, Harvard University Press, 1960.

Israel, John. *Student Nationalism in China, 1927-1937*. Stanford, Stanford University Press, 1966.

James, William. "Pragmatism's Conception of Truth," *Essays in Pragmatism*. New York, Hafner Publishing Co., 1957.

Jen-min chiao-yü 人民教育 (People's education). 1951-1955.

Jen Shih-hsien 任時先 . *Chung-kuo chiao-yü ssu-hsiang shih* 中國教育思想史 (A history of Chinese educational thought). Taipei, The Commercial Press, 1964.

Kao Lin-yin. "Academic and Professional Attainment of Native Chinese Students Graduating from Teachers College, Columbia University." Unpublished Ph.D. dissertation, Teachers College, Columbia University, 1951.

Kao Yin-tsu 高蔭祖 , ed. *Chung-hua min-kuo ta shih chi* 中華民國大事記 (A chronology of events in Republican China). Taipei, Shih-chieh shu-chü, 1957.

Karier, Clarence. "Liberalism and the Quest for Orderly Change," *History of Education Quarterly* XII.1 (Spring 1972), 57-80.

Kasanin, Marc. *China in the Twenties*. Moscow, Central Department of Oriental Literature, 1973.

Keenan, Barry. "Educational Reform and Politics in Early Republican China," *Journal of Asian Studies* XXXIII.2 (February 1974), 225-237.

Kiang Wen-han. *The Chinese Student Movement*. New York, King's Crown Press, 1948.

Kilpatrick, William. *K'o-po-chueh chiang-yen chi* 克伯屈講演集 (Kilpatrick's lectures). Tr. Ch'ü Chü-nung 瞿菊農. N.p., Wen-hua she, n.d.

KMEM. See Kuo Ping-wen, *In Memoriam*.

Kobayashi, Victor N. *John Dewey in Japanese Educational Thought*. Ann Arbor, University of Michigan Press, 1964.

Koo, V. K. Wellington. "Problems and Difficulties of Returned Students," *The Chinese Students' Monthly* XIII.1 (November 1917), 20-28.

KTST. See Chiang Meng-lin, *Kuo-tu shih-tai chih ssu-hsiang yü chiao-yü*.

Kuan Su-jen 關素人 . "Shih-yen chu-i ti che-hsueh" 實驗主義的哲學 (The philosophy of experimentalism), *Tung-fang tsa-chih* XVIII.3 (October 1921), 49-67.

Kuang-ming jih pao 光明日報 (Kuang-ming daily). See Union Research Institute.

310

Kuhn, Philip A. "Tao Hsing-chih, 1891-1946, An Educational Reformer." Papers on China XIII. Cambridge, Center for East Asian Studies, Harvard University, December 1954.

"Kuo-li tung-nan ta-hsueh" 國立東南大學 (National Southeastern University), Chiao-yü tsa-chih XVII.2 (February 1925), 8-9.

Kuo Ping-wen 郭秉文 "Chi Ou-Mei chiao-yü chia t'an-hua" 記歐美教育家談話 (Account of discussions with American and European educators), Hsin chiao-yü II.2 (October 1920).

———"Higher Education in China," Bulletins on Chinese Education, 1923. Peking, Chinese National Association for the Advancement of Education, 1923.

———"Liu Po-ming hsien-sheng shih-lueh" (An account of Liu Po-ming), Hsueh heng 學衡 ("The Critical Review") XXVI (February 1924), Appendix 1-4.

———"China's Revolt Against the Old Order: The Cultural and Social Background," Current History XXVI.3 (June 1927), 372-378.

———In Memoriam: Kuo-Ping-wen hsien-sheng chi-nien chi 郭秉文先生紀念集 (A commemoration for Mr. Kuo Ping-wen). Taipei, Chung-hua hsueh-shu yuan, 1971.

Kwok, D. W. Y. Scientism in Chinese Thought, 1900-1950. New Haven, Yale University Press, 1965.

Lasch, Christopher. The New Radicalism in America 1889-1963: The Intellectual as a Social Type. New York, Vintage Books, 1963.

Levenson, Joseph. "The Abortiveness of Empiricism in Early Ch'ing Thought," Far Eastern Quarterly XIII (1954), 155-165.

———"The Day Confucius Died," Journal of Asian Studies XX (1960-1961), 221-226.

———"The Intellectual Revolution in China." *The Far East: China and Japan*. Toronto, University of Toronto Press, 1961.

Levin, N. Gordon, Jr. *Woodrow Wilson and World Politics: America's Response to War and Revolution*. New York, Oxford University Press, 1968.

Levine, Daniel. "Randolph Bourne, John Dewey and the Legacy of Liberalism," *Antioch Review* XXIX.2 (1969), 234-245.

Li Chi 李濟 "Wo tsai Mei-kuo ti tu-hsueh sheng-huo" 我在美國的大學生活 (My life as a college student in America), in *Ta-hsueh-sheng ti hsiu-yang* 大學生的修養 (The cultivation of a college student). Taipei, Cheng-chih ta-hsueh, 1963.

Li Chien-nung. *The Political History of China, 1840-1928*. Ed. and tr. Ssu-yu Teng and Jeremy Ingalls. Stanford, Stanford University Press, 1956.

Li Shou-yung 李壽雍 "Kuo-li chi-nan ta-hsueh" 國立暨南大學 (Natural Chinan University), in Chang Ch'i-yun, ed., *Chung-hua min-kuo ta-hsueh chih*. Taipei, Chung-hua wen-hua ch'uan shih-yeh wei-yuan-hui, 1954.

Lin Yu-sheng. "Radical Iconoclasm in the May Fourth Period and the Future of Chinese Liberalism," in *Reflections on the May Fourth Movement: A Symposium*. Ed. Benjamin Schwartz. Cambridge, Harvard University Press, 1972.

Link, Arthur. *Woodrow Wilson and the Progressive Era, 1910-1917*. New York, Harper and Row, 1954.

Lippmann, Walter. *A Preface to Politics*. London, T. Fisher Unwin, 1913.

Liu, C. H. "Introduction of Modern Science into China," *The China Journal* XXXIV.2 (February 1941), 120-125; 5 (May 1941), 210-219.

Liu Chun-jo. *Controversies in Modern Chinese Intellectual History: An Analytic Bibliography of Periodical Articles Mainly of the May Fourth and Post-May Fourth Era.* Cambridge, Harvard University Press, 1964.

Liu Po-ming 劉伯明 "Shih-yen ti lun-li hsueh" 試驗的論理學 (Experimental logic), *Hsin chaio-yü* I.1 (February 1919), 15-19.

———"Tu-wei chih lun-li hsueh" 杜威之論理學 (Dewey's logic), *Hsin chiao-yü* I.3 (April 1919), 269-273.

———"Tu-wei lun Chung-kuo ssu-hsiang" 杜威論中國思想 (Dewey on Chinese thought), *Hsueh-heng* 學衡 ("The Critical Review"), 5 May 1922.

Lo Chia-lun 羅家倫 "Che-hsueh kai-tsao" 哲學改造 (Reconstruction in philosophy), *Hsin ch'ao* III.2 (March 1922), 53-71.

Luh, C. W. Review of *The School and Society* by John Dewey, *Hsin ch'ao* II.1 (October 1919), 187-191.

———Review of *Moral Principles in Education*, by John Dewey, *Hsin ch'ao* II.1 (October 1919), 191-194.

———"China's New System of Education," *Bulletin on Chinese Education 1923*, II.8 (1923), 1-17.

Ma Hsu-lun 馬敘倫 *Wo tsai liu-shih sui i-ch'ien* 我在六十歲以前 (My life before sixty). Shanghai, Sheng-huo shu-tien, 1947.

Mai Ch'ing 麥青 *T'ao Hsing-chih* 陶行知 (T'ao Hsing-chih). Hong Kong, Sheng-huo, Tu-shu, hsin-chih, 1949.

Mao Tse-tung. *Selected Works of Mao Tse-tung.* 4 vols. Peking, Foreign Languages Press, 1969.

Mayer, Arno J. *Politics and Diplomacy of Peacemaking: Containment and Counterrevolution at Versailles 1918-1919*, New York, Alfred A. Knopf, 1967.

Mei-chou p'ing-lun 每週評論 (Weekly critic). December 22, 1918–August 31, 1919.

Mei Hua-chuan. "The Returned Student in China," *The Chinese Recorder* XLVIII.3 (March 1917), 158-175.

Meisner, Maurice. *Li Ta-chao and the Origins of Chinese Marxism.* Cambridge, Harvard University Press, 1967.

Millard's Review. 1919-1921.

Mills, C. Wright. *Sociology and Pragmatism: The Higher Learning in America.* Ed. and intro. Irving Horowitz. New York, Oxford University Press, 1966.

Monroe, Paul. "Address to the Kiangsu Educational Association," *Chinese Students' Monthly* IX.2 (December 10, 1913), 126-130.

―――*A Report on Education in China for American Authorities.* New York, Teachers College, Columbia University, Institute of International Education, 1922.

―――*China: A Nation in Evolution.* New York, The Chautauqua Press, 1927.

"Nan-ching kao-shih huan-ying Tu-wei po-shih chi" 南京高師 歡迎杜威博士 (Nanking Teachers' College welcomes Dr. Dewey), *Chung-hua chiao-yü chieh* IX.5 (May 15, 1920), 12-14.

Needham, Joseph. *Science and Civilization in China.* 7 vols. Cambridge, Cambridge University Press, 1954.

Neugebauer, Ernst. *Anfänge pädagogischer Entwicklungshilfe unter dem Völkerbund in China 1931-1935* (The beginnings of assistance for educational development under the League of Nations in China 1931-1935). Hamburg, Mitteilungen des instituts für Asienkunde, 1971.

The North China Herald. 1919-1921.

Oral History Project of Columbia University. See Hu Shih, "Dr. Hu Shih's Personal Reminiscences," 1958.

314

Pai Ju 百如 "Chi Tu-wei po-shih" 記杜威博士 (A sketch of Dr. Dewey), *Hsueh teng*, May 2, 9-12, 1919.

P'an K'ai-p'ei 潘開沛 . *T'ao Hsing-chih chiao-yü ssu-hsiang ti p'i-p'an* 陶行知教育思想的批判 (A Critique of T'ao Hsing-chih's educational thought). Peking, Ta chung shu-tien, 1952.

Peake, Cyrus. *Nationalism and Education in Modern China*. New York, Columbia University Press, 1932.

———"Some Aspects of the Introduction of Modern Science into China," *Isis* XXII (December 1934), 173-219.

Pei-ching ta-hsueh jih-k'an 北京大學日刊 (The Peking University daily), March 18, March 28, 1919.

Peking Daily News, May 1919.

P'ing-min chiao-yü 平民教育 ("Democracy and Education"). October 1919-1922.

Pou Hui Er. "Those Returned Students," *Millard's Review* XIV.11 (November 13, 1920), 573.

Racine, Nicole. "The Clarté Movement in France, 1919-21," *The Journal of Contemporary History* II.2 (April 1967), 200-201.

Rankin, Mary. *Early Chinese Revolutionaries*. Cambridge, Harvard University Press, 1971.

"Red Letter Years at Teachers College," Second Series, No. 43. New York, Library Consultant Service Leaflet, 1962.

Reinsch, Paul S. *An American Diplomat in China*. Garden City, Doubleday, Page & Co., 1922.

Remer, C. F. "John Dewey in China," *Millard's Review* XIII.5 (July 3, 1920), 266-268.

———"John Dewey's Responsibility for American Opinion," *Millard's Review* XIII.6 (July 10, 1920), 321-322.

Republic of China, Chiao-yü pu (Ministry of education). *Chiao-yü pu kung-pao* (Bulletin of the ministry of education), 1918-1924.

Rice, Edward. "The Campaign to Criticize Lin Piao and Confucius," *Pacific Community* VI.1 (October 1974), 94-107.

Robinson, James H. *The New History*. New York, The Free Press, 1965.

Rucker, Darnell. *The Chicago Pragmatists*. Minneapolis, University of Minnesota Press, 1969.

Russell, Bertrand R. "The Happiness of China." Letter from China, October 28, 1919, published in *The Nation* (London) XXVIII.15 (January 8, 1921), 505-506.

———*The Problem of China*. London, Allen & Unwin, Ltd., 1922.

———*The Autobiography of Bertrand Russell 1914-1944*, Vol. II. Boston, Little, Brown and Company, 1968.

Russell, Dora W. B. R. *The Tamarisk Tree: My Quest for Liberty and Love*. New York, G. P. Putnam's Sons, 1975.

Saitō Akio 齊藤秋男 . *Chūgoku gendai kyōiku-shi* 中國現代教育史 (The history of modern Chinese education). Tokyo, Kokudo sha, 1962.

Schilpp, Paul A. *The Philosophy of John Dewey*. 2nd ed. New York, Tudor Publishing Co., 1951.

Schneider, H. W. "John Dewey and His Influence," *New Era* (London) II (January 1921), 136-140.

Schneider, Herbert. *A History of American Philosophy*. 2nd ed. New York, Columbia University Press, 1963.

Schneider, Laurence. *Ku Chieh-kang and China's New History: Nationalism and the Quest for Alternative Traditions*. Berkeley, University of California Press, 1971.

Schram, Stuart. *The Political Thought of Mao Tse-tung*. Revised and enlarged ed. New York, Praeger Publishers, 1969.

———*Mao Tse-tung*. London, Penguin Books, 1970.

Schwartz, Benjamin. "Ch'en Tu-hsiu and the Acceptance of the Modern West," *Journal of the History of Ideas* XII (1951), 61-74.

———*Chinese Communism and the Rise of Mao*. New York, Harper and Row, 1967.

———*In Search of Wealth and Power: Yen Fu and the West*. Cambridge, Harvard University Press, 1964.

Shao-nien Chung-kuo 少年中國 (Young China). July 1919– May 1924, monthly.

Sheridan, James. *Chinese Warlord: The Career of Feng Yu-hsiang*. Stanford, Stanford University Press, 1966.

Shu Hsin-ch'eng 舒新城, ed. *Chin-tai chung-kuo chiao-yü shih liao* 近代中國教育史料 (Historical materials on modern Chinese education). 4 vols. Shanghai, Chung-hua shu-chü, 1923.

———*Chin-tai chung-kuo liu-hsueh shih* 近代中國留學史 (The history of study abroad in modern China). Shanghai, Chung-hua shu-chü, 1927.

———*Chung-kuo chiao-yü kai-k'uang* 中國新教育概況 Shanghai, Chung hua shu-chü, 1928.

———*Chin-tai Chung-kuo chiao-yü ssu-hsiang shih* 近代中國教育思想史 (History of educational thought in modern China). Shanghai, Chung-hua shu-chü, 1929.

Sizer, Nancy. "John Dewey's Ideas in China, 1919 to 1921," *Comparative Education Review* X.3 (October 1966), 390-404.

"Social and Political Philosophy" Course 31. Handwritten notes by James Gutmann, with typewritten syllabus. Columbia University, 1917-1918. Ninety-seven pages in Private Collection of James Gutmann.

Spelman, Douglas. "Ts'ai Yuan-p'ei, 1868-1923." Unpublished Ph.D. dissertation, Harvard University, 1974.

Stuart, John Leighton. *Fifty Years in China*. New York, Random House, 1954.

"Suh Hu Speaks Up," *The Post-Standard* (Syracuse), March 1,
1915. Reprinted in the Williams Letters of the Hu Shih
Collection at Academia Sinica, Taiwan.

Sun Te-chung 孫德中, ed. *Ts'ai Yuan-p'ei hsien-sheng i-wen
lei-ch'ao* 蔡元培先生遺文類鈔 (Writings of the
late Mr. Ts'ai Yuan-p'ei classified by subject matter). Taipei,
Fu-hsing shu-chü, 1966.

Sun Yat-sen 孫逸仙 *Hsin-li chien she* 心理建設 (On
psychological reconstruction). *Sun chung-shan chüan chi*
孫中山全集 (The collected works of Sun Yat-sen).
4 vols. 8th ed. N.p., San min kung-ssu, 1928.

*A Survey of Chinese Students in American Universities and Colleges
in the Past One Hundred Years.* New York, The China Institute
in America, 1954.

Tai Chen Hwa. "A Critical Study of the Resolutions of the Chinese
Federation of Educational Associations, 1925-1926." Unpublished Ed.D. project, Teachers College, Columbia University,
1954.

[Tai] Po-t'ao 戴白韜. *T'ao Hsing-chih ti sheng-p'ing chi ch'i
hsueh-shuo* 陶行知的生平及其學說 (T'ao
Hsing-chih's life and thought). Peking, San Pien shu-tien,
1949.

Tao Chih 導之. "Tu-wei ti chiao-yü che-hsueh yü she-chi fa"
杜威的教育哲學與設計法 (Dewey's educa-
tional philosophy and the project method), *P'ing-min chiao-
yü* 平民教育 ("Democracy and Education"), No. 43
(January 10, 1922).

T'ao Hsi-sheng 陶希聖 *Chung-kuo she-hui chih shih ti fen-hsi*
中國社會之史的分析 (An analysis of the history of
Chinese society). Taipei, Ch'uan-min ch'u-pan she, 1954.

318

———Interview, July 29, 1967, Taipei.

T'ao Hsing-chih 陶行知 "Shih-yen chu-i yü chiao-yü 實驗主
義與教育 (Experimentalism and education), *Hsin Chao-
yü* I (February 1919); *Chung-kuo chiao-yu kai-tsao*, pp. 1-7.

———"Chieh-shao Tu-wei hsien-sheng ti chiao-yü hsueh-shuo" 介·
紹杜感先生的教育學說 (Introducing Pro-
fessor Dewey's educational theory), *Hsin Chung-kuo* I.3
(July 15, 1919), 271-272.

———"Tui-yü ts'an-yü kuo-chi chiao-yü yun-tung ti i-chien" 對於
參與國際教育運動的意見 (The idea of
participating in the international education movement), *Hsin
chiao-yü* IV.3 (March 1922), 521-523.

———"Chung-hua chiao-yü kai-chin she ti i-tz'u nien-hui pao-kao
shu"中華教育改進社第一次年會報告啟
(First annual report of the National Association for the Advancement of Education), *Hsin chiao-yü* V.3 (October 1922),
337-341.

———"China" in *Educational Yearbook of the International Institute
of Teachers College, Columbia University, 1924*. New York,
The Macmillan Company, 1925.

———"Chung-kuo chiao-yü cheng-ts'e chih shang-chio"中國教育
政策之商榷 (A discussion of Chinese educational
policy), *Hsin Chiao-yü* XI.2 (September 1925), 204-206.

———"Nien-hui kan-yan" 年會感言 (Special comments on the
occasion of the annual convention of the Chinese National
Association for the Advancement of Education), *Hsin chiao-yü*
XI.2 (September 1925), 147-148.

———"Chiao-hsueh tso ho-i" 教學做合一 (Combining teaching and learning), dated Nov. 2, 1927, in *T'ao tsing-chih
chiao-yü lun-wen hsuan-chi*, Fang Yü-yen, ed. Peking, Sheng-
huo, tu shu, hsin chih, 1949.

———*Chung-kuo chiao-yü kai-tsao* 中國教育改造 (Reconstruction in Chinese education). Shanghai, Ya-tung t'u-shu-kuan, 1928.

———*Chih-hsing shu-hsin* 知行書信 (The letters of Chih-hsing). Shanghai, Ya-tung t'u-shu kuan, 1929.

———"Education in China," *Educational Yearbook 1938*. New York, International Institute of Teachers College, Columbia University, 1938.

———*T'ao Hsing-chih chiao-yü lun-wen hsuan-chi* 陶行知教育論文選集 (An anthology of T'ao Hsing-chih's articles on education). Ed. Fang Yü-yen. Peking, Sheng-huo, tu shu, hsin chih lien-ho fa-hsing-so, 1949.

———"Sheng-huo chi chiao-yü" 生活即教育 (Life is education), in T'ao, *Wei chih-shih chieh-chi*. Peking, Hsin Pei-ching ch'u-pan she, 1950.

———*Wei chih-shih chieh-chi* 偽智識階級 (The false intelligentsia). Peking. Hsin Pei-ching ch'u-pan she, 1950.

T'ao Hsing-chih hsien-sheng chi-nien chi 陶行知先生紀念集 (A commemoration of Mr. T'ao Hsing-chih). N.p., T'ao Hsing-chih hsien-sheng chi-nien wei-yuan hui, 1949.

Teng Ssu-yü and John K. Fairbank. *China's Response to the West: A Documentary Survey, 1839–1923*. New York, Atheneum, 1963.

TFTC. See *Tung-fang tsa-chih*.

Theses and Dissertations by Chinese Students in America. Bulletin No. 4. New York, China Institute in America, 1927.

Thomas, Milton H. *John Dewey: A Centennial Bibliography*. Chicago, University of Chicago Press, 1962.

Ti Chun-ch'ien 瞿俊千 . "Tu-wei lun shih-yen chu-i" 杜威論實驗主義 (Dewey on pragmatism), *P'ing-lun chih p'ing-lun* 評論之評論 ("The Review of Reviews") I.4 (December 15, 1921).

Ting Chih-p'in, 丁致聘 , ed. *Chung-kuo chin ch'i-shih-nien lai chiao-yü chi-shih* 中國近七十年來教育記事 (Events in Chinese education during the last seventy years). Shanghai, The Commercial Press, 1935.

Tong, Hollington K. "The Increase of French Influence in China," *Millard's Review* XXX.5 (July 3, 1920), 265-266.

———"A National University at Nanking," *Millard's Review* XIV.7 (October 16, 1920), 332-333.

———"Confucius and John Dewey: The Bankruptcy of the East and the West," *The Chinese Students' Monthly* XVI.8 (June 1921), 539-541.

Ts'ai Yuan-p'ei 蔡元培 "Tui-yü chiao-yü fang-chen chih i-chien" 對於教育方針之意見 (Views on the aims of education), *Chiao-yü tsa-chih*, No. 11 (February 1912), reprinted in translation in Teng Ssu-yü and John Fairbank, eds. *China's Response to the West*. New York, Atheneum, 1963.

———et al. "Wo-men ti cheng-chih chu-chang" 我們的政治主義 (Our political beliefs), *Hu Shih wen-ts'un* II.iii, 27-34.

———*Ts'ai Yuan-p'ei hsien-sheng ch'üan-chi* 蔡元培先生全集 (The collected works of Mr. Ts'ai Yuan-p'ei). Taipei, The Commercial Press, 1968.

Ts'ao Fu 曹孚 *Tu-wei p'i-p'an yin-lun* 杜威批判引論 (An introduction to the criticism of Dewey). Peking, Jen-min chiao-yü ch'u-pan she, 1951.

Tseng-ting chiao-yü lun wen so-yin 增訂教育論文索引 (Index of articles on education, revised). Comp. T'ai Shuang-ch'iu 邰爽秋 , et al. Revised and enlarged by P'eng Jen-shan 彭仁山 . Shanghai, Min-chih shu-chü, 1932.

Tseng Yueh-nung 曹約農 . Interview, July 25, 1967, Taipei.

T'so Shun-sheng 左舜生 . *Chin san-shih nien chien wen tsa-chi* 近三十年見聞雜記 (Interesting events of the past thirty years). Hong Kong, Tzu-yu ch'u-pan she, 1954.

Tsur, Y. T., ed. *Who's Who of American Returned Students*. Peking, Tsinghua College, 1917.

"Tu-wei lun fei chih-yeh k'o" 杜威論非職業科(Dewey on non-vocational courses), *Chiao-yü yü chih-yeh* 教育與職業 (Education and vocation), No. 57 (August 31, 1924).

"Tu-wei lun shou-kung chiao-hsi" 杜威論手工教練 (Dewey on manual training), *Chiao-yü yü chih-yeh*, No. 57 (August 31, 1924).

"Tu-wei po-shih chiang-lai yu wo kuo" 杜威博士將來遊我國 (Dr. Dewey's coming trip to our country), *Hsueh teng*, March 14, 1919.

"Tu-wei po-shih lai Hua chiang-yen chi-wen" 杜威博士來華講演紀聞 (An account of Dr. Dewey's arrival and lectures), *Chiao-yü ch'ao* I.2 (June 1919), 75-76.

"Tu-wei po-shih tao Hu" 杜威博士到滬 (Dr. Dewey arrives in Shanghai), *Hsueh teng*, May 1, 1919.

Tung-fang tsa-chih 東方雜誌 ("The Eastern Miscellany"), 1904-1949.

Twiss, George Ransom. *Science and Education in China*. Shanghai, The Commercial Press, 1925.

Tyau, Minchien T. Z., ed. *China in 1918*. 2nd ed. Shanghai, The Commercial Press, 1919.

Ubukata Naokichi 幼方直吉 "Kirisutokyo" キリスト教 (Christianity), in *Gendai Chugoku Jiten* 現代中國辞典 Tokyo, Gendai chugoku jiten kankokai, 1954.

Union Research Institute, Hong Kong. Card catalogue index to clippings from newspapers and magazines in the People's Republic of China, 1950-1962.

U.S. President, 1901-1909 (Roosevelt). *Remission of a Portion of the Chinese Indemnity: Message from the President*. Washington, D.C., U.S. Government Printing Office, 1909.

322

Wang Chih-p'ei 王之培 "Tu-wei po-shih tui yü shih-yeh chiao-yü chih i-chien" 杜威博士對於實業教育之意見 (Dr. Dewey's views on vocational education), *Chiao-yü ts'ung-k'an* 教育叢刊 (Educational journal) I (December 1919).

Wang Feng-gang. *Japanese Influence on Educational Reform in China from 1895 to 1911.* Peiping, Authers [*sic*] Bookstore, 1933.

Wang Mou-tsu 汪懋祖 "Meng-lu po-shih chih lai Hua yü shih-chi chiao-yü tiao-ch'a she chih yuan-ch'i" 孟祿博士來華與實際教育調查之緣起 (Dr. Monroe's visit to China and the origin of the practical education survey society), *Chiao-yü ts'ung-k'an* 教育叢刊 (Educational journal) II.8 (October 1921).

———"Chung-hua chiao-yü kai-chin she yuan-ch'i chi chang-ch'eng" 中華教育改進社緣起及章程 (The origin and by-laws of the Chinese National Association for the Advancement of Education), *Hsin chao-yü* V.3 (October 1922), 343-344.

Wang, T. L., comp. *The Handbook of the Chinese Students in the U.S.A.* Chinese Students' Alliance, 1922.

Wang Tsi C. *The Youth Movement in China.* New York, The New Republic, Inc., 1927.

Wang, Y. C. *Chinese Intellectuals and the West, 1872-1949.* Chapel Hill, University of North Carolina Press, 1966.

Wang Yu 王玉 "Tu-wei chih chiao-yü hsüeh-shao" 杜威之教育學說 (Dewey's educational theory), *Chung-hua chiao-yü chieh* XII.4 (April 1923), 1-17.

Wang Yü-ch'uan. "The Development of Modern Social Science in China," *Pacific Affairs* XI.3 (September 1938), 345-362.

Weber, Max. "The Chinese Literati," in *From Max Weber: Essays in Sociology.* Ed. Hans H. Gerth and C. Wright Mills. New York, Oxford University Press, 1958.

"Wei huan-ying Tu-wei po-shih tao Chiang-su chiao-yü hui han"
為歡迎杜威博士到江蘇教育會函 (Letter
telling of Dewey's welcome at Kiangsu Education Association), *Chiao-yü ch'ao* I.1 (April 1919), 106.

Wei, T. S. "Political Progress and Our Present Educational Policies," *The Chinese Students' Monthly* XIII.4 (February 1918), 221-227.

White, Morton. *Social Thought in America: The Revolt Against Formalism*. Boston The Beacon Press, 1957.

Whiting, Allen. *Soviet Policies in China 1917-1924*. Stanford, Stanford University Press, 1968.

Who' Who in China. 6 editions. Shanghai, The China Weekly Review, 1918-1950.

Who's Who of the Chinese Students in America. Berkeley, Lederer, Street and Zeus Company, 1921.

Wieger, Père Leon. *Chine Moderne*. 10 vols. Hopei, Hsien-hsien, 1921-1931.

Wilhelm, Richard. "Intellectual Movements in Modern China," *The Chinese Social and Political Science Review* VII.2 (April 1924), 110-124.

Wright, Mary, ed. *China in Revolution: The First Phase, 1900-1913*. New Haven, Yale University Press, 1968.

Wu Chün-sheng (Ou Tsuin-chen) 吳俊升 . *La Doctrine Pédagogique de John Dewey* 2 ed. Paris, Vrin, 1958.

―――"Tu-wei chiao-yü ssu-hsiang ti tsai p'ing-chia" 杜威教育思想的再評價 (A reappraisal of Dewey's educational thought), *Chiao-yü yü wen-hua* 教育與文化 (Education and culture), No. 251 (January 1961), 26-39.

―――Interview, December 30, 1966, Kowloon, Hong Kong.

―――*Chiao-yü sheng-ya i-chou chia* 教育生涯一周甲 (A sixty year cycle in the educational profession). Taipei, Chuan-chi wen-hsüeh ch'u-pan she, 1976.

———"Yeh shih Kuo Hung-sheng hsien-sheng chiao tse chui-ssu lu"
業師郭鴻聲先生敎澤追思錄 (Retrospective
thoughts on the seminal teaching of Mr. Kuo Hung-sheng) in
In Memoriam: Kuo Ping-wen . . .

Wu K'ang 吳康　Interview, June 13, 1967, Taipei.

Wu-ssu ai-kuo yün-tung tzu-liao 五四愛國運動資料
(Source materials for May Fourth patriotic movement). 3 vols.
Peking, K'o-hsueh ch'u-pan she, 1959.

Wu-ssu shih-ch'i-k'an chieh-shao 五四時期期刊介紹
(An introduction to periodicals of the May Fourth period).
3 vols. Shanghai, Jen-min ch'u-pan she, 1958-1959.

Yang Ch'eng-pin 楊承彬. *Hu Shih che-hsueh ssu-hsiang*
胡適哲學思想(Hu Shih's philosophic thought). Taipei,
The Commercial Press, 1966.

———*Hu Shih ti cheng-chih ssu-hsiang* 胡適的政治思想
(Hu Shih's political thought). Taipei, The Commercial Press,
1967.

Yang Hsing-fo 楊杏佛　*Yang Hsing-fo yen-chiang chi* 楊杏
佛演講集(Collected lectures of Yang Hsing-fo). Shanghai,
The Commercial Press, 1927.

———"Yü Tung-ta t'ung-hsueh lun chun-fa, yü chiao-yü shu"與
東大同學論軍閥與敎育敍　(A discussion of
warlords and education with students at Southeastern University), in *Yang Hsing-fo wen-ts'un* (Collected writings of
Yang Hsing-fo). Shanghai, P'ing-fan shu-chü, 1929.

———*Yang Hsing-fo wen-ts'un* 楊杏佛文存　(Collected
writings of Yang Hsing-fo). Shanghai, P'ing-fan shu-chü, 1929.

Yi-yi. "The Problem of Returned Students," *Chung-hua chiao-yü
chieh* XIII.10.

Yin Chih-ling. *Reconstruction of Modern Educational Organizations
in China*. Shanghai, The Commercial Press, 1924.

Yip, Ka-che. "The Anti-Christian Movement in China." Unpublished Ph.D. dissertation, Columbia University, 1970.

Zen, H. C. "Science, Its Introduction and Development in China," in *Symposium on Chinese Culture*. Shanghai, China Institute of Pacific Relations, 1931.

GLOSSARY

Ch'en Fu-ch'en 陳黻宸
Ch'en pao 晨報
Ch'en Shou-yi 陳受頤
cheng 政
cheng-chih 政治
cheng-chiao 政教
Ch'i Hsieh-yuan 齊燮元
chiao-yü 教育
Chia-yin jih-k'an 甲寅日刊
Chia-yin tsa-chih 甲寅雜誌
Chiang Ch'i 姜琦
chiang-hsueh she 講學社
chiao 教
chiao-hsueh-tso ho-i
　　　教學做合一
chiao-yü hui 教育會
chih-shih chieh-chi
　　　智識階級
chinputang 進步黨
chin-shih 進士
chü-jen 舉人
Ch'üan-kuo chiao-yü hui lien-
　　ho hui
　　全國教育聯合會
chueh-wu 覺悟
Chung-hua chiao-yü kai-chin
　　she 中華教育改進社
Chung-hua chih-yeh chiao-yü
　　she 中華職業教育社

erh-shih nien pu t'an cheng-
　　chih; erh-shih nien pu kan
　　cheng-chih
　　二十年不談政治
　　二十年不幹政治

Fan Chi-ch'ang 樊際昌
Fan Yuan-lien 范源濂

Hsiao-chuang 曉莊
hsien chang 縣長
Hsin chiao-yü kung-chin she
　　新教育共進社
hsueh-ch'ao 學潮
hsueh-feng 學風
hsueh-shu chiang-yen hui
　　學術講演會
Hsueh-ts'ui 學粹

Ichiko Chūzō 市古宙三

jen 仁
Jen Hung-chun 任鴻雋

Kaizo 改造
ken-pen 根本
Kiangsu sheng chiao-yü hui
　　江蘇省教育會
ko-hsing chu-i 個性主義

327

Kuang-ming jih pao 光明日報

kung-chü 工具

kuo-ch'eng 過程

kuo-chia chu-i 國家主義

kuo-chia chu-i ti chiao-yü 國家主義的教育

kuo-chia kuan 國家觀

kuo-hsueh pao-ts'un hui 國學保存會

lien-huan chiao-hsueh fa 連環教學法

min-chu chu-i 民主主義

Nankao 南高 (Nan-ching kao-teng shih-fan hsueh-hsiao) 南京高等師範學校

Nan she 南社

nung-min kan-k'u hua 農民甘苦化

Peita 北大 (Pei-ching ta-hsueh) 北京大學

p'ing-min 平民

P'ing-min chiao-yü ts'u-chin hui 平民教育促進會

p'ing-min hsueh-hsiao 平民學校

p'ing-min tu-shu ch'u 平民讀書處

po-shih 博士

pu-hsi chiao-yü 補習教育

San-min chu-i 三民主義

shang-chih hsueh-hui 尚志學會

shao-nien Chung-kuo hsueh-hui 少年中國學會

she-hui chi hsueh-hsiao 社會即學校

sheng-huo chiao-yü 生活教育

shih-chi chiao yü tiao-ch'a she 實際教育調查社

shih-yen chu-i 實驗主義

ssu-t'ung pa-ta 四通八達

T'ang Erh-ho 湯爾和

tang-hua chiao-yü 黨化教育

t'i-kao hsueh-shu 提高學術

ti-tzu 弟子

T. K. Tong 唐得剛

Tsinghua (Ch'ing Hua) 清華

Tu-wei 杜威

Tuan Ch'i-jui 段祺瑞

Wang 王

wei 威

wei chih-shih chieh-chi 偽智識階級

yuan 元

INDEX

Babbitt, Irving, 117
Barbusse, Henri, 137
Bentley, Arthur, 146
Bourke, Paul, 55, 284n54
Bourne, Randolph, 146, 155-156
Boxer remission payments: by U.S.,
    15; by several in 1924, 97
Brandauer, Lucy Dewey, 31,
    244n1

Cavour, 138
Chang Ch'i-yun, 247n16
Chang Chien, 67
Chang Hsi-jo, 102
Chang Shih-chao, 27, 95
Chang Yu-chuan, 17
Ch'ang Tao-chih, 58, 251n52
Ch'en Fu-ch'en (Ch'en Chieh-shih),
    116
Ch'en Ho-ch'in, 57
Ch'en pao fu-k'an (Morning post
    supplement), 22
Ch'en Tu-hsiu: 144; founder of
    Hsin Ch'ing-nien, 25-26; Dean
    at National Peking University,
    26; work with Hu Shih, 27;
    split with Hu Shih, 74, 153-
    154; experimentalism, 152-154;
    affiliation with *The Tiger*, 153
Cheng Tsung-hai: translator of
    Dewey's work, 35; at National
    Southeastern, 57
Cheng-chiao, 60, 120
Ch'eng Ch'i-pao, 57
Ch'i Hsieh-yuan, 114, 116
Chiang Ch'ien, 67
Chiang Meng-lin (Monlin Chiang):
    invitation to Dewey, 11, 55;

at Teachers College, 12; interpre-
    ter for Dewey, 12; acting Chan-
    cellor at National Peking Uni-
    versity, 12, 58; Ed. D. from
    Teachers College, 20; interpre-
    tation of May Fourth, 25, 72-73;
    spearhead of new education
    reform movement, 59; editor
    of *Hsin chiao-yü*, 60; educational
    thought of, 62-64; reforms at
    National Peking University, 64;
    relationship to Ts'ai Yuan-p'ei,
    66, 265n66; views compared
    with Hu Shih's, 70; social action
    education, 70-72; reference to
    Russian Revolution, 71; coopera-
    tion with Hu Shih, 72-73, 285n65;
    manifesto, 1920, 76; *t'i-kao hsueh-
    shu*, 78; and Paul Reinsch, 81;
    sponsorship of T'ao, 82; on in-
    tellectuals in early Republic,
    120-123; problems with student
    activism, 112; chicken and egg
    puzzle, 121, 150; returned student
    elitism, 122, 124; "paper tiger"
    intellectuals, 123
Chiao-yü hui (public education
    societies), 61
"Chicago School," 146
Chihli clique, 114
Ch'in dynasty legalism, 68
China Foundation for the Promotion
    of Education and Culture, 97
Chinese Communist Party, 2, 113,
    137
Chinese Education Club, Teachers
    College, 19
Chinese Movement to Study Abroad,

329

National Federation of Education Associations (Ch'üan-kuo chiao-yü hui lien-ho hui), 31, 61-62, 267n1

National Humiliation Day, 95

New education reform movement 55-127; institutions feeding in, 56-58; origins, 58-61; initial aims, 61-64; Dewey's contributions to, 61-64; School Reform Decree, 1922, 65-66; classical legacy evaluated, 66-69; diverse composition of, 66-67; natively-trained reformers, 67; its place in New Culture movement, 69; T'ao's emphasis on investigation, 83-86; Monroe, McCall, Twiss, 84-86; Chinese National Association for Advancement of Education, 84, 111; T'ao and informal education, 86-111; leadership at end of 1920s, 111, 120-127; frustrations, 159-160; relationship to rising middle class, 264n49

New Republic, The, 3, 24; Dewey's articles from China, 23-25, 130, 146; identification with experimentalism, 136; liberal editors, 142-143; response to WWI, 154-156; Deweyan experimentalism tested, 154-156

Nietzsche, Friedrich, 147

Northern Expedition, 104

Ono Eijirō, 9

Painlevé, Paul, 17

Parkhurst, Helen, 85, 269n20

Peake, Cyrus H., 262n29, 273n56

Peking Higher Normal School (Peikao, later called Peking Teachers' College), 23, 58

P'eng Yun-i, 89

"Problems and isms," 143-146

Public peace police law, 1920, 75

Reinsch, Paul, 16, 81

Remer, C. F., 156

"Restore educational rights," 96

"Returned Students" from the United States, 14-21; at Dewey's arrival in China, 3; relationship to 1911 Revolution, 26, 115-117, 158; response to May Fourth Incident, 28; T'ao's comments on, 90, 93, 104, 124; students of Babbitt, 117; elitism of, 122-124; Chiang Meng-lin's conception of his role as, 122; origins of reform commitment, 157-158. *See also* Dewey, John: followers in China

Robinson, James Harvey, 37

Rolland, Romain, 136

Russell, Bertrand, 33

Schneider, Laurence, 279n17, 281n8, 287n87

Science Society, Chinese, 115-116

School Reform Decree of 1922, 65-66, 77, 111

Shanghai, American population of, 17

Shatskii, Stanislav Theofilovich, 106-107

Shen En-fu, 62

Smith, T. V., 146

Social history controversy, 102

Society for the Promotion of New Education (Hsin chiao-yü kung-chin she): foundation, 59-61; influence of Dewey's ideas on, 60, 64-66; nature of sponsors, 67; May Fourth Incident, 69, 72; absorbed into Chinese National Association for the

HARVARD EAST ASIAN MONOGRAPHS